Verdict on '

The Inside Story
of the
Cop Case
that Ignited Miami's
Deadliest Riot

by
John Dorschner

This is a work of nonfiction. It is based on public documents, newspaper reports, television clips, books, government reports, and interviews with the participants and observers. No anonymous sources were used. All information has been fact-checked as to the greatest extent possible. All quotations are the opinions solely of the person speaking. All major figures in this narrative still living at the time of the research for this book were given the opportunity to comment if they so desired. For a complete list of sources, see Sources and Notes.

© 2020 by John Dorschner

All rights reserved. No part of this book may be reproduced or used in any manner without written permission of the copyright owner except for the use of quotations in a book review.

Cover Design: Greg Aunapu / New-Media Gurus

E-formatting: Greg Aunapu / New-Media Gurus

For Kathy Martin,
who stood by me all these years

ABOUT THE AUTHOR

John Dorschner was a staff writer for the Miami Herald for four decades, much of that time with Tropic, the Sunday magazine. In his later years, he covered mostly healthcare economics. He is the winner of two National Headliner Awards and the Green Eyeshade Award and was a finalist for the Pulitzer Prize. He is co-author of "The Winds of December," a book about Cuba in 1958, and author of "How Florida Got Its Shape." His writing has been anthologized in several college textbooks, including "Telling Stories Taking Risks" and "Textures: Strategies for Reading." In 2001, he was a Senior Fulbright Fellow, teaching journalism and studying the post-Communist economy in Timisoara, Romania. He lives in Miami Shores with his wife, Kathy Martin.

For more information about the book, Miami in 1980 and the author, see Miami1980.com.

Foreword
By Patrick Malone

Arthur McDuffie was not the first, and far from the last, unarmed black man killed at the hands of white police officers. He died four days after a savage beating that fractured his skull in multiple places. When the officers indicted for his death were acquitted in fewer than three hours by a jury of white men, a vast swath of mostly black neighborhoods in Miami burned and 18 people were killed in two days of bitter rioting by black residents: young, old, criminal and previously law-abiding. But now, four decades on, McDuffie's name is hardly remembered, his grave unvisited, the scars in Miami's soaring cityscape long paved over. Why revisit this painful episode in an American city's past that its leaders would as soon forget?

What happened in the McDuffie case, as John Dorschner's book brilliantly unspools, is nothing less than an unraveling of the basic social compact that binds human societies together. We live in peace because we make a promise to each other: We stop the cycle of blood, end the back-and-forth of private revenge and personal retribution, in return for our governments bringing public justice to calm the fires of violence. We do this through norms we call laws and their neutral application through rules that we all agree on: procedures that guarantee fairness to the accused and penalties that are proportional to the offense, among other conventions. Law and order puts an end to anarchy, and that brings prosperity for all. That, at least, is the theory of civilization.

Law and order versus anarchy: Both took their turns in the McDuffie story at different times – anarchy on the late-night street when club-wielding cops beat a black man to death after stopping him for speeding through a string of red lights, law and order in the investigation and prosecution, then anarchy again with the riots when the law proved incapable of bringing any justice to McDuffie's death.

Is there something unique about black males and white cops and the criminal justice system? Over and over, stories not dissimilar to McDuffie's have happened in the decades since: Black male is killed in an episode that starts with a trivial offense, then white cop walks. Did 12-year-old Tamir Rice deserve to be fatally shot for displaying a BB gun outside a recreational center in Cleveland? Or Alton Sterling, who was selling CDs outside a Baton Rouge convenience store when he was shot? Or Eric Garner, choked to death by a New York city cop after he was found selling untaxed cigarettes? And Freddie Gray, arrested on a charge of possessing a knife, placed in the back of a Baltimore police van, and given a "rough ride" that snapped his spinal cord? In each of their cases, as in McDuffie's, no criminal charges ever stuck, although the families in some instances received multimillion-dollar civil settlements and some of the officers were fired. Riots and protests followed.

In these cases, I was a bystander like most Americans, but with some extra knowledge of how jury trials work because of my career as a trial lawyer for the last 35 years. In the McDuffie case, I had a more direct, albeit small, role in the reporting as part of my job at the time as medical writer for the Miami Herald. That brought me to a seat across the desk from the deputy chief medical examiner one day in December 1979 as he showed me the autopsy photographs and the diagrams of multiple fractures to McDuffie's skull. I wrote a piece detailing the forensic evidence for the Herald. It ran December 29, 1979, at the top of the first page, just above the story about the indictment of the officers.

To me, the evidence was clear: Someone had murdered this man and then had taken clumsy steps to try to make it look like an accidental crash of McDuffie's motorcycle. A few months later, when six white men on the jury pronounced all the McDuffie defendants not guilty, I, too, was stunned by the acquittals. What happened? Many observers reached for racism, pure and simple, as the explanation. "All-white jury acquits." End of story. Or was it?

Now, looking back at this case after more than three decades as a trial lawyer, I know that dramas in the courtroom can be much more complex than simplistic narratives of race. Readers of this book will learn that race certainly flowed as an undercurrent from start to end, but much, much more was going on. Dorschner shines a spotlight that illuminates, as never before, the intricacies of fact and personalities that together spelled the doom of the McDuffie prosecutions: for starters, a naïve chief prosecutor (later the attorney general of the United States) who had never tried a case and who made fateful missteps in the first days of the investigation, pressured by a felt need for quick action to placate a restive minority community skeptical of the ability of the justice system to deliver.

In the end, this important book teaches an old but valuable lesson: When law enforcers become law breakers, the justice system is put to its ultimate test. For all of our sakes, we must demand the highest level of mature judgment and simple competence from our prosecutors. The many mistakes that marred the McDuffie prosecutions did not have to happen. These are hard, hard cases to win, but a better, more peaceable result may have been possible. Trial lawyers console themselves after losing a case they thought they should have won by telling each other, "We did all that any lawyers could have done." In the McDuffie case, no reader of this book could honestly say that of the prosecution. They labored in good faith but clearly lacked the experience and judgment to perform at the level required. The outcome was for the individuals on both sides, as well as an entire city, nothing short of an epic tragedy.

Fifteen months after the McDuffie verdicts, Patrick Malone left the Herald and enrolled in Yale Law School. He became a trial lawyer *based in Washington, D.C., representing injured people and their families in civil lawsuits for medical malpractice, defective products, police brutality and other wrongs.* *Chapter Notes

Chapter 1
Prologue: "A Shock to Everyone"

The incident took 11 minutes. Ultimate cost: 19 dead, more than 400 injured, $100 million in property damage.

The basic, indisputable facts: At 1:51 a.m., on Monday, December 17, 1979, in the heart of Miami's Liberty City, a white police officer in a squad car began chasing a speeding black motorcyclist. More squad cars joined the chase. For eight minutes, the motorcyclist evaded capture, roaring through the streets of Miami.

Near the entrance to a freeway ramp, the chase ended. At least a half-dozen patrol cars slammed to a halt around the motorcyclist. Two minutes and three seconds later, an officer called for an ambulance, which arrived in four minutes. The paramedics found the motorcyclist unconscious, with severe blows to his head. He died four days later.

Six white officers were charged with killing the motorcyclist, Arthur McDuffie, 33, or attempting to cover up the way he died. The judge dismissed charges against one officer shortly before the trial began. Five others went on trial in Tampa, because the judge didn't want a "time bomb" going off in Miami.

The trial took 48 days. Fellow officers testified that some of their colleagues used nightsticks or heavy flashlights to hit McDuffie, even when he was on the ground and in handcuffs. A medical examiner told the jury that McDuffie's autopsy showed clearly that he had been murdered. His head must have been on the pavement or against the wall when his skull was smashed with brutal force by a nightstick or large flashlight. McDuffie's hands and arms showed no scratches or bruises that would indicate he was trying to defend himself.

In mid-trial, the judge dismissed charges against one defendant. On Saturday, May 17, 1980, the jury deliberated for two hours, 44 minutes — roughly one minute for every 50 minutes of testimony and arguments they heard. Their verdicts: The remaining four were not guilty on all counts.

The acquittals stunned most people in Miami. They believed newspaper and television accounts had shown clearly that McDuffie was beaten to death.

"It was a shock to everyone," recalled Maurice Ferre, then mayor of Miami. "We were all caught off guard."

Dewey Knight Jr., the black deputy manager of Dade County: "My expectation — as was the expectation of everyone in the black community — was that those men would be convicted of killing McDuffie. To us the evidence appeared to be overwhelming."

Several hours after the verdict, the rioting started. Mayor Ferre was at a symposium at Princeton University, along with the executive editor of the Miami Herald. The county manager was having dinner at a Key Biscayne restaurant. No Miami leader had prepared for a possible riot, because none thought there would be acquittals.

A Herald editorial expressed the community's astonishment: "The jury in Tampa mocked justice. For reasons unknown, the system went awry." The afternoon Miami News said the verdict was "simply numbing, impossible to comprehend."

What happened in that courtroom? That question remains as crucial today as it was in 1980, especially in high-profile cases in which there is intense pretrial publicity about the defendant, often with groups demanding "justice" — a conviction — while the defense remains largely silent before trial. That often makes for the appearance of an "open and shut case," leading to public shock at the acquittals. The evidence against O.J. Simpson seemed overwhelming. Trayvon Martin was a kid returning from a store with a bag of Skittles when he was chased and gunned down by George Zimmerman. How could Zimmerman and O.J. be found not guilty?

Truth is, a jury sees and hears a different reality than that portrayed in the media. Sometimes jurors hear more, sometimes less, but it is always different. In cases involving intense pretrial media attention, the stakes can get very high, with heavy pressure on prosecutors to satisfy public expectations. That's particularly true when white police officers are charged with killing unarmed black men. Riots erupt from Baltimore to Ferguson, Missouri, to St. Paul. Minnesota. What reason can there be to kill an unarmed civilian? Plenty, according to jurors. It remains hard in America to convict an officer for something he did on duty.

This book takes a deep look inside one such police brutality case. It happened 40 years go, but the situation — death of unarmed black man, public outrage, pressured prosecutors, shock at unexpected verdict, riots — could happen again tomorrow in any large city in America.

The reader will learn how Dade County State Attorney Janet Reno, later attorney general of the United States, led a team that made hasty decisions at the very outset — decisions that led to disasters in the courtroom. The first four witnesses for the state contradicted each other in major ways. One witness, granted immunity by the state, admitted on the witness stand that he had done so many bad deeds that prosecutor Hank Adorno had to tell the jury in his final argument, "I agree he is bad."

Years later, the lead homicide detective, Marshall Frank, admitted he had profound concerns about the state's case: "Had I been on that jury, I might have had those same doubts."

Even Marvin Dunn, a Miami black activist who frequently protested police brutality, acknowledged there were problems in the trial. In a book he co-authored on the riots, he put it this way: "The evidence presented by the state was so confusing and contradictory that the six white male jurors who heard the case, though themselves selected through an arguably racist process, could hardly be blamed, considering the rules they were told to follow, for finding the police officers not guilty."

In 1980, a few minutes after the verdicts, jury foreman David H. Fisher was picked up by his wife at the courthouse. "How'd it go?" she asked.

"They're all innocent," Fisher replied.

"You've got to be kidding," she said. She'd been following the trial through Tampa media.

As Fisher stated to the Tampa Tribune: "She just couldn't believe it from what she had read in the newspaper and seen on the television. They just didn't get the full picture."

In the ensuing decades, most journalistic accounts attribute the verdicts to an "all-white jury," as if that were sufficient explanation. The Miami Herald alone has mentioned the "all-white jury" 187 times from 1982 through 2019 in describing the McDuffie case, often without further examination of the not-guilty verdicts.

As I write this in the spring of 2020, a documentary has just debuted on McDuffie and the riots. Called "When Liberty Burns," it gives excellent insights into Arthur McDuffie's life and the long-festering racial problems in Miami. But its coverage of the trial is reduced to several seconds of silent clips of witnesses demonstrating how the deadly blows were struck, plus two short clips with sound, one of a prosecutor's opening remarks and one of a prosecutor's closing statement. Then a black woman who was on the stand briefly said the white jury seemed bored and not paying attention.

Edna Buchanan, the legendary Herald crime reporter who broke the McDuffie story, summed up the trial this way in an interview at Pulitzer.org: "They sent the case off to Tampa, off to redneck country with an all-white jury and they came back pretty quickly with an acquittal."

Of course, there are many different kinds of whites, and this book will describe how among the prosecution's mistakes was selecting the type of white men who were least likely to convict police officers.

High-profile criminal trials are complex, often messy dramas. Big publicity can lead to big pressure for police and prosecutors to make arrests and get convictions. As happened in the McDuffie case, the pressure on law enforcement can become a theme for defense attorneys, who decry the "rush to judgment." In the O.J. Simpson case, the defense essentially put Detective Mark Fuhrman on trial, exploiting past racist remarks and creating doubts about everything he claimed to have found in his investigation. All the pretrial publicity, including leaks from police and prosecutors, pointed overwhelmingly to Simpson's guilt. Only in the courtroom did the Fuhrman problem come up, and it proved to be decisive. So it went in Tampa. By the end of the trial, jurors were convinced that the guiltiest parties were the state's own witnesses.

When Zimmerman was charged with manslaughter in Florida for killing Trayvon Martin, Martin's family and black activists demanded that the charge be raised from manslaughter to second-degree murder. Prosecutors did so. The jury didn't buy it. That same scenario played out in McDuffie: A juror said afterward that the second-degree charge was an "effrontery" to the jurors' intelligence.

After the Tampa trial, Verne Williams of the Miami News wrote: "The case crumbled. Not like a house of cards, all at once. More like a big three-story frame hotel caught in a hurricane. First the windows, then pieces of the roof, then the porches washing away. Inside, the occupants — the prosecution — ran around frantically boarding things up."

How did the prosecution go wrong in the McDuffie case? How much did political-media-community pressure contribute to rushed, bad decisions? How much of a factor was it that the lead prosecutors, a mere six years out of law school, were facing much more experienced defense attorneys, some of whom had once been their supervisors and mentors?

And what lessons do the problems in the McDuffie case extend to all the other cases over the years when police officers are accused of killing unarmed citizens? Are there ways for prosecutors to make better cases?

To give an expert legal perspective to this book, I've asked James B. Lees, a nationally renowned trial attorney, to read a draft of this book. I've inserted his comments into the chapters. His background gives him unique qualifications to look at this case: Lees began his career as a police officer in Ocean City, Maryland. He was an assistant district attorney in Pittsburgh, for six years, during which he handled 44 first-degree murder cases. Overall, he has litigated over 400 jury trials to verdict throughout the courtrooms of America. He has also conducted 1,400 focus groups as a consultant to attorneys wanting to hone their persuasion strategies. And he frequently teaches the psychology of persuasion and trial tactics in seminars and law schools nationwide.

In recent years, there have been indications that body cams and cellphone videos make it more likely that officers can be convicted. But not necessarily. In 2015, Michael Slager, a white officer in South Carolina, shot an unarmed black motorist, Walter Scott. He had stopped Scott for a broken taillight. Scott ran away. The officer, with a Taser in hand, said he chased Scott. They got in a fight. Slager said he was in "total fear." He shot and killed Scott. A spectator's video showed Scott running away from the officer. He was at least 17 feet away when Slager shot at him eight times, hitting him in the back. A trial in state court ended with a hung jury. Was there a way that case could have been made better?

In the McDuffie case, three months after the verdicts, CBS broadcast an hour-long special on the trial. "What seemed to many to be an open and shut case," host Ed Bradley said, "still raises questions about our criminal justice system.... The tragedy reaches beyond McDuffie's death and the riots in Miami. Across the country blacks are many times likely to be killed by policemen than are whites suspected of the same crimes. When too many Americans believe that the criminal justice system — the police, the prosecutors, the courts — does not dispense justice, then chaos and disorder may be the result, and that is a threat to us all."

Decades later, that statement still holds true. *<u>Chapter Notes</u>

Chapter 2
"The Damage Was Fake"

Offense-incident report filed about a John Doe on December 17, 1979, by Officer Charles Veverka of the Public Safety Department. Veverka was to become the state's lead witness at the trial. His report was approved by Sergeant Ira Diggs, who was to become a defendant:

CHARGES:
1. Reckless Driving.
2. Willfully Fleeing.
3. Leaving Scene of Accident
4. Battery on Police Officers
5. Resisting Arrest with Violence

REMARKS:

"At approx. 1:51 a.m. Monday December 17 1979, Unit 2120 Sgt. Diggs observed the above unidentified subject operating the above vehicle at an excessive rate of speed. Sgt. Diggs then actuated his emergency red lights and siren in an attempt to effect a traffic stop.

"The subject continued north then attempted to negotiate a left turn, west onto NW 38th Street, at which time he lost control of the motorcycle, struck the curb along the north side of N.W. 38th St. and was seperated [sic] from the vehicle.

"Upon initial impact with the curb, the subject's helmet came off, after which the subject fell to the pavement, landing on his head. The subject immediately [sic] jumped up on his feet and struck an unidentified officer who approached him. At this time, this writer, Officer Veverka, attempted to restrain the subject during which time a fight ensued. As officers arrived they attempted to help subdue the subject as he fought violently. Sgt. Diggs was kicked to the ground sustaining injuries to his right knee and thigh. The subject was eventually subdued and was handcuffed.

"Miami Fire Rescue arrived and per their instruction the handcuffs were removed for the treatment of the subject's injuries. The subject again became violent and had to be physically restrained during treatment of his injuries. The subject was transported to Jackson Memorial Hospital."

• • • •

SEVERAL HOURS LATER, at 6 a.m., Sergeant Herbert Evans called the pager of the on-duty Internal Affairs officer, Sergeant Linda Saunders. She was at home. Evans said he was following protocol by informing Internal Affairs that he was filing a "use of force" report about a motorcyclist who had been injured during an arrest. Saunders went to the Central District headquarters and interviewed four officers who had been at the scene. All said the motorcyclist had crashed his bike during a chase, which may have caused his head injuries. After the crash, he battled officers, who had to use force to subdue him.

Four days later, at 2 p.m., Friday, December 21, Arthur McDuffie died without regaining consciousness.

That same day, Edna Buchanan, the Miami Herald's police reporter, received a call from a "familiar" voice. The source said a black motorcyclist was either dead or about to die, "brutalized by white Public Safety Department officers after a chase. They beat him with their heavy flashlights, called Kel-Lites, then faked a traffic accident to explain his fatal injuries."

Buchanan began investigating. At age 40, she was already something of a legend in Miami. A blue-collar gal from Paterson, New Jersey, she'd worked at a Western Electric plant until a writing class excited her and she landed a job with a small newspaper, the Miami Beach Sun. She found she loved crime stories and had a special talent for communicating with cops. For a while she was married to one. A later portrait of her in the New Yorker began: "In Miami, a few figures are regularly discussed by first name. One of them is Fidel Castro. Another is Edna Buchanan."

After getting the tip, she made a flurry of calls. One went to Charlie Black, a division chief in the county police, formally known as the Public Safety Department (PSD), and sometimes called Metro. Black told her he knew nothing about the case. When he hung up, he called the home of a buddy, Captain Marshall Frank, commander of the homicide unit. "What do you know about an Arthur McDuffie?" Black sounded angry. Frank said he'd never heard of him. "Edna Buchanan just asked called asking questions," Black said. "This McDuffie guy is at the morgue."

Marshall Frank, raised in Miami, was an anomaly among cops, a cultured fellow whose off-duty pastime was playing the violin with local classical orchestras. He had climbed the PSD ladder fairly quickly, mostly within the homicide bureau, where he started as a detective in 1966. He transferred out for a while after being promoted to lieutenant, then was brought back in 1979 to lead the department in the wake of a scandal that linked several of its detectives with drug dealers. Over the years, he headed more than 1,000 homicide investigations.

Frank knew Buchanan as "a tenacious crime reporter," he wrote in his memoir "From Violins to Violence." "Dealing with Edna was like being plugged into an electric outlet. She could be a colossal nuisance.... I'd seen her dozens of times at crime scenes standing behind the tape, pad in hand, dressed handsomely, her hair coiffed perfectly while I admired her sultry curves. I never knew anyone who could ask more questions in less time."

On this Saturday before Christmas, Frank called the reporter, who told him about the tip. Frank understood the implications: A Herald reporter knew about a possible homicide before the homicide commander did. That didn't sit well with him, and he figured it wasn't going to sit well with his superiors, who were already battling media accusations they tried to cover up police brutality accusations.

What happened next illustrated the intense pressures and divisions within the county police – pressure that were to haunt the entire McDuffie investigation.

Here's Frank's version from his memoir: "Written orders had long been established stating that any incident in which a citizen is killed by police, or where death was imminent after injuries were sustained at the hands of police, was to be investigated by Homicide. Not Internal Affairs. I started off at a major disadvantage, picking up the pieces six days late."

He learned that the case was sitting on the desk of Linda Saunders in Internal Affairs. She'd been in the department just a few weeks. "She had no investigative background at all. She should not have worked any case, much less this case.... She may have followed the lead of experienced supervisors, had they bothered to lead her. Such was not the case. During those first six days, Saunders — and her boss — had not even inspected the most crucial item of physical evidence available: The motorcycle. When I inquired of its location, she didn't know. She thought McDuffie's next-of-kin might have it. The motorcycle had been impounded."

The Internal Review sergeant, now Linda Saunders Finney, disputed Frank's entire assessment. "I had a lot of experience," she said in an interview for this book. She had been in Internal Affairs for several years as an officer-detective, transferred to homicide, then went back to Internal Affairs a short time before the McDuffie case, when she was promoted to sergeant. "I never talked to Frank." She said she wasn't permitted to. Internal Affairs was supposed to be insulated from other sections of the county police so that it could do an independent investigation.

Officers involved in an investigation were required to talk to Internal Affairs, Saunders said. "Our interviews couldn't be shared outside Internal Affairs," especially not with detectives who might charge officers with crimes. "These officers had the right not to incriminate themselves." Ordinarily, she would also have interviewed the person injured, but she was told McDuffie was comatose.

In retrospect, Saunders said, she realized the officers used the time between the incident at 2 a.m. and her getting called at 6 a.m. to get their stories straight. That's why she found all their tales consistent. It wasn't her duty to notify homicide, she said. Among other things, when she launched her investigation, McDuffie wasn't dead. She knew where the motorcycle was. Its location was mentioned in the police reports. She didn't look at it: "I was not an accident investigator."

Frank, however, immediately thought the motorcycle was key. Accompanied by detective Robert Archer, who specialized in traffic homicides, he went to Barbon Wrecker Services, where the motorcycle had been impounded. They found that the Kawasaki 900 had a smashed speedometer, dented gas tank, dented fenders, smashed headlight, broken taillight. All the damage looked like it been made by a nightstick or rock. "There was no major damage to the front, which there should have if the motorcycle had slammed into something at a high speed. Nor were there any striations that should have been evident if the motorcycle skidded on its side. The obvious stared us in the face. There had been no accident.... The damage was obviously fake."

• • • •

TRIAL CONSULTANT JAMES Lees, the former police officer and prosecutor, commented for this book: "There are certain 'red flags' that should automatically trigger a review by the Internal Affairs. Battery on police officers and resisting arrest with violence are two such triggers, particularly when accompanied by a 'willfully fleeing' charge. Any seasoned police investigator would know from these charges that a civilian allegedly fled the scene of an accident, was caught by police officers, and some type of fight or violence ensued. This is the textbook example of a situation in which police officers are overcome with anger and frustration when chasing down a fleeing individual, and such emotions have been known to lead to incidents of excessive force. Thus a prompt and professional review of these situations is mandatory.

"The fact that standing orders dictated that the deaths of civilians at the hands of Public Safety Department officers was to be investigated by the Homicide Division of the PSD is troublesome," Lees wrote. "The role of Internal Affairs is to be a separate agency within the police department and not tied to any of the officers in the department. If Internal Affairs, by standing order, is determined not capable of handling investigations of this manner, then the investigation should have been referred completely outside of the department and to a statewide agency. The appearance of one department inside the PSD investigating officers within that same police department will never pass the fairness and unbiased test in the minds of the general public."

• • • •

ON MONDAY, CHRISTMAS Eve, Buchanan's story appeared under the headline: "Cops' Role in Death Probed."

She recounted Veverka's report about an accident but said a crash "does not account for all the injuries suffered by McDuffie and all the damage done to the orange-and-black Kawasaki." Ronald Wright in the medical examiner's office said some of McDuffie's head injuries could have been caused by an accident, but several other head wounds may have been the work of a police flashlight. She noted that the officers said McDuffie was "combative."

Christmas Eve is generally the start of an unofficial two-day holiday, especially for government workers, but Buchanan's story spurred county police into action. Bobby Jones, the PSD's acting director, called a meeting of top brass and homicide. He wanted the McDuffie case handled quickly, and he wanted Frank to lead the investigation personally.

Frank picked two homicide detectives and began assembling information. The dead man, Arthur McDuffie, was an associate sales manager at Coastal States Life Insurance. He had a clean criminal record but some gnawing traffic problems. He paid a $35 ticket with a bad check. That's why his license had been suspended for the past year. Six weeks before, a cop slapped him with two more tickets: for failure to exhibit a driver's license and driving while under suspension. That's probably the reason he'd fled when he heard a squad car turn on its siren.

Frank learned that several City of Miami officers had seen McDuffie being beaten by officers of the county force, the Public Safety Department. The City of Miami police department was a completely different entity than the county — separate chiefs, different uniforms (blue for the city, brown for the county).

One of the city officers was John "Jerry" Gerant, 30, a graduate of Kansas State College in Pittsburg, Kansas, who spent his downtime on the late shift studying to become a pilot. On Christmas Eve, he was home, off work, helping entertain his wife's relatives who had arrived from the Midwest. The doorbell rang. A Miami police sergeant and some county detectives came in, "stomping around," he recalled, "not quite terrorizing" his guests. They wanted him to go to county headquarters to talk to Frank. He did.

"You say his motorcycle was parked?" Frank asked him.

"Yeah, it was on its kickstand."

He saw the motorcyclist lying flat on his back. "He wasn't doing anything. Even when they were hitting him, he wasn't hitting or anything." Officers were smashing McDuffie with Kel-Lites — large, heavy flashlights with up to seven batteries that some officers used as nightsticks. Gerant said he saw a county officer smash the Kawasaki's headlight with a Kel-Lite.

Gerant said he didn't know any of the county officers by name. He wasn't certain who smashed McDuffie's head with the worst blows.

Another city officer at the scene was Richard Gotowala, an 18-year veteran, who was so traumatized by what he saw that he resigned the night of the incident. "There had been too many incidents, too many bad things" in Liberty City where he might have died. "My time was coming."

Gotowala's neighbor was Jack Rafferty, head of the county's Internal Affairs division. Several days after the incident, he told Rafferty about what he'd seen and asked what happened to the motorcyclist. "Well, he died," Rafferty said.

Frank interviewed Gotowala on Christmas day at PSD headquarters.

"Q: Did someone hit him in self-defense?

"A: No, they hit him in pure vengeance....

"Q: He was handcuffed when you saw him get hit?

"A: Yeah.

"Q: Both hands?

"A: Both hands were handcuffed."

He saw an officer kick the Kawasaki and it fell down. Then the officer smashed out the red taillight. Another officer jumped in a squad car and ran over the motorcycle. "I said to myself... 'They are going to make it look like an accident.'"

Frank now had two independent officer-witnesses who saw county cops pummel an unresisting McDuffie as he lay on the ground. But neither identified the officers who hit the man or smashed the motorcycle.

On Christmas Day, after the Gotowala interview, Frank talked with Hank Adorno, chief assistant to Dade County State Attorney Janet Reno. Frank said he was now certain that McDuffie had been murdered.

The police reports of officers at the scene included one that raised a lot of red flags. Michael Watts, 30, had been the lead subject of a front-page Herald story five months before as part of a lengthy, multiday series on police brutality. He was a hefty guy — six-foot-three, 200 pounds. In a one-month span, he'd sent two men to the hospital after he stopped them for traffic violations.

One was Enrique Baradat, a musician stopped on suspicion of an invalid decal when driving home from a gig playing guitar at a Holiday Inn. He later told Internal Affairs that one officer asked him if he'd been drinking. "No, have you?" Baradat shot back. Watts and another officer told him he was under arrest for not having a valid tag. They put his hands behind his back and handcuffed him. Watts' partner opened the guitar case. Baradat asked him not to touch the instrument. "I felt a club on my head as Watts started beating.... Watts picked me up by the throat and had my head back against the roof of the police car and said, 'This is what we get paid to do, to run assholes like you off the street.'" Baradat needed six stitches on his head.

In another case, Roy Marvin Stevens, 53, a Pan Am skycap, parked in the driveway of his home in a black area of South Dade. Watts had followed him in a patrol car. He jumped out and accused Stevens of drunken driving. Watts then started hitting the skycap for no reason, Stevens said in a complaint. Stevens needed two brain surgeries.

In another complaint, a woman with an expired tag said Watts stopped her car, grabbed her by her boots, dragged her out of her car and pounded her head on the concrete pavement. His report said she refused to show her driver's license and tried to kick him.

In each instance, Watts denied the accusations. The complaints were not sustained. Two months after the Herald report, Watts was transferred to the Central District, the low-income black area where the McDuffie chase started.

He ranked very low in his September 1979 evaluation: On a scale of 1-9, with 9 being the highest, he scored 1.5 for attitude, 3.5 for dependability and 3.5 for initiative. "Officer Watts must drastically improve his initiative, dependability and attitude if he is to become an effective officer as he once was," his supervisor stated.

Watts was one of the officers who admitted to hitting McDuffie that night, according to Sergeant Evans, the acting lieutenant supervising the Central District for that shift. Watts said he was simply subduing the combative motorcyclist.

Alex Marrero, who was to become the chief target in the state's investigation, told Evans that he, too, hit the battling McDuffie — six to 10 times. Marrero was 25, with four years on the force. He had been a star baseball player in high school and was part of the St. Louis Cardinals farm system until an injury ended his career. He'd been in the Central District for a year and a half. He and a partner shared Officer of the Month honors for reducing the crime rate in the district, solving the robbery and beating of a 90-year-old woman, arresting a man accused of committing a dozen armed robberies, and apprehending a man who had shot a teacher.

In an October 1978 evaluation, his supervisor noted: "Although courteous, his firm approach when dealing with the public in past traffic situations had resulted in some friction. He was advised, and did become more lenient while maintaining control," the report noted. On the night of the incident, he was driving an unmarked car looking for burglars.

On Wednesday, December 26, after Frank talked to the prosecutor, the PSD suspended Watts; Marrero; Charles Veverka Jr., who wrote the accident report and admitted he hit McDuffie; and Sergeant Ira Diggs, supervisor of the squad that night. *Chapter Notes

Chapter 3
The Race for Immunity

Hours after he was suspended, Charles Veverka Jr. appeared at Frank's homicide office. He said he wanted to cooperate, making him the first to step over the blue line of silence that separated cops willing to turn on their colleagues from those who stand up for their buddies no matter what.

Veverka's dad was a PSD lieutenant who knew Frank. Veverka, 29, had been named Office of the Month by a club in the southern part of the county. Transferred to Central only three weeks before the incident, he told Frank that his superiors, Sergeants Diggs and Evans, picked him, the newest squad member, to write a false report stating there had been an accident. In fact, there had been no accident.

Frank understood what Veverka was doing: "Veverka had seen the writing on the wall and was prepared to preempt everyone else with his own mea culpa."

Veverka told him that while he'd been chasing the speeding motorcyclist, he'd heard two or three shots. That sound apparently caused McDuffie to stop at North Miami Avenue near the ramp leading up to the elevated State Road 112 freeway. Veverka grabbed him off the Kawasaki. At first McDuffie resisted fiercely. Veverka said he hit him as hard as he could with his fist. Officer Mark Meier arrived, followed by others. Meier didn't touch McDuffie, but the others pummeled him with Kel-Lites or nightsticks. McDuffie stopped fighting, but still the blows kept coming. Veverka said he heard Marrero say, "Easy, one at a time." He saw Officer William Hanlon strike McDuffie, perhaps in the chest. Then Marrero hammered McDuffie in the skull with a nightstick or Kel-Lite. McDuffie lay motionless.

Sergeant Evans appeared on the scene and organized a coverup, Veverka said. Evans told them they should make the scene look like an accident by adding damage to the Kawasaki.

"I believed most of Veverka's story, but not all," Frank wrote in his memoir, published in 2007. He thought back to the two city officers who saw the Kawasaki parked on its kickstand. "If McDuffie had parked his motorcycle on its [kickstand], that indicated intent to surrender. It made no sense that McDuffie would give up, then throw a punch at a uniformed officer. More likely, Veverka's adrenaline had pumped to overload after eight long minutes of a harrowing chase and he simply charged after McDuffie like a bull, causing the man to pull away or resist. When other cops arrived, they saw Veverka in a scramble with McDuffie in what appeared to be a resisting mode. That's when they all piled in with nightsticks and flashlights. Veverka — I thought — had to come up with McDuffie's 'first punch' scenario to cover his own ass. In my opinion, Veverka was the cop who sparked the chaos that followed. Had he and Meier simply taken the man into custody, the name McDuffie would never have been a household word in Dade County."

Those thoughts came later. As it was, on this day after Christmas, Frank scrambled to get more information from cops who'd been at the scene, while Veverka rushed over to the state attorney's office. He won the race to get cooperating status that would lead to immunity — a get out of jail free card, as it were. He was now accompanied by his lieutenant father, Charles Veverka Sr. They were met by Denis Dean, general counsel for the Dade Police Benevolent Association. Dean recalled that the senior Veverka had "some influence" on his son and urged him to cooperate. The son told Dean he had "information that would blow the whole thing open." Dean talked with prosecutor George Yoss, whom he knew. He said Yoss told him, "We want to know what he can testify to, and we can offer immunity."

With that, Veverka gave a sworn statement.

Back at PSD headquarters, Frank kept interviewing officers. As many as a dozen county cops had been at the scene, plus four from the city. Some insisted they hadn't seen anything because they arrived late. Others said they'd witnessed an accident and/or McDuffie battling cops.

Sergeant Evans said he first accepted the officers' account that McDuffie's injuries had been caused by an accident, but he later went to Jackson Memorial, where doctors told him that some blows couldn't have been caused by a crash. He then accepted the participants' stories that McDuffie had resisted arrest and they'd had to strike him to subdue them him. Evans concluded from their statements that "the officers used only that force necessary to subdue the subject," as he stated in his formal report. And he stuck with that story when talking to Frank. He denied doing anything to further a coverup.

Between interviews, Frank kept talking to Wright, the deputy chief medical examiner. Wright had gone to the tow yard to see the Kawasaki for himself, and he had visited the alleged crash site with Reno's top trial assistants, Hank Adorno and George Yoss. They saw no pole or wall that McDuffie could have crashed into that would have caused such severe fractures to his skull. Wright's preliminary autopsy report had said the death was due to a traffic accident. But he estimated that the impact on the skull was about 90 times the force of gravity. These were horrendous blows. The worst one had been right between the eyes, but there were others, including two to the back of the head. If McDuffie had been standing, his head would have snapped back and the impact of the blows wouldn't have been that severe. He must have been lying on the pavement or sitting against a wall when hit. If he was battling, or defending himself, his hands should have shown injuries. There were none. Wright was certain: McDuffie had been murdered.

Frank ordered a Metro mobile crime laboratory to the scene, along with two other police vans. Working late into the night, with flares lighting the scene, they searched for evidence. Technicians cut squares of the pavement. They were examining the area nine days after the incident. Eula Bell McDuffie, the motorcyclist's mother, had been there long before, after seeing her comatose son in the hospital. She had found the chin strap from a helmet, smashed sunglasses, a watch strap and an officer's distinguished marksmanship pin.

Back at homicide headquarters, Frank and his team also worked late. They asked Officer Mark Meier to come back. He had been at the scene, and he'd already given one statement that day, sticking with the story that there had been an accident and McDuffie resisted arrest. He was a bookish guy, 28, who looked more like a schoolteacher than a cop, and he had a clean record in his two-and-a-half years in the department, unlike many of his colleagues that night. Veverka had told them Meier hadn't touched McDuffie.

At 10 p.m., Meier was interviewed by Frank and Captain Dale Bowlin, commander of the Central District. Frank spewed a stream of obscenities at Meier. He said he knew Meier had lied earlier. Someone down the hall was making a statement about what really happened. Meier asked to talk to him. "I did not want to be the first person to flip," he said later. That would have dangerous consequences. "If I was to get in trouble and needed help in a hurry, a lot of officers would simply say,... Let's take our time and let him get his clock cleaned.'"

He met Veverka in the hallway. Veverka said he was cooperating. He urged Meier to do that same. Late that night, Meier started talking.

• • • •

ON THURSDAY, DECEMBER 27, prosecutors started to prepare criminal charges as the PSD suspended four more: Sergeant Evans and officers William Hanlon, Meier and Ubaldo Del Toro, 26, a Cuban-American who had been on the force for 18 months. Evans was 33, on the force for eight years. Hanlon, 27, was a six-year veteran. The county gave no reason for the suspensions, but Veverka had named Evans for the coverup and Hanlon for hitting McDuffie. He had not mentioned Del Toro.

Del Toro had a clean record. He was bright, skipping his last year of high school because he was bored and wanted to get a head start on a degree in business administration from Florida International University. His father, a pharmacist, was upset when he decided to be a police officer. Del Toro said he did it because he thought the work was "rewarding and challenging." On Wednesday, December 26, Frank had a brief 15-minute interview with him. Del Toro said he'd arrived at the scene after the action was over because he had a flat tire. Frank had a vague suspicion that Del Toro knew more than he was saying but hadn't had time to question him further. For reasons never explained, the PSD decided to suspend him. He was about to become the nearly invisible man at the defense tables in Tampa.

While investigators kept racing, the McDuffie family's new attorney, Carol King Guralnick, held a press conference to announce the filing of a $5 million lawsuit against Dade County and the Public Safety Department.

McDuffie's mother and sister appeared with the lawyer in her office to give reporters details about Arthur's life. He had been living with his sister in a modest home in Northwest Dade, where a wall was filled with his awards and honors as a Marine and an insurance salesman. He'd been born in Culmer, a black area near downtown, and went to Booker T. Washington High, where he played the tuba. After serving in the Marines as a military policeman, he'd married his high school sweetheart, Frederica. They had two daughters and then divorced. Recently they'd started seeing each other again, and he'd taken her to an office Christmas party. He had just won a major sales contest and Frederica was telling people that he had planned to take her on an all-expenses-paid vacation to Hawaii.

McDuffie's sister, Dorothy, told reporters that he left their house about 5 p.m. on Sunday, Dec. 16. She didn't know where he'd been before the wild police chase early Monday morning. She had visited him at the hospital: "His head was like a basketball. His eyes were swollen out of his head."

The mother, Eula Bell, was overwhelmed with emotion. "I feel terrible. They beat my child to death. All they had to do was arrest him. They didn't have to kill him. They hate black people. That's why they beat him."

The attorney showed journalists the helmet strap and other things she'd found at the beating scene. After the family left the room, she brought out Arthur's blood-splattered clothes to show reporters. A plastic bag contained a navy blue knit cap, faded jeans with spots of dried blood, a navy-blue shirt, a light blue T-shirt, black boots and a black leather jacket, all of which the hospital had returned to the family.

When prosecutor Adorno saw the press conference on the television news, he sent an investigator over with a subpoena to seize the clothing and the items found by McDuffie's mother.

James Lees, the former police officer-prosecutor, commented for this book: "Commander Frank's comments in his memoir that he 'believed most of Veverka's story but not all' illustrate the problem with a police department being investigated by one of its own internal divisions, particularly when that division is not the Internal Affairs Division. Commander Frank should not have been in a position where he determined who and what to believe. Either an outside police department or a grand jury should have been making these decisions from the outset of this investigation.

"The initial conversation," Lees went on, "between prosecutor George Yoss, the general counsel for the Dade Police Benevolent Association, Veverka and Veverka's father who was also a member of the department, if true, violated just about every standard for negotiations by and between prosecuting attorney's offices and suspected criminals. No respectable prosecutor — at the initial stages of such an investigation and with such limited knowledge gleaned in whole from an investigation of this police department by this police department — would ever offer immunity at such an early stage.

"If indeed Veverka's sworn statement was given at this juncture of this already tainted investigation pursuant to a promise of immunity," Lees wrote, "this act would clearly be the linchpin for the downfall of this entire prosecution. Why? Because it was simply too soon, it was based on incomplete information, and it was based on information that was gathered by people within the very department that was being investigated. This was the quintessential Rush to Judgment.

"When the attorney for the victim's family held a press conference to announce the filing of a $5 million lawsuit, Commander Frank and his Homicide Division, despite their best intentions, should have stood down. The prosecuting attorney's office should have demanded they stand down and either turned over the case to an outside agency or referred the matter to an investigating grand jury."*Chapter Notes

Chapter 4
"The Cops Weren't His Friends"

On the sixth day of Frank's investigation, after working through Christmas Eve and Christmas Day, the Dade State Attorney's office was racing toward indictments in what was to become the most explosive criminal case in Miami's history. That speed was to become a major point of attack by defense attorneys in the upcoming trial.

The defense, the media and eventually even a Tampa juror said the reason for that rush could be traced back to February 12, 1979, when county police — five plainclothes detectives and one uniformed officer — burst into the house of a black sixth-grade teacher, Nathaniel LaFleur. They cracked his skull, broke his ribs and beat up his 20-year-old son. The cops, all white, were on a drug raid. They had gone to the wrong address.

LaFleur opened the door to see several police officers, including one "pointing a gun that looked like you use to shoot elephants." He slammed the door, locked it, raced to the bedroom and called 911. "[I] told the police that the police were breaking into my house." The cops broke the door down. LaFleur's girlfriend asked what they were looking for. Narcotics, the cops said. "You've got the wrong place," she said. The police beat LaFleur and spent more than two hours looking for drugs. They didn't find any.

After the Herald published an interview with LaFleur, PSD Director E. Wilson Purdy apologized to the LaFleurs and suspended three detectives for 10 days and another for three days. One of the detectives was already being sued for beating a man and his friend.

Black leaders, fed up by repeated incidents of police brutality, demanded criminal charges against the cops. For two months, Janet Reno, the state attorney, reviewed the case before deciding not to file charges. The black community complained loudly. Reno stewed about the matter for another week, then sent the LaFleur files to the grand jury.

In May, three months after the incident, the grand jury said the cops erred in inexcusable ways but didn't commit crimes. The panel of lay community members said that LaFleur could have avoided the incident if he hadn't slammed the door.

Why would a law-abiding teacher slam the door on police and then call 911? The Miami media didn't speculate. LaFleur certainly should have understood police procedures. One of his sons was a police officer in a small Florida town. His brother was a county officer killed in the line of duty in 1961. Rick Katz, a Reno prosecutor at the time, thought he understood the situation: "The cops weren't his friends, and he couldn't count on them to be his protectors. He was afraid of them."

The anger of black residents turned against Purdy, the head of the PSD for 13 years, accusing him of repeatedly ignoring black concerns. Only 7.2 percent of Metro's officers were black and 10.5 percent Hispanic, compared with the county population that was 15 percent black and 35 percent Hispanic. The U.S. Commission on Civil Rights had complained about Purdy's hiring practices as well, and black officers filed a lawsuit claiming discrimination. The county's top black police officer, Lieutenant Willie Morrison, had passed the captain's exam four times but hadn't been promoted. Another black officer, Willie Kirkland, passed exams to become a sergeant three times but wasn't promoted. His black colleagues suspected it was because Kirkland had testified against two white officers accused of beating a black suspect. Kirkland passed three polygraphs. The accused officers refused to take them. They were cleared of any wrongdoing.

County Manager Merrett Stierheim had his own complaints against Purdy, including his refusal to let the public know about officers' disciplinary and Internal Review records. For Stierheim, the last straw was Purdy ignoring his advice and announcing a one percent pay raise. It was worth $750,000, in a tight budget year. He and Purdy had agreed to hold that raise back, so they had a bargaining chip with the union. On May 25, 1979, Stierheim fired Purdy and announced a national search for a new PSD leader. As an interim, he named Bobby L. Jones, 43, a cautious bureaucrat who had been in charge of administrative services.

By the time McDuffie died, the PSD had gone seven months without a permanent head. Because of all the accusations of racial prejudice during the Purdy era, the PSD leadership didn't want any new accusations popping up. The tepid Internal Review to start the McDuffie case had been part of the old Purdy style. Acting Director Jones wanted to correct that — and fast.

• • • •

JANET RENO WAS IN A similar situation. In office fewer than two years when McDuffie died, she faced repeated criticism by the media and the black community — and also from the police, her partners in law enforcement.

While some critics charged that she was overly sensitive to media criticism because her parents were journalists, those who worked for her said that accusation was misdirected. "I think she was very sensitive to the Herald. And the News," said prosecutor Yoss. "But she was very sensitive to every complaint. It didn't make a difference whether it was the editor of the Miami Herald or Georgia Ayers [a black activist].... Janet was sensitive no matter who you were — to a fault."

What's more, said Tom Petersen, her chief administrative assistant, "She really wanted the police to like her. She was perceived as a left-leaning woman [but] the nature of the system is that prosecutors and police officers are not totally objective about crimes by police officers. And that's always been the problem — you're asking a partner to prosecute a partner."

Reno's mother, Jane, who once wrestled alligators, wrote for the Miami News, first doing a home-improvement column, later serving as an investigative reporter. Her father, Henry, worked for the Herald, mostly as a police reporter, for more than four decades. Janet grew up in a ramshackle, un-air-conditioned Cracker house in southern Dade that was built mostly by Jane. The site was originally 21 acres, sometimes with horses, cows, chickens and donkeys. Except for the years she worked out of town, Janet Reno lived in the house her entire life.

At six-foot-two, she always stood out, majoring in chemistry at Cornell, then graduating from Harvard Law. She worked briefly at Miami law firms before becoming an aide in the Florida Legislature, helping draft laws remaking the state's courts. She ran for the Legislature and lost. In 1972, Richard Gerstein, the Dade state attorney, hired her. He was a veteran politician who endured a testy relationship with the Herald, especially its investigative reporters who wondered if he was connected to criminal elements, partly because of his fondness for hanging around horse-racing tracks.

Gerstein hired Reno at least in part to try to repair relations with the Herald, or so some on his staff believed. She became a top assistant without ever having been a trial lawyer. Her main achievement was reorganizing Gerstein's staff. She then went into private practice with a large law firm connected with Sandy D'Alemberte, a former legislator.

When Gerstein resigned in December 1977, many expected his successor to be Ed Carhart, his top assistant and an accomplished trial lawyer. But several well-connected Democrats, including D'Alemberte, urged Governor Reubin Askew to appoint Reno.

Askew, too, remembered fondly her work in the Legislature. In January 1978, he picked Reno, at age 39, to lead 95 prosecutors who dealt with 15,000 felonies and 40,000 misdemeanors annually.

Single, living at home, she was a workaholic, often in the office by 7 a.m. and staying well past 7 p.m. For years, she didn't own a television. When she won election in November 1978, she went to the home of friends to watch the returns on their set.

"She didn't see the state attorney's office as a chance to line her pockets and go to the racetrack every day," said Abe Laeser, who worked in her office for more than a decade. "She saw this as an opportunity to help those people who feel they have been wronged to have one more opportunity to get a voice, to have somebody listen to them and have somebody see if there was something they could do for them."

That desire was to be tested severely in the McDuffie case, especially when Carhart, her rival for the state attorney's job, decided to represent one of the cops she charged in the case. [*Chapter Notes]

Chapter 5
"A Rush to Judgment"

By Thursday, December 27, five days after Frank started looking into the case and three days after his first eyewitness interview, reporters were hearing that prosecutors were preparing indictments to be announced Friday. This was astonishing speed for such a major, complex case.

In many critical cases, prosecutors or detectives polygraph key witnesses before offering them immunity or any kind of deal. In the rush to indict, that didn't happen in this case. Prosecutor Yoss acknowledged that Reno's office felt "some expediency, given Edna's story... There's no question that we rushed. There's no question we worked a lot of overtime and stayed up a lot of nights trying to get the charges filed as soon as we could. Mr. McDuffie dies on December 21, and we filed our information on December 28. But I don't think anything would have changed if we had waited.... That's the way the case laid out. You gave a deal to Veverka. He told us what happened. You found corroboration. You grabbed Mark Meier and made a deal with him, and then you move on. It wasn't going to get any better.... We were convinced that he [McDuffie] was killed. I don't think there's any doubt that's what these guys did."

Almost as soon as the trial was over, lawyers and others launched a wave of criticism, charging Reno's office had worked way too fast to bring indictments, making mistakes that were to haunt prosecutors throughout the trial. These criticisms were hindsight.

"If there was a real rush — and this was discussed a lot —it was the media pressure, and the public pressure, and the pressure from the black community," Frank, the homicide commander, said in an interview for this book. "They wanted to see results. They didn't want it to drag on forever."

It didn't look any better inside Reno's offices. Abe Laeser should know. At the time, he was Reno's chief of felony crimes, near the start of a 37-year career as a Dade County prosecutor, some of them as Reno's chief assistant. When he retired in 2009, the Herald reported he was "credited with sending more men to Death Row than any other prosecutor in the state." He also supervised every homicide case for 28 years. Laeser wasn't directly involved in the McDuffie case, but it was going on all around him, and he witnessed the overwhelming sense of urgency.

"I know that in one or more of the meetings LaFleur was specifically mentioned," Laeser said, citing the outrage over the sixth-grade teacher beaten in a mistaken raid. "Whether or not we put enough effort into it to make a decision in rapid enough fashion that the community felt we cared." With McDuffie, "it was 'Come on, come on.' It was 'Is there anything else we absolutely have to do? If not we're ready to go.'"

Yoss acknowledged the rush, but didn't recall LaFleur being a reason.

Laeser said he sat in on some early meetings on how to handle the McDuffie case. "Everybody wants justice. 'Let's do it quickly. Let's prove to them we can try police officers for killing a black man, and we can do it expeditiously and correctly,'" Laeser said. "Those last two words bump into each other. Expeditiously and correctly don't always mesh. And this was fast. This was not as thought-out as it could have been.... Over the years, as I've gotten some perspective on it, I think the longer investigations work better. Long investigations allow you to do what's necessary and nail down every possibility before you make a charging decision. And McDuffie was sort of on the far end of that. McDuffie was — and I hate to quote Mark Lane — but it was a 'Rush to Judgment.'"

Neal Sonnett, a former federal prosecutor who represented William Hanlon in the early stages of the McDuffie case, said in

1980 after the trial: "They charged much too hastily. The state spends months, usually, investigating cases as complicated as this one. But they wanted to show people they had the situation under control. And their effort to calm the public backfired. When you overcharge or mischarge some of the defendants, it spills over and makes the jury less likely to convict any of the defendants." Sonnett certainly had experience in bringing charges: He had once overseen all federal criminal cases in southern Florida.

The issue was not only whom to charge, but whom to give immunity to. The choice of Veverka, in particular, was questioned.

"We didn't polygraph him [Veverka]," Frank, the homicide commander, told me. "But I just don't believe him. I believe he was just as wound up as the other cops were, and he just happened to be the first to arrive. And in my opinion — no one knows this for sure — in my opinion he [McDuffie] was surrendering."

This is no small point: Veverka, the man who was to become the state's main witness, the first witness at the trial, not only signed the first, admittedly false police report, but in the opinion of the lead homicide investigator started the brutal pounding that led to McDuffie's death.

When I contacted Veverka by phone and asked for an interview, he said, "I'm not interested." I had sent him an email and a letter about Frank's comments concerning his actions that evening. Had he seen Frank's comments? "I did." Did he want to respond to Frank? "Nope." Still, it should be noted that he spent two grueling days of cross-examination in Tampa and at another trial in federal court, and he continued to maintain under the most intense questioning that McDuffie had battled at the start and that's why Veverka had to hit him.

At the time, Frank passed along his reservations to prosecutors, he said in an interview for this book. "I told Yoss that I seriously doubted that McDuffie threw a first punch, but there was no way to discount Veverka's account.... I figured Veverka threw that in to have us see him as a victim, in self-defense mode. But it was totally illogical."

Yoss did not respond to a question about whether he recalled hearing about Frank's concerns.

Laeser was also concerned about who should get immunity. "Part of the internal fight that we had about charging decisions really was an evaluation of who we were going to be good to and who we were going to put in the dock. Veverka really wins the lottery. He's the first one in the door.... There was a knock-down, drag-out fight for a day or two or three, I don't remember how long, about whether or not that was a good decision within the office....

"The only person I remember on my side was Kurt Marmar, who passed away years ago. He was chief of our appellate unit. And we tried to sort of draft out what the elements of the crimes were, and what immunity decision making should be about. And Janet read it closely, studied it, asked us questions, called Hank [Adorno] in and Hank says basically 'Pshaw. I've thought about this already. Here's my take on it.'"

Yoss disputed Laeser's anecdote about the memo with Marmar. "I am shocked to hear that. I've never heard that before. You find the memo? Does Abe have the memo? No? OK."

Yoss said Marmar "was my best friend at the end of law school" and early in his prosecutorial career. He found it hard to imagine that Marmar would have written a memo about one of Yoss' cases without letting Yoss know.

Laeser said Reno invariably accepted Adorno's advice: "She relied upon him to make so many day-to-day decisions, that she decided he was not likely to be wrong in his decision." Eventually, the team gave immunity to three witnesses: Veverka, Meier and later Hanlon. "They just threw out immunity like it was going on the carousel and you get the gold ring as you go by."

Laeser said that, in nearly three decades, he may occasionally have given immunity to a minor player or a secondary co-defendant. "But not without a polygraph and an unshakable written contract which involved their serious punishment as part of the deal, and a revocable decision to go after them if they lied on the stand." Most emphatically, he wrote in an email: "NEVER did I give or approve complete immunity for a potential major participant in a crime.... Jurors hated those persons.... That is why I was so bothered by the fact that we knew so little of the beginning of the McDuffie beating and we chose to believe the two persons who rushed for a deal — long before any deal made sense...."

"Two or three of us were absolutely certain that Veverka had done a hell of a lot more than he was admitting to investigators. My guess is he's the guy who knocked his helmet off. He's the guy who hit him first, I don't know. And deep down, I'm sure by the time it gets to the trial in May, there are a lot of jurors thinking the same thing. If this guy's the bad guy, why are we convicting the others?" Laeser said.

Adorno disagreed utterly with that assessment, and Laeser acknowledged in an interview that he and Adorno didn't get along.

Tom Petersen, another top attorney in Reno's office at the time: "A lot of people didn't like Adorno. He was abrasive." Reno viewed him differently. "Personalities meant a lot to Reno. Everybody knew Adorno was her favorite." Petersen didn't know about any discussion about Veverka and immunity, but "she was always going to listen to Adorno. It would surprise me if she ever listened to Laeser over Adorno."

Adorno, 32, was born in Havana and moved with his mother to New York, then to Miami, where he was a star quarterback at Miami High. After getting a law degree from the University of Florida, he joined Gerstein's office in 1974. He rose quickly over three years, then left to go into private practice for about a year. When Reno was appointed, he jumped to her office and soon became her top assistant.

Yoss, two years younger than Adorno, was born in the Bronx and went to the University of Miami law school. He was known as Adorno's top aide and best buddy. "Sometimes detractors call the two prosecutors Mutt and Jeff," wrote Verne Williams in a Miami News profile. "Tall, slim like a rapier. That's skier and racquetball ace Adorno. Short, stocky, a Roman short sword. That's Yoss, 30, right-hand man to Adorno and skiing partner, too. They work together. They play together. They got married together — on Sept. 8, 1978. Dade Judge Ellen Morphonios Gable tied the knot.... No question who is the boss, the strategist, the man who calls the shots. That's Adorno, proud, sometimes called arrogant. But Yoss is a man of action, not a go-fer. He moves out front, aggressive, energetic, laughing. He puts the case together."

Their biggest success together was convicting Rolando Otero, an anti-Castro militant accused of planting bombs at the FBI building and other places. Federal prosecutors lost their case against Otero. Adorno and Yoss won theirs in a three-week trial.

Both were a mere six years out of law school. In the upcoming trial, they were to face attorneys who were not only much more experienced, but in some cases had been their supervisors and mentors.

The News profile described Adorno as "a fiery personality." That trait did not endear him to some in Reno's office. "Hank heard his own drum beat all the time, and it was always saying 'Hank,'" said Laeser.

Adorno didn't respond to numerous requests for interviews for this book, but in 1980, he explained to Ed Bradley of CBS that he needed to immunize witnesses to make a case. "None of the officers who testified in this particular case are what you would call willing participants or willing witnesses. I think it's quite obvious that I had to draw out from them every bit of evidence that in any way incriminated their fellow officers. And I think that's natural. Once we found out what had happened, we made every effort to try to get witnesses we could try to put on the stand."

Yoss, his co-lead counsel, who gave two substantial interviews for this book, is adamant that they had no choice but to offer Veverka immunity. "Without him, there was no way to prove this case at all."

Frank, even with his reservations about Veverka, backed up Yoss on the need to have someone cooperate: "There's no cameras rolling. There is no other evidence.... The only witnesses are policemen. And the only way you're going to get a conviction is by getting cops to testify against other cops.... And you just can't have one. They'll destroy one. You have to have a corroborative witness." That witness was Meier.

James Lees, the former officer-prosecutor, observed: "Predictably, these initial choices — keep the investigation inside the Public Safety Department, promise a potential defendant immunity before you know all the facts — lead to chaos in the charging and prosecution to follow. Participants soon begin to pass the blame like a hot potato. Sides are chosen, and the blame games begin by blaming the media, the public, and the black community for the rush to judgment when in fact the blame falls squarely on two initial choices that should have been seen as terrible mistakes at the time: Keeping the investigation within the department and promising immunity to a potential defendant way too early in the investigation.

"Virtually any major police investigation that begins with these two major mistakes," Lees wrote, "will lead to a botched process and a lack of ultimate justice."[*Chapter Notes]

Chapter 6
Why Not a "Dress Rehearsal"?

If prosecutors had not been in such a rush, critics suggested, there was another way Reno's office could have gone: They could have presented their evidence to a grand jury, a group of 18 to 24 community members who could hear the evidence, listen to witnesses, ask questions of witnesses and prosecutors and then decide who should be charged and with what crimes. As a bonus, the process would lock in the eyewitness' stories given under oath and would expose early on where the key contradictions and weaknesses lay.

Before Reno, Gerstein had picked his own grand jurors: "Gerstein's Christmas card list" was the in-house joke. They tended to be civic and business leaders whose judgment Gerstein trusted. Reno changed to choosing a panel at random from voter rolls, but the concept remained the same: A test of what those in the community thought of the state's case.

After the Tampa trial, a blue-ribbon panel appointed by Governor Bob Graham thought Reno might have avoided the trial disaster if she'd had a grand jury giving her "the insights of a civilian body.... We believe that the state attorney's office acted in haste in this matter. The facts were so repulsive and the incident so shocking as to catapult the state attorney's office into filing the charges approximately one week from the time that the matter came to its attention. We believe such haste did not allow an adequate amount of time to properly investigate and evaluate all of the parties and the evidence."

The National Law Journal agreed with that assessment, adding that a grand jury "would have given them a chance to catch the inconsistencies in their witnesses' statements."

That view was shared by Ed Carhart, Gerstein's former chief assistant who was about to battle Adorno and Yoss as a defense counsel in Tampa: "The problem, I thought frankly, was the case was mishandled from the very beginning," he said in an interview for this book. "There was a rush to charge.... The grand jury was not utilized."

Under Gerstein, Carhart had presented plenty of cases to grand juries. "They were pretty astute with their evaluation of cases, and I had cases I presented, thought there was sufficient evidence, ... cases ready to charge police officers, school board member, etc., and the grand jury wouldn't indict. I thought it was the wrong decision, but it was kind of like the community's decision."

The theory was that if a prosecutor couldn't convince a grand jury, without the defense making its case, then he was unlikely to convince a trial jury that would hear not only from prosecutors but also from defense attorneys. "It's kind of a pretrial rehearsal," even though the defense is not represented," Carhart said. The grand jurors "can question the witnesses. And they can question the prosecutor presenting the case. It's very vigorous. You really have to have your act together. Gerstein thought that an extremely important aspect of the criminal justice system, and literally believed the grand jury was both the sword and the shield: a shield to protect innocent citizens from perhaps overreaching by prosecutors."

Laeser knew Reno didn't like grand juries: "She really did feel that was shirking responsibility.... If she was going to do something, she was going to make the decision....

"I think in the back of Janet's mind [was] 'If I go with the grand jury, first of all it's secret,'" Laeser said. "Nobody gets to see any of the statements or the testimony, and if [the grand jurors] come up with a result that makes the community unhappy, they're still going to do whatever they're going to do," including rioting. "Except they're going to think we pulled a fast one on them. And she wanted to be able to say, 'Listen, here's everything, all the statements, all the reports, all the pictures. I put some really good lawyers on it, a trial jury figured it out — the end.'"

Decades after the case, Yoss remained adamant: "There was no reason to take this case to a grand jury. This is not a hard question to me. In those days you went to a grand jury when you had issues, or you wanted civilians to give you their input on whether or not you have sufficient evidence to prosecute a case. In this instance. there was no issue. McDuffie was dead. Clearly, he was killed by the police officers. And our witnesses, whom we believed for the most part, were absolutely convinced to what they saw and what happened. There was no reason to go to a grand jury."

• • • •

THE DEBATE ABOUT USING grand juries in cases where police are charged in a killing continues. In 2014, the New York Times published an analysis headlined "Grand Jury System, With Exceptions, Favors the Police in Fatalities." In quite a few cases, the Times reported, the grand jury is simply paying attention to the law: "Most states give officers wide discretion to use whatever force they reasonably believe is necessary to make an arrest or to protect themselves, a standard that hinges on the officer's perceptions of danger during the encounter, legal scholars and criminologists say. The whole process is really reluctant to criminalize police behavior." So are most people who sit on trial juries. That means that a fairly short, quiet grand jury session may be less likely to raise public ire that a protracted, highly publicized trial that ends in acquittals.

Or maybe not. In the Ferguson, Missouri, case where Officer Darren Wilson shot 18-year-old Michael Brown in 2014, the grand jury refused to indict. Angry blacks responded with riots in Ferguson and other cities. Still, a detailed federal case study by the Obama administration debunked witness accounts that Brown raised his hands in surrender and was shot in the back. Brown was moving toward the officer, the feds found, concluding Wilson's use of force was justified.

That meant that a jury trial ending in acquittal would have just created a new set of problems.

Carhart acknowledged that grand jurors are reluctant to criticize an on-duty officer: "Jurors for the most part are law-abiding citizens who have great respect for police and they give them, I think, a lot of slack, and unless you have a really tight case against them, you don't get an indictment returned. But I once convicted five police officers of raping a prostitute. I presented that case to the grand jury with Mr. Gerstein, and the grand jury accepted my advice not to indict for rape, [but for] false imprisonment and crime against nature," Carhart said. By not charging rape, the "prostitute's character didn't come into play so severely. And they were convicted. So I found a grand jury to be a useful tool, though it made you work hard to do your job. But it was a check on the executive, so to speak."

James Lees, the former police officer and prosecutor, offered this blunt assessment of their value: "Any prosecutor who claims they do not need the help of 16 or more level-headed citizens in sorting through the complexities of a case such as this is either suffering from a severe case of God complex or is a complete idiot."

Petersen, the Reno assistant who presented cases to grand juries for eight years, countered: "I am not a fan of grand juries because I think they are too susceptible to manipulation by prosecutors.... In the movies you get '16 or more level-headed citizens.' In reality, you get eight who deeply resent being there or are bored or indifferent, four who are biased for or against certain demographics, and four reasonable people capable of making a rational decision."

Still, Reno came to value grand juries. After McDuffie, Petersen noted, "she sent all the cop cases to the grand jury. She made nonpolitical an art form."

• • • •

WITHOUT A GRAND JURY in the McDuffie case, the Reno prosecutors were all-in with Veverka. The top homicide investigator and a top prosecutor may have doubted his statements, but without him they felt they didn't have a case. That put them in a tough spot even before the indictments were announced. "It was a very difficult case to win," Yoss acknowledged.

The profound concerns felt by law enforcement were not shared with the public at the time. Reporters saw only the prosecution rushing ahead on what appeared to be a clear case of angry officers beating to death a motorcyclist they'd caught speeding. *Chapter Notes

Chapter 7
"As Vigorously as Possible"

By Friday, December 28, the McDuffie story was consuming the media. The funeral home visitation was slated for that evening, a prelude to Saturday's planned memorial march through black neighborhoods followed by the funeral. The Herald had a team of reporters talking to police, prosecutors and the medical examiner's office in preparation for a huge package of stories in Sunday's newspaper.

Before any of this, Reno held a noon press conference to announce charges against five officers: Alex Marrero, Michael Watts, Ira Diggs and William Hanlon were charged with manslaughter and tampering with evidence. Sergeant Herb Evans was charged with accessory after the fact and tampering with evidence.

The charging documents were backed by an affidavit from Frank: "In the process of arresting and handcuffing him, McDuffie's helmet was removed and he was thrown to the ground. Officers Ira Diggs, Michael Watts, William Hanlon and Alex Marrero... proceed to strike McDuffie in and around the head and chest with flashlights and nightsticks.... During this time the defendants used their flashlights and nightsticks to repeatedly strike the motorcycle upon which McDuffie had been riding and which, at the time he was initially apprehended, was undamaged. At the instructions of Sgt. Herb Evans the defendants subsequently reported that the injuries McDuffie and damage to motorcycle were the result of a motorcycle accident. There was no motorcycle accident."

Stepping to a bank of microphones, Reno said: "His death is one of the most tragic events in this county's history.... We will prosecute these cases as vigorously as possible."

Hanlon was vacationing in New York. Frank booked the four others into the Dade County Jail, where they were immediately released on bond.

• • • •

THE ARRESTED OFFICERS had been through a lot together in the Central District, which some cops called "the combat zone." The cops there were accustomed to sticking up for each other. A month before their arrests, Hanlon, Evans and Marrero had gotten into a brawl trying to end a loud party near a housing project. Evans was knocked out when a partier hit him in the head with a wooden statue. Marrero rescued Evans. Hanlon was so enraged that he knocked out every window of the partiers' house.

Hanlon, 27, was a college graduate and a member of the PSD's elite Special Response Team, a SWAT-type unit with hostage negotiation training. In his six years on the force, he'd been the subject of 23 civilian complaints. Three were sustained. He'd also received letters thanking him for giving mouth-to-mouth resuscitation to a girl who overdosed on drugs and in another case for halting a sexual battery.

In one evaluation, a superior wrote that he needed improvement with civilian relations. Another time, a supervisor wrote that Hanlon projected an image of over-aggressiveness because of his "exceptional enthusiastic approach toward his job." He'd been transferred to the Central District in February 1979. Behind his back, some colleagues nicknamed him "Mad Dog."

Ira Diggs, 31, the sergeant of the squad that night, had been on the force four-and-a-half years. Formerly a cop in a small New Jersey town, he'd earned a bachelor of arts degree studying photography while with the PSD. In May, he was transferred to the Central District, where he'd injured his right knee during a struggle with a man resisting arrest.

One job review stated that Diggs "demonstrates high ethical and moral standards," but "unfamiliarity with district procedures, numerous personnel complaints, a lengthy disciplinary action and the multiple demands of the unit did not afford him the opportunity to adjust to his new role."

Sergeant Herbert "Skip" Evans, 33, charged with the coverup but not the murder, was the oldest of those charged, and he'd been in the Central District the longest — almost two-and-a-half years. He was married to a Miami Beach police officer. She was pregnant with their second child. He'd been on the force for eight years and had a bachelor's degree. In an April 1979 evaluation, he was rated satisfactory – a 5 on a scale of 1 to 9. He was criticized for "his failure to assume a leadership posture because of a lack of confidence."

At least one prosecutor wondered why Evans had been indicted. "I don't know for sure, but I think that there's a good guy in this whole story who got screwed," Laeser said in an interview for this book. "I think that Skip Evans... figured out that something stunk, and I think he's the guy who goes to supervisors and says something stinks." His first report was what officers on the scene told him. "Later he went to the hospital, and he learned it couldn't have just been a motorcycle accident. And he told his supervisor. If anybody in this wide panoply of idiots should have gotten an immunity deal because he had done no crime, it should have been him."

In fact, Frank said he urged Evans to cooperate, but Evans stuck to the group's story about McDuffie resisting and needing to be restrained. Carhart, defending Evans, later summed up the situation to the jury: "He was offered an opportunity on December 25 to hand up his men. Just as he wouldn't cover up for his men, he wouldn't hand them up to save his own skin and testify falsely."

Laeser was friends with Rick Katz, one of Evans' lawyers in the McDuffie case, which meant he was hearing the defense's position on the sergeant's case. Still, the fact that someone in Reno's office would later question why Evans was charged showed how weak the case against him might be.

• • • •

AFTER THE CHARGES, the PSD conducted a review that the media and black leaders had been demanding for years: Trying to identify problem officers. Major Robert Senk reviewed records of the 2,200 PSD officers and found 35 to 40 potential problem officers. On the list were three of the indicted cops: Diggs, Watts and Marrero.

Diggs had 15 personnel complaints, which were filed by civilians. One involving harassment was sustained. One physical force report was not sustained. He had filed 10 use-of-force reports since 1975.

Marrero's file had seven personnel complaints against him, four of them involving physical force. Three were "not sustained." During his four years, he had filed 11 use-of-force reports. All were justified, the department reported.

Watts, the lead subject of a Herald police brutality series published five months before McDuffie died, had filed 10 use-of-force reports since 1972. He had been subject of seven personnel complaints and three Internal Review complaints, which are generally more serious than personnel complaints filed by civilians. None were sustained at the time. But Watts apparently got on this list because of the vehemence of the citizens' complaints about being beaten for traffic violations.

Bowlin, commander of the Central District, said he knew Watts' reputation when he arrived and warned him that he would be watched closely. Bowlin also criticized Diggs, saying he showed "weak leadership." He warned him: "Sergeant, if you don't straighten up and realize what sergeant's stripes mean, some of your men will land jail."

From a larger standpoint, the Central District's primary problem was that it was the dumping ground for some of the worst officers on the force. Sending problematic officers to a problematic area made for explosive confrontations. In the McDuffie case, the primary example was Michael Watts.

Years later, Captain Dale Bowlin, commander of the district at the time, admitted the problem: "It's a very busy area. It's a very volatile area. There's a lot of serious calls in that area. It was not a pleasant place to work for most of our white officers. And so, in my opinion, it was used as a punishment area." He didn't mention Watts by name, but when he heard that the lead subject of a police brutality article was coming to his district, "I said, 'Of all the people we don't need here is this officer who has a history of problems around use of force and having to fight with citizens and so forth.'... I was told he was going to be put there because he had fell out of [favor] with some of the people in top management."

Said Frank, the homicide commander: "While hindsight is always 20/20, it boggles the mind how and why these kinds of men were assembled in one squad unharnessed, harassing citizens night after night with their personal brand of street justice."

Black activists like Marvin Dunn, a Florida International University professor of psychology, knew these "bad apples" were bound to hurt black areas. "The senior best white cops were out patrolling avocado groves in South Dade. The ones who were rookies, the ones who were inexperienced, the ones who were problematic, were sent to Liberty City and Overtown especially. And this created tension.... There evolved... the view that white officers didn't want to be there. They didn't take their breaks in the black community. They'd drive out of Liberty City when they were on break, come back after. That they preferred to stay in their police cars as opposed to coming out and walking among the people and making the contact with people, and so in a sense they were isolated in attempts to building relations with the community and there were hostile feelings about that."

• • • •

SEVERAL HOURS AFTER the charges were filed, the visitation for McDuffie began at the Range Funeral Home. About 2,000 people filed past the open casket to see McDuffie dressed in his Marine uniform.

Many expressed outrage. Some linked the LaFleur and McDuffie cases. "I finally figured out why I wasn't screaming mad," said H.T. Smith, a young black criminal defense lawyer. "It was like the second time they dropped the atomic bomb. It wasn't quite as shocking."

The next day, hundreds came to the funeral in Liberty City. "His mother screamed and his little girl, bewildered and tearful in white ruffles, called out 'Daddy!' as a Marine honor guard bore his flag-draped casket into Jordan Grove Missionary Baptist Church," Edna Buchanan wrote. "'I'll fly away,' the choir sang, as the engines of a local motorcycle club escorting the hearse thundered outside the church."

Dunn, the professor-activist, recalled: "At the funeral, I remember there was dramatic photograph of McDuffie's mother, Eula McDuffie, in total despair.... She was saying, 'Leave it to God. It's all in God's hands.' This had a very, very strong impact on the black community. Mind you there was no riot after the funeral. People didn't take to the streets then. There was a plea to wait for justice. 'Let the system work.' Well, the system didn't work." *Chapter Notes

Chapter 8
Pressure in the Second-Degree

The three months before the trial sped by, with the defendants assembling the best legal talent they could get, followed by flurries of pretrial motions and the taking of depositions of dozens of potential witnesses. Lenore Nesbitt, who had a reputation as a stern judge, insisted there be no delays under the belief that the community needed to get finished with this explosive case.

The depositions were a key part of the defense's preparation. Florida law allows attorneys to question at length any potential witness in a criminal case, including the case's investigators, with prosecutors present. The one exception: Defendants cannot be required to give a deposition because of the Fifth Amendment provision that no one shall "be compelled in any criminal case to be a witness against himself."

James Lees, the former officer-prosecutor: "Almost no other state in America permit depositions of witness to be taken in criminal cases, nor does the federal criminal justice system. Defense attorneys receive grand jury testimony about three to five days before trial and also generally get access to police reports and other evidence, but no depositions."

The Florida system opens vast opportunities for defense attorneys. They can spend many pretrial hours probing the state's key witnesses: what they saw, what they didn't see. When a lawyer in Tampa asked a key state witness, "You wouldn't bet your life on it," the lawyer knew that witness had already said he wouldn't bet his life on it. And if by chance, the witness suddenly changed his story in the courtroom, the lawyer could challenge him by citing his deposition statements.

• • • •

MEANWHILE, BLACK LEADERS kept up the pressure. Decrying the manslaughter charges as too lenient, groups of up to 300 demonstrated frequently in front of the Metro Justice Building, which housed Reno's offices and the criminal courts.

Joyce Knox, a member of the Dade County School Board and president of the Black Lawyers Association, told a reporter: "I think they are undercharged. The state attorney's office should amend the charges [for] second-degree murder."

Marvin Dunn, the FIU professor, viewed manslaughter as "inadequate, unacceptable and unfair.... The black community has become even more enraged since those manslaughter charges were filed." He feared the defendants wouldn't get proper punishment. "I think they will get off. I think their lawyers will ask for change of venue. They'd be stupid if they didn't. I think this case could be tried in North Florida. I think in another community they could be given a very light sentence. A couple of years on each count with good behavior. Because police certainly know how to act good in jail. They could be out and back in the streets in less than a year or two." He vowed to place the blame on Reno if there were acquittals.

But in the Miami News, an anonymous lawyer suggested Reno needed to be cautious about the charges. In Florida, second-degree murder required "evincing a depraved mind regardless of human life." That meant the state's trial strategy would need to be shaped, from opening arguments through each witness, to convince jurors that "a depraved mind" existed.

Reno responded stiffly to her critics, as always: "Based on the evidence, the charges that were filed were appropriate." Still, a week later, as the demands for second-degree charges persisted and groups continued to demonstrate, her tone softened, and she suggested that, if new evidence emerged, she'd consider adding a second-degree murder charge.

To make sure the pols and civic leaders knew what was at stake, Benjamin Hooks, national director of the NAACP, came to Miami and took aim at tourism, the area's premier industry. "As I move around the country, I will make it my business to let it be known that tourists making their way here ought to be watchful to see how the ruling powers of Miami react to police brutality."

Certainly, politicians were in a reform mood. Barbara Carey, a new black county commissioner appointed by the governor after her predecessor was indicted on gambling charges, introduced proposals requiring psychological testing of police applicants as well as stress tests and counseling for existing officers. She demanded PSD records be more accessible to the public. The county commission passed both measures.

Meanwhile pressure continued to build for county leaders to pick a permanent PSD director after more than a half-year of a national search. Acting Director Bobby Jones, who had earlier said he didn't want the permanent job, changed his mind. It was because of the McDuffie case, he said. "The sobering effect of that investigation and the ongoing problems of the department have brought me a sense of purpose which was not present before."

Some black leaders thought the department needed an outsider to clean things up, but Dunn from FIU believed Jones would be excellent "precisely because of the way he handled the McDuffie incident."

County Manager Stierheim picked Jones for the full-time job. Jones in turn quickly promoted a black man, an Hispanic man and a white non-Hispanic woman to the top ranks. He demoted Chief Charlie Black, Frank's buddy and head of the police division, which supervised all uniformed officers, and replaced him with Bowlin, the Central District commander at the heart of the McDuffie incident. Not noted by any of the media: the black, Hispanic and female promotions concerned secondary departments. The biggest promotion went to Richard Smith, a white non-Hispanic who leaped from captain to assistant director, essentially Jones' right-hand man. And Jones' No. 3 was Bowlin, another white non-Hispanic.

Bowlin's promotion was to become an issue during the McDuffie trial, with the defense arguing that he was rewarded for moving against the officers involved in the incident. Also rewarded: Linda Saunders, a black officer who initiated the Internal Affairs investigation of the McDuffie cops, such as it was. She was promoted from sergeant to commander. That promotion too would become defense fodder.

Meanwhile, the county, looking to settle the McDuffie family lawsuit, announced it would take of care of McDuffie's $13,834 bill at Jackson Memorial Hospital.

• • • •

IF ALL THESE EVENTS were not putting enough pressure on Reno, the Herald added an extra push on January 21, with the publication of another Edna Buchanan scoop: A white state trooper, Willie Thomas Jones, had molested an 11-year-old black girl in his squad car. The charges could have led to a prison sentence of up to 15 years. Jones offered to plead no contest to a charge of lewd and lascivious or indecent assault upon a child if he were granted probation. A Reno prosecutor told the judge behind closed doors that the state attorney's office had no problem with probation but would not say so in open court. The judge put Jones on probation.

When Buchanan revealed what had happened, Miami's black community added that to the LaFleur wrong-house raid and other cases as reasons Reno and the cops couldn't be trusted. The Miami News and television stations picked up the trooper case, and black leaders questioned loudly whether prosecutors would have been so lenient if the trooper had been black and the girl white.

After all these denunciations of Reno's office, on Friday, February 1, prosecutors brought a second-degree murder charge against Marrero. Another officer was also charged, Ubaldo "Eddie" Del Toro, accused of failing to disclose "observations and personal knowledge" of facts in the case. New aggravated battery charges were added against Watts, Diggs and Hanlon, while one charge was dropped against Watts: Tampering with or fabricating physical evidence.

In a court hearing on the charges, Veverka and Meier were formally granted immunity. Each took the stand. Each said they had lied at first to investigators but now were telling the truth. Each said they saw Marrero swing a Kel-Lite or nightstick at McDuffie's skull as he lay defenseless on the ground. Veverka testified that Marrero told him later that "when they [the other officers] backed away that gave me a clear shot at him."

Meier had the most astonishing revelation: He heard McDuffie say, "I give up!" when he stopped his motorcycle on the side of the street. Meier had not revealed that in his statements a month before in his interviews with Frank in homicide or in the prosecutors' offices.

Yoss and Adorno told the judge the second-degree charge was based on the statements of these officers. Judge Nesbitt said no bail was allowed for second-degree charges. She ordered Marrero jailed.

The Miami News reported "Marrero started for the exit, but his wife blocked his path. Choking back tears, she removed a gold cross from her husband's neck and hugged him as hard as she could. The jailer stepped back, visibly uncomfortable with his role.... [Marrero] was believed to have become the first Metro police officer ever to be put behind bars."

Ed O'Donnell, Marrero's lead attorney, was outraged: "They were reacting to public pressure. I thought it was vindictive. I thought it was an attempt to get Alex to fold," to plead guilty, perhaps to manslaughter, "which he would never do."

Even decades later, Yoss, the prosecutor, insisted "There was no political reason to up his charges. It was based on the evidence, that we felt what he did deserved that charge. I feel strongly about that."

After the trial, one of the jurors, David L. Draper, 39, wrote a letter to the governor complaining about the prosecution's choices, including the second-degree charge. "That charge was added to the information in the case without any additional evidence to indefensible—as is the effrontery of the state to assume that a jury could support it with a 'guilty' verdict."

James Lees, the ex-officer/prosecutor, sees it differently: "The black community's complaints that the defendants were undercharged has merit, particularly when this prosecution is compared to most other prosecutions in America. In most cases, prosecutors prefer to overcharge, not undercharge, so that they can later plea bargain away the more serious charges if needed to achieve a fair and just outcome while avoiding a trial.

"Looking at this case from the outside, 99 per cent of veteran prosecutors in America will say these defendants were undercharged. As to why they were undercharged the answer is obvious: They were police officers.

"When Meier testified in the court hearing to new information that was not in his original statement, that act in and of itself would have been grounds to violate his immunity deal with prosecutors," Lees wrote. "All immunity deals contain clauses that if the defendant is not completely forthright and honest in statements and testimony, such lack of honesty would be grounds to take away the immunity. When this officer suddenly remembered the victim saying 'I give up,' a timeout should have been called and the notion of revoking the grant of immunity should have been on the table. How did he forget in his original 'honest' interview that the victim said 'I give up' before he was beaten?

"In Veverka's deposition he stated that McDuffie fought like hell," Lees wrote. "When Meier, the other immunized witness, testified that McDuffie said 'I give up,' how in the world could the prosecutors not realize they had a major problem?"

• • • •

THE OTHER ISSUE WAS the sudden adding of charges against Del Toro. After the trial, Draper, the juror, also decried the charge against Del Toro, calling it "the most blatant example of the carelessness of the State Attorney's office in preparing this case."

Frank, the homicide commander, was bothered as well. "Yoss and Adorno, great lawyers each, seemed under the gun to charge as many cops as possible." He thought Del Toro may have kicked McDuffie one time, "but [that] couldn't be verified. And he may have participated in some of the motorcycle coverup, but the reports were iffy. I thought the case against him was weak, at best, but they wanted him charged as well."

That was a mistake, Frank believed. "I always felt that Del Toro should not have been charged. I didn't think that was going to be a winner." He recalled telling one of the prosecutors that he thought the Del Toro case was "very weak. But they decided to go with it anyway. Who knows…. maybe they were trying to squeeze Del Toro for testimony against the others."

That's exactly what they were doing. Twice after Del Toro was charged, prosecutors approached Del Toro's lawyer and offered a deal in return for his cooperation. Del Toro insisted that he had nothing to reveal since he arrived late at the scene with a flat tire. Still, the state never dropped the charge against Del Toro, probably because the black community and the media would have seen that as a sign of Reno's leniency on bad cops.

Bowlin, commander of Central District, recalled he too had doubts: He didn't cite Del Toro by name, but he must have been thinking of him when he said: "I expected a not guilty verdict with some of the officers because I think there was overkill. I think... too many officers were charged.... Not an effective tactic. I made my feelings known there."

In an interview for this book, Yoss said he couldn't recall why Del Toro was charged.

• • • •

ALONG WITH THE NEW charges, the PSD announced it was firing the six indicted officers, plus two others who were at the scene and claimed to have seen nothing.

One was Frank Mungavin, 30, who said he arrived late and spent his time helping Sergeant Diggs, who injured a leg during the melee. The other was Eric Seymen, 30, who also said he arrived after the action. But Hanlon told investigators that Seymen said to him, "Skip [Evans] says we have to make this look like an accident." Then Seymen gouged the road with a tire iron in an attempt to fake an accident, Hanlon said, adding that later Seymen climbed a fence at the wrecking service where McDuffie's motorcycle was taken that morning and took a part off the Kawasaki to make it look more like it had been in an accident.

Veverka and Meier were forced to resign, and they didn't like that at all. Reporters found them outside the Central District office after they'd turned in their resignation letters.

The News: "They stood in disgrace before the cameras, misery etched in their faces. Two young men, both large and strong, admitting their lies for all to see.

"Mark Meier, 28, tall and blond with blue eyes: 'I helped to cover it up. I lied to Internal Review. I've felt sick ever since I did it.'

"Charles Veverka, 29, dark and husky and full of life: 'I covered up, tampered with physical evidence. The fact I lied is no one's fault but my own. This was a killing.'

"Meier seemed the more emotional of the two. His demeanor tended to affirm the sworn statement of his former supervisor, Sergeant Herbert Evans, who said that Meier 'would be the type of individual that can be broken.... If anything went wrong, he would just spill his guts.'"

Both said they were angry they were forced to resign. Veverka said he was ordered to write phony reports to cover up the beating. He then told investigators the truth. Still, he was threatened with a manslaughter charge if he didn't resign. The only evidence against him, he said, was his own statements.

Meier said he was a victim of "the department's decision to placate the community outcry, and had the community outcry not been so great, my disciplinary action may not have been so severe."

As the state prepared for trial, its two main witnesses were angry at how they had been treated.

• • • •

ON FEBRUARY 27, AFTER almost a month in jail, Marrero was ordered released on a $75,000 bond by U.S. Magistrate Herbert Shapiro, who agreed with Marrero's attorneys that keeping him in jail violated federal protections against unlawful incarceration: "The killing of Arthur McDuffie was a tragedy and cannot be overlooked," the magistrate said, "but [Marrero] has certain constitutional rights which must be observed. Bond is not imposed as a punishment."

Marrero was held in isolation for all 28 days. His relatives said he'd lost nearly 30 pounds. "That was not ill treatment," said O'Donnell, his attorney. "That's just something that happens to people in jail."

Marrero celebrated with apple pie and devil's food cake, brought by O'Donnell for him to eat as they sat through Veverka's day-long deposition. O'Donnell thought it went very well. Veverka insisted that McDuffie fought like hell, which was exactly what Marrero maintained. "After the deposition of Veverka," O'Donnell said years later, "I knew we won." *Chapter Notes

Chapter 9
"Inexcusable and Insensitive"

As if the McDuffie prosecutors weren't under enough pressure before, other racially tinged cases were percolating in the background, and Reno was taking the blame for all of them.

One involved Larry Shockley, a policeman in the Miami suburb of Hialeah, who shot and killed a 22-year-old black man named Randy Heath. The officer said he suspected Heath of robbing a warehouse, they scuffled, and the officer fired in self-defense. Heath's family said he'd gone outside a bar to urinate. Paramedics found him with urine-stained pants which were unzipped, his penis exposed. A county judge decided that "there is reasonable ground that the crime of manslaughter has been committed." Reno did nothing. Five months later, the family filed a lawsuit. The feds started investigating. Shockley changed his story: He'd accidentally shot Heath. Almost half a year after the incident, Reno sent the case to a grand jury, which concluded there was not enough evidence to indict. Later, a governor's panel found Reno's slowness to act was "inexcusable and insensitive."

If Reno's office was showing leniency to white cops' treatment of black men, it showed no mercy for the highest-ranking black official in Miami: Johnny Jones, superintendent of schools, was caught using school funds to buy gold-plated bathroom fixtures for a high school plumbing class that didn't exist. A contractor in Naples, Florida, said those fixtures were intended for Jones' new vacation home in that posh Gulf resort town. This case Reno passed to a grand jury, which indicted Jones on Saturday, February 23, on charges of second-degree grand theft.

The facts of the case appeared irrefutable, but many black people felt Jones somehow had been set up. A hundred black protestors went to the Herald building to complain about the newspaper's coverage of what was called the "Gold Plumbing Caper." One protestor complained: "The media degraded him with just circumstantial evidence. Nothing is logical, and nothing proven."

The Herald responded with a massive Sunday package of stories about the black community, its anger and poverty. Dewey Knight, an assistant county manager who was the highest-ranking black person in government after Jones, said: "I think the system —government, private and all the rest — has got to give black folks some significant victories."

• • • •

ALL THIS PRESSURED Reno's office to show what a great job they were doing on the McDuffie case in the months leading up to the trial. One way to do that was to release an extraordinary amount of information about what was happening behind the scenes.

A key hearing involved Parker Thomson, attorney for the Miami Herald, demanding that Judge Nesbitt release more prosecution material. Defense attorneys objected strenuously. "If the information that the media is seeking is released," warned Philip Carlton, representing Watts, "and if it is spread across the kitchen countertops of Dade County... you can be sure [the defendants] will not receive a fair trial."

Adorno told the judge that Reno favored the press getting more information: "Since the documents were given to the defense, that made them a public record."

Nesbitt decided to release statements made to investigators and to allow the press to cover the depositions, in which defense attorneys questioned the key prosecution witnesses.

Both the Herald and News ran lengthy stories on these witnesses' statements. The Miami News account opened on the front page and went inside over two full pages. The Herald's 1A story said witnesses reported McDuffie was "handcuffed behind his back when he was fatally beaten by Metro officers." Channel 4 sent cameramen and reporters to the taking of depositions and telecast excerpts on the nightly news.

"I think this just about guarantees our getting a change of venue," said attorney Terry McWilliams, representing Diggs. "I just don't see how we can get a fair trial if the information has been disseminated."

From the start, the defense had been pushing to get the trial moved out of Miami. At every hearing, lawyers complained about the overwhelming coverage of the prosecution's side the case.

On Friday, February 29, Judge Nesbitt held a final hearing about whether to change the location. Defense attorneys took four hours to make their case. They complained that the media and the black community were tying the wrong-house LaFleur raid to the McDuffie cops. "Reams of publicity on both cases have led people to accept many of the accusations as facts," Carlton said.

Tom Goldstein, an assistant county attorney, testified that the county itself was seeking a change of venue in the civil suit in which the LaFleur family was suing for damages.

Gerald Kogan, a veteran attorney and former prosecutor representing Del Toro, said the McDuffie publicity exceeded that of several other sensational Miami cases, including the 1964 trial of Candace Mossler, accused of killing her millionaire husband while having an affair with her nephew. "Never have I ever seen a reaction in any case as I have in the McDuffie case," Kogan told the judge. "I tell people I'm defending an officer in this case and they look at me like I'm a leper."

Neal Sonnett, representing Hanlon, said finding Dade residents who hadn't seen or heard all the McDuffie publicity would mean getting "a jury of the deaf, the blind and the completely ignorant."

In the afternoon, the judge made her decision: The trial would take place elsewhere. "I am concerned by the state of unrest in the community. I don't want a time bomb exploding in the courtroom or in the community."

She said she'd received bags filled with mail, including letters from Cuban groups supporting Marrero. "My observations as a citizen and a jurist is that the general state of mind is so affected that jurors chosen here could not put the extensive pretrial publicity out of their minds. McDuffie has become a byword for terrorism. The notoriety of the case permeates the community.

"From the beginning it has been a case of black and white," Judge Nesbitt went on, "fed by racists, a case of police officers being charged as liars, a case in which there was such an outcry against the state attorney that the original low charges were increased in one case."

Indeed, with that comment, she acknowledged publicly what the defense maintained: The second-degree murder charge against Marrero was the product of public pressure.

Most black leaders were angered. Miami, in the southern part of the Florida, was a mixture of people who'd come from all over the country. Cities in northern Florida tended to be more like the old Deep South of the Confederacy. "I don't see how we can hope to go into some of the northernmost counties," said one black leader, "and hope to get a fair trial."

Several days later, Judge Nesbitt announced the trial would start March 31 in the Hillsborough County Courthouse in Tampa. The chief judge there said he had a large courtroom available, and the city's demographics were roughly similar to Dade County.

• • • •

AFTER THE TRIAL, THE move to Tampa became a huge matter of debate, starting two hours after the verdict when defense attorneys celebrated in a hotel bar. Attorney Carlton raised a glass: "Here's to change of venue!"

The governor's panel blamed Reno: "The State Attorney herself failed to participate even in part of the prosecution of this case.... We do not believe that the State Attorney vigorously opposed the defendants' application for change of venue, nor did she present any evidence in opposition to the motion for a change of venue. We do not know whether or not venue would have been changed regardless of the opposition of the State, but this case demanded a personal appearance by the State Attorney and a vigorous opposition to the application for change of venue; this she failed to do."

Laeser, the prosecutor, said the location of the trial was a hot topic in the office: "How hard do we fight against the change of venue? Do we want to make Nesbitt happy? We wanted a happy judge.... I saw her 20 years later at a bar meeting, and she said, 'The worst decision I ever made was to move the trial.' Because she thought it would be calm in Miami if the trial was far away, and the truth was this could have been tried in Siberia. When the news [of the verdict] hit on that Saturday afternoon, the world exploded."

Carhart and other former assistants of Reno's predecessor, Richard Gerstein, said the venue hearing was the kind of situation where Gerstein would have made a personal appearance, loudly defending the ability of Miami to produce fair jurors. Even if his posturing failed, it would send a signal to the community, particularly black residents, that he was fighting hard for them.

Yoss responded : "I could see Gerstein coming down there, walk in the courtroom, and then bitch at the judge so that when [a reporter] wrote the story about the change of venue, he'd write that Gerstein came into the court himself.... But that's not what Janet did.... Reno, as far as I know, appeared once in a courtroom. She wasn't a courtroom prosecutor. She wanted to prosecute a bingo case, as I recall. And as it happened, in the middle of the case, we sent someone in there to try the case with her.... She wasn't a trial lawyer. There wasn't any reason for her to be in there."

James Lees, the ex-officer and prosecutor, commented: "Whether the dissemination of details about the case was prompted by the actions of Janet Reno or the judge is irrelevant. What is relevant is that any seasoned prosecutor or judge would have to know that having details of this case, including witness statements, out in the public domain prior to trial would virtually guarantee a change in venue for the trial."

• • • •

THE WEEK BEFORE THE trial was filled with defense motions, including directed verdicts of acquittal. These are usually pro-forma arguments in just about any criminal case, but in this one Judge Nesbitt spent considerable time listening to the lawyers argue why Del Toro and Hanlon shouldn't go to trial.

For Del Toro, Kogan argued that his name had rarely come up in the depositions of the main witnesses because he arrived late with a flat tire. The attorney said he'd made a statement to Frank in homicide under duress and that statement should be suppressed.

Frank testified for the state. Though he privately thought Del Toro shouldn't have been charged, he told the judge that "as Del Toro was talking to me, I became suspicious that he did know more than he was telling me."

After several days of consideration, the judge rejected Kogan's motion. Del Toro was going to trial.

Hanlon was a different matter. His attorney, Sonnett, argued that Hanlon had given statements to investigators without being warned he was a target of a criminal investigation. Sonnett was also concerned about statements Hanlon made in early January to prosecutors and a polygraph operator when he was seeking to be immunized as a cooperating witness. Hanlon had talked to Yoss after receiving the prosecutor's promise that he would not use his statements in court unless Hanlon testified differently during a later trial.

Hanlon talked with Yoss, then met with a polygraph examiner. In an interview before putting Hanlon on the machine, the examiner found some of Hanlon's statements "vague or less than fully responsive." Hanlon said he was tired and had missed some meals. The examiner rescheduled the test for the next day. Hanlon came back in, redid the pretest interview, then the polygraph. The examiner said his responses indicated deception. Hanlon admitted that he struck McDuffie in the back with a nightstick and "intended to hurt him" when he choked McDuffie.

Sonnett argued that Hanlon believed all the statements he had given during those two days were covered by Yoss' pledge. Prosecutors maintained because he'd been caught lying, his post-test statements were not covered by the agreement.

On Friday, March 28, three days before jury selection was to begin in Tampa, Judge Nesbitt dropped a bombshell: She was dismissing charges of manslaughter and aggravated battery against Hanlon because investigators and prosecutors had not informed him of his Miranda rights. She left two minor charges: tampering with evidence and joining in the coverup by falsifying reports.

The next day, in open court, Adorno offered Hanlon immunity for the remaining two charges in return for his testimony. Hanlon refused. Adorno then told the judge the state was going ahead without Hanlon's cooperation. It was dropping the minor charges, granting Hanlon immunity from any prosecution in the McDuffie case. Adorno said he planned to subpoena Hanlon as a state witness and asked the judge to order Hanlon to testify.

The judge agreed. She said to Hanlon: "I therefore compel you to answer [Adorno's] questions.... Should you fail to answer those questions, you will be in direct contempt of this court, and I can sentence you to jail for an indeterminate period of time. Do you understand the court's ruling?"

Hanlon: "Yes, I understand."

Nesbitt: "Are you now going to answer Mr. Adorno's questions?"

Sonnett, his attorney: "Yes, your honor.... He will comply with that order."

Later, a WTVJ reporter talked to Hanlon outside the courthouse.

"A tremendous burden has been lifted," Hanlon said, stammering for words. "Uh, for both myself and my family. Uh, it's been very, very difficult emotionally, psychologically and financially, and now that this has occurred, I am very, very grateful to my attorney, Mr. Sonnett, who's done an excellent job."

Black leaders were incensed. "I feel insulted but it doesn't surprise me," said Dunn of FIU. "I've been saying these people are going to get off and Hanlon is the first one to do so. The black people aren't going to forget this. This is a deep wound that won't heal.... When I was organizing the demonstrations in front of the Justice Building, some people would come up to me and tell me to let justice take its course. But justice is not done in a case like this."

• • • •

MIRANDA RIGHTS, OF course, are an important part of American legal protections. The right to remain silent, the realization what you say can be used against you, the right to an attorney: those reminders have protected over the decades many poor black people, along with everyone else. But the Miami media reports offered no explanations of how these rights played into the decision to offer Hanlon immunity from prosecution.

The broader concern was Hanlon himself. Both prosecutors and defense attorneys had Hanlon on record saying he'd enjoyed hitting McDuffie and wanted to hurt him, and he had committed "pure vandalism" on McDuffie's possessions at the scene.

Eric Saltzman, a Harvard law professor who served as producer of the hour-long CBS Report on the trial, viewed immunizing Hanlon as "a very bad mistake. They immunized some who are among the worst, worse than the guys they put on trial. That's never palpable to a jury. Just stupid."

Frank said he sometimes questioned whether immunizing Hanlon "was the right thing.... I think Reno was trying to shore up [the case]. When Hanlon is immunized and starts giving a statement, well, he's just as guilty as Marrero. So that doesn't look good. That's probably one of the reasons that the jurors came back with the verdict they did."

That was also Carhart's view: "Juries start out with prejudice and hostility against immunized witnesses. It's the great American way. You don't fink on your friends.... I think they immunized one too many witnesses in this case."

Yoss countered: "I assume Carhart's bitch is we immunized Hanlon. We worked out the deal with Hanlon because candidly our case wasn't a great case. It was what we had. My recollection is that by the time we got to that point we knew that between Veverka and Meier we had a prima facie case, but it was a very weak case because of all the negative aspects of both of their testimonies....

"We debated the issue and we finally made a decision, right or wrong, that we needed a third witness, regardless of how poor that witness was, with all the baggage he had," Yoss said. "We had no other choice." Looking ahead, even before jury selection, Yoss knew some admissions by the immunized witnesses were going to turn off jurors. "These are bad guys."

James Lees, the ex-officer/prosecutor, wrote: "The dismissal of the case against Hanlon three days before jury selection was stunning, not because of the basis for the ruling but because of the need for the ruling. If it is true (and I assume it was) that neither the Dade County police investigators nor the prosecutors ever obtained a signed waiver of Miranda rights from Hanlon or had a tape recording in which they clearly informed Hanlon of those rights, it is virtually incomprehensible that something like that could happen if indeed Hanlon was even suspected of any criminal activity prior to being interviewed...

"To give Hanlon immunity after his dismissal was sheer stupidity and elevated incompetence to a new level. Again, if true that Hanlon was on record at that point saying he intended to hurt McDuffie, granting him immunity borders on insanity. How in the world did prosecutors believe Hanlon's testimony would be received in the context of a trial in which prosecutors are seeking to put officers in jail for the exact same conduct? Above all else, trials involve fundamental fairness and American citizens are very good at understand and applying the concepts of fundamental fairness in such situations."

Underlying the prosecutors' reasoning was that for weeks they had been seeing the problems with the state's case as the first two immunized cops, Veverka and Meier, went through lengthy depositions, enduring intense probing by defense attorneys that served as dress rehearsals for the trial. The prosecutors knew the questions the defense was asking and the witnesses' responses were. And Yoss didn't like what he was hearing.

He and Adorno were convinced they needed another eyewitness to convince a jury. Instead, they were just deepening their problems. O'Donnell, the attorney for Marrero, had felt very good after the Veverka deposition. Then came the Hanlon flip. "They called him Mad Dog. He was going to be a state witness. That was a bonus."

Hanlon was to present profound problems for the prosecution when he took the witness stand, but at that moment, just before the start of jury selection, most members of the defense were more focused on the timing of the flip, happening just before the weekend that the attorneys needed to move to Tampa and set up accommodations for what looked like a lengthy trial.

"We weren't ready for trial," Carhart said. "The judge set up a brutal schedule." Hanlon needed to be deposed at length. Other depositions were still to be done. Carhart's co-counsel, Rick Katz, would have to do the Miami depositions while Carhart did other depositions at night in Tampa. "That's how jammed we were for trial," Carhart said. "There were more than 100 witnesses."

What was Hanlon saying in private to the prosecutors? That wasn't likely to come out in the deposition. For three months, he knew everything about what the defense thought, what their strategy was for various witnesses, how they viewed their own weak spots. "It was a great concern to us," Carhart said. "I assumed he had spoken honestly with the prosecutor, so he would have given insights on the nature of the people involved, etc." *Chapter Notes

Chapter 10
"A Rigidly Segregated Place"

Over the weekend of March 29-30, the lawyers and defendants moved to Tampa. Most stayed in hotels. O'Donnell and Marrero rented a condo near the courthouse, as did Watts and his parents. Carhart and Evans saved money by staying in Carhart's mother's home in St. Petersburg, a 30-minute drive away.

A prominent Tampa criminal defense attorney offered a conference room to the defense team. For the Dade prosecutors, E. J. Salcines, the Hillsborough County state attorney, volunteered to go over the lists of prospective jurors to explain what their addresses might reveal about their socio-economic status.

Hillsborough had about a third the population of Dade. The 1980 census, which was being compiled as the trial started, showed the county had 76 percent non-Hispanic white residents, compared with Dade's 46.4 percent. Hillsborough had 13.1 percent non-Hispanic black residents, Dade 16.6 percent. For all Hispanics, Hillsborough was 9.9 percent, Dade 35.7 percent. Among registered voters, the pool that jurors were to be chosen from, the numbers showed 10 percent of Hillsborough's rolls were made up of black residents, compared with 15.4 percent in Dade. There would be less chance, in other words, to get a black person on a Tampa jury.

Numbers, of course, don't tell the entire story.

Joe Oglesby, a black reporter/columnist for the Herald, was born and raised in Tampa, and he had a low opinion of the place. "Miami compared to Tampa in those days... was an extremely progressive place. Tampa in my opinion was racially a very, very different place. When I left Tampa, probably in 1965, I vowed I was not going back there. I think it was highly racially segregated. As a child growing up, I had incidents where I had been denied service or actually abused from time to time by whites, in my opinion, for no good reason, and I think the overall background and cultural atmosphere in Tampa made it a much more rigidly segregated place than Miami ... much more harsh in its racial attitudes."

Yvonne Shinhoster was a black reporter for the Tampa Tribune who at the time of the trial had lived there for two years, mostly covering courts. She recalled: "It was a divided town. Blacks lived in certain places, Hispanics, whites in certain places. To me, it had that kind of racial division. Miami was a whole different thing. I was surprised they brought the case to Tampa."

"Look at Tampa's history," said Maurice Ferre, Miami mayor. "In my opinion, of all the cities in Florida, there's no more racist city than Tampa." He pointed to the difficulties that Cubans had moving into the city's Ybor City neighborhood after a failed revolution in the 19th Century, and black militants who were kicked out of New Orleans and struggled to gain equality in Tampa. "The history of Tampa and racism is rampant."

James Lees, the ex-officer and prosecutor, who lives in Venice, Florida, about an hour's drive south of Tampa, disagrees. "I do not believe the history of Tampa, the demographics of Tampa, or whether Tampa was a more segregated city than other places in America mattered in the eventual outcome of this trial. What matters in trial are whether the investigators are fair and unbiased, whether the prosecutors are competent and whether seeking true justice was the goal as opposed to politics and press relations and the myriad of other issues that clearly plagued this case from the outset."

At the time, black civic leaders in Tampa feared the McDuffie trial would heighten racial tensions in the already troubled city. Bob Gilder, a member of the advisory committee of the U.S. Civil Rights Commission, said Tampa was "noted for letting people go, particularly police, when they kill a black person." He complained that prosecutors often ruled police killings of black people as "justifiable homicide" and don't prosecute.

Al Davis, a member of the local NAACP, told a reporter before the trial began: "I certainly would recommend that they be very careful in selecting a jury and not exclude blacks.... That bomb might just go off here — because the Johnson case is still connected to a powder keg."

He was referring to a case a few months before that was quite similar to the McDuffie case: A white Tampa police officer, John Hundley, chased a black motorcyclist, John Alexander Johnson, through 50 intersections before catching up to him. The officer pulled out his revolver and confronted Johnson, shooting him in the head. The jury consisted of four men and two women, all white.

The prosecution said Johnson was unarmed and did nothing wrong. He was just straddling his motorcycle. It was manslaughter. The defense said Hundley's gun went off accidentally: "A police officer has to confront a citizen who violates the law. He never knows what to expect in retaliation.... Being a police officer is unlike any other job in our society."

Unlike McDuffie, Johnson had a criminal record; he was found guilty in 1963 of manslaughter after a barroom brawl. Also unlike the McDuffie case, civilian witnesses watched the encounter. One saw Johnson just sitting on his motorcycle. "Words were exchanged." There was a shot. "The officer seemed like he was angry." A woman watching through a window saw the officer shaking his gun at Johnson. "He had the gun in the man's face. He was only a foot away."

The prosecution maintained the officer had no right to pull his gun on someone suspected of a misdemeanor violation. A Tampa police sergeant and a captain testified that officers are trained not to pull their guns in traffic cases. Still, under cross-examination, the captain acknowledged a motorist could be dangerous. "They can hide weapons anywhere. They hide them in their waistbands, pockets, boots and leg holsters.... Yes, sir. An officer can pull their weapon when their lives are in danger."

Defense attorneys maintained that Hundley was justified in pulling his gun because he indeed felt his life was in danger. Three defense eyewitnesses said they saw Johnson make moves that could have alarmed the officer. A man sitting on a swing saw the officer point the gun at Johnson's head. "The motorcyclist took his helmet off, and swung back, swung the pistol away." A fellow officer also testified that Johnson swung his hand to move the gun away from his face. Hundley testified in his own defense: "All I wanted to do was stop him. Get him to the ground and cuff him. I did not intend to shoot him." He said Johnson yelled at him: "Get your motherfucking hands off me, pig."

The verdict: Not guilty.

As the McDuffie trial was set to open in Tampa, Hundley's prosecutor, Anthony Guarisco, told United Press International, "I kind of question having the case here in Tampa. I don't know if they knew we had a similar case." But, the UPI story added, "he said he thinks a fair trial can be conducted in Tampa because it [the McDuffie case] is a much stronger case than he had in the Johnson case." *Chapter Notes

Chapter 11
Too Much Knowledge

On the morning of Monday, March 31, the lawyers and defendants assembled in Courtroom 2 in the main courthouse of Hillsborough County, in downtown Tampa. It was a drab, wood-paneled place with linoleum floors. Four hundred citizens had been summoned for possible jury duty.

Judge Nesbitt had been expecting to find people who knew nothing about an incident that happened on the other side of the state. She learned quickly that she was mistaken. Protesters were waving signs outside the courthouse as the prospective jurors entered. One was held by a white university student: "If you saw five people beating a helpless man, what would you do? Call the police, perhaps?"

On Sunday night, a Tampa station had carried an hour-long special on the trial, including graphic photographs of McDuffie's swollen head at the autopsy. On Monday morning, the Tampa Tribune carried a front-page story headlined "Police Brutality Case Begins Today." The lead: "Arthur McDuffie's alleged crime was running a stop sign. His penalty was death."

The article was by Yvonne Shinhoster, whose brother Earl was the NAACP man in Miami. She offered Tampa readers a primer of Miami's racial history, including the LaFleur case, the state trooper who didn't go to jail for molesting the 11-year-old, and the recent arrest of school superintendent Johnny Jones that "fanned the flames of community outrage." She picked up a Frank quote from a Herald story about how "the real horror story" was yet to unfold.

If prospective jurors missed that story, they might have seen the one in the St. Petersburg Times, which also circulated in the Tampa area. The Times story described the details of the McDuffie case and had an interview with Dade County Chief Judge Edward D. Cowart, who said Tampa was selected because it was the only metropolitan area in the state that could accommodate a trial that might last up to six weeks. He said he wasn't aware of the Hundley case, but it didn't matter. "I don't think there is a racial issue in the trial. The question is whether or not a man committed a crime. It's a simple question of guilt or innocence."

In the courtroom, Judge Nesbitt listened to an hour of defense attorneys' complaints that they weren't ready for trial and needed time to depose Hanlon. The judge didn't buy it. "The law as I understand it in the state of Florida says the defendants should be aware that a co-defendant may be granted immunity and should prepare for that eventuality."

The courtroom wasn't crowded. About 20 journalists outnumbered others, including several black representatives of civil rights groups.

Of the first 18 prospects, 12 knew about the case. A woman said the article she read made the defendants seem guilty. Another woman said, "I realized what I read in the press was a very one-sided picture." When a defense attorney asked if she'd made up her mind, she said she hadn't.

Three of the first 18 potential jurors were black people. Five defense attorneys grilled a black woman about her knowledge of the case as they tried to get her to admit bias. She said she knew the officers were white, the victim black, but hadn't formed an opinion.

A black man had. "I don't like police brutality," he said matter-of-factly. He said he'd seen a newspaper story. He remembered "a big coverup.... It seems they wouldn't print it, if it weren't true." He believed McDuffie was a "victim of police brutality.... I don't think I can give the defendants a fair trial." Off he went.

The defense filed a barrage of motions, including a demand for change of venue, the first of many dozens of attempts to get objections into the record in case they were needed for appeal. When the lawyers persisted in their need for time, the judge snapped, "Don't argue with me."

After the lunch break, some jurors said they'd seen eight demonstrators carrying signs in front of the courthouse and at a nearby mall. The defendants were called "murderers" and suggested the trial would be a "whitewash." The judge ordered the panelists to ignore them.

A second group of 18 was brought in. Most knew about the case. A black woman said several black co-workers told her about the case at work. Under questioning from Carlton, she said she knew the victim was a black man and the police officers were white. Her co-workers said the incident was "something that could have been prevented."

Did she feel the same way?

"Well, yes."

Off she went.

In the afternoon, an attorney for Tampa television stations requested that the Hanlon deposition be open to reporters. The defense attorneys objected, and this time Adorno did too. The judge agreed with them: There was already too much news in Tampa reaching the jury pool. *Chapter Notes

Chapter 12
"The Thumpers and Non-Thumpers"

If the lawyers were intent on watching the prospective jurors, some courtroom observers were looking equally intently at the lawyers. Gilder, the Tampa black activist, thought the defense crew was "probably the sharpest I've ever seen in a court. You can tell they must have a hundred years combined experience between them."

Gilder was not so impressed by the prosecutors: Adorno and Yoss in their early 30s and Stuart Adelstein, 29, who had been a trial lawyer fewer than two years but knew the area well from his days as an undergraduate at the University of South Florida in Tampa. "The entire crew seemed very young, very inexperienced," Gilder concluded. "I just hope the state is putting its best foot forward in prosecuting these people."

Roy Fauntroy, a Miami representative of the Southern Christian Leadership Council, agreed about the prosecution: "They seem too young." That's what Eula Bell McDuffie, the motorcyclist's mother, thought too: "The prosecution is so young and inexperienced. I just hope that they are able to do their job and get convictions up here."

The quality of lawyers, of course, can be a major factor in shaping any trial. In the McDuffie case, the defense team was not only older, but four of the five were veterans of the state attorney's office. They knew how the office worked, and in some cases they had been mentors of the prosecutors they were opposing.

Most of the defendants had started out with other lawyers, then switched to experienced criminal attorneys. They gravitated toward former prosecutors at least in part because they had good reputations among police officers. It's probable that at least some of the defendants had police buddies who had worked on criminal cases with the attorneys when they were prosecutors.

The best criminal defense attorneys often have a certain swagger about them: The lone gun slinger walking into a saloon where everyone hates him. Carhart thought that an apt analysis, especially in the McDuffie case. "When you represent a pariah, you get the same mantle.... This was not a popular case in Dade County," he said with considerable understatement.

Carhart, 42, was the most celebrated of the defense team. He grew up in St. Petersburg and was briefly a reporter with the St. Petersburg Times before going to the University of Florida law school.

He started in the Dade State Attorney's Office under Gerstein in 1963, slowly climbing through the ranks until he became chief assistant. Unlike Reno, he established a reputation as an accomplished trial lawyer, convicting everyone from a corrupt hospital administrator to cops who raped a prostitute. "The best prosecutor I ever saw in my life," said Phil Hubbart, once chief Miami public defender and later a judge.

In Gerstein's office, Carhart and Reno were a Mutt-and-Jeff pair: Reno at six-foot-two, Carhart considerably shorter, with a pronounced limp, due to a debilitating genetic disease called Charcot-Marie-Tooth, which affects the nerves that control muscles.

When Gerstein stepped down, many in the office assumed Carhart would take over. After the governor appointed Reno as state attorney, Carhart went off to private practice, to commence a career that was to achieve almost legendary proportions.

"Ed Carhart is one of the two or three finest trial lawyers that I've ever seen in a courtroom," said Laeser, who worked with Carhart in the Gerstein era. "I watched him do some things that I did my best to steal over the years and emulate. There was a thought process and a smoothness to him that I rarely saw anywhere else."

Tom Petersen, another top assistant under Reno, praised Carhart for his "sensitivity to the human part of what the criminal justice system was about, and [for] his incredible integrity."

Saltzman, the Harvard law professor who produced the CBS report on the trial, praised Carhart as "really smart."

In the courtroom, Carhart generally had a gentle demeanor, sometimes slightly sarcastic in cross-examining state witnesses, tending toward the cerebral.

"Soft-spoken" is the way Miami News reporter Verne Williams described him. "Carhart is deceptive in the courtroom. His diffidence with a hostile witness is disarming. He will smile and preface an innocent question with: 'And isn't it so, sir,' as he pursues his objective. Then the trap springs and a dumbfounded witness will often find himself caught in a lie, discrepancy or mistake."

[For an example of Carhart's achievements see the Addendum about how he represented Johnny Jones, the former school superintendent, in Jones' second trial.]

• • • •

AMONG THE OTHER LAWYERS, Edward O'Donnell — almost everyone called him Eddie — had the toughest task, representing Alex Marrero, charged with second-degree murder and named by the three immunized witnesses as the one who had struck the most vicious blows.

O'Donnell, 35, had also been a top prosecutor in Gerstein's office, starting straight out of law school and rising to head of the Major Crimes division. He went into private practice in August 1977, a few months before Carhart. While Carhart probed gently, O'Donnell often shouted. "The most physically imposing of the defense attorneys," Williams noted. "A big Irishman with a courtroom manner that ranges from mildly persuasive to thundering denouement."

Laeser, who worked with and against O'Donnell over the years, recalled that "he had a knack of finding that one thing that he's going to concentrate on, didn't seem to pay attention to a whole lot of the rest of the trial, and just honed in on what he thought was crucial. And was very personally persuasive."

O'Donnell said he came to represent Marrero because "I had a girlfriend at the time named Kathleen Walsh who worked in the state attorney's office. She was a paralegal and she knew a lot of police officers." Marrero had been calling him. "I'd read the Herald. I really didn't want to return his call. This is all true. But Kathy said to me, 'Will you please just call the guy, because these police officers are giving me a hard time.' And I told her, 'I don't think I want to get involved in this case. I've read the Herald and this is a very troublesome case.' That's a terrible thing to do and say as a defense attorney. It truly was, and it's the last time I've ever done it, but it's not the last time I've ever thought about it. So I said, 'OK, you're right. I'm not being the kind of lawyer I think I am.'" He met Marrero. "He told me what happened. And that was it. I knew he was innocent."

That kind of anecdote is often used by criminal defense attorneys to justify representing an unpopular client, but O'Donnell's scenario — how someone in Reno's office was involved — reveals how intertwined the defense was with the state attorney's office.

• • • •

TERRY MCWILLIAMS, 37, representing Sergeant Ira Diggs, started working for Gerstein in 1968, serving subpoenas while awaiting the results of his bar exam. Like O'Donnell, he also was head of Major Crimes for a while. Williams of the News saw him as "an aggressive man with courtroom demeanor of an Airedale chasing a rat. He seldom smiles, never gives up." For 20 years, his hobby had been motorcycles.

As a prosecutor, McWilliams' most publicized case involved convicting Jim Morrison of the Doors, charged with indecent exposure (showing his penis to the audience) and open profanity during a 1969 concert in Miami. In another case, McWilliams teamed up with O'Donnell to prosecute Rick Cravero, a drug kingpin who led a gang dubbed the Dixie Mafia, suspected of 35 murders and disappearances in the drug trade during the late 1960s and early 1970s. They won a conviction of him for murdering a rival.

"McWilliams had always been very close to the police," Carhart said. "We didn't ask him to prosecute police officers. And I'm sure that's one of the reasons Ira went to him." McWilliams was so proud of his police connections that in the Tampa trial, he wore a tie clasp shaped like a pig.

Laeser described McWilliams as being "more shoot from the hip" than plodding analysis. Rick Katz, Carhart's co-counsel for Evans, who worked with McWilliams as a prosecutor and remained close to him afterward, said, "Terry is someone who absolutely always wore his emotions on his sleeves about everything." In Tampa, he broke down in tears in giving his summation defending Diggs.

Gerald Kogan, 46, representing Del Toro, had served as Gerstein's head of Major Crimes before McWilliams and O'Donnell. A University of Miami law graduate, he was known as a polite, cerebral attorney. In March, as he was preparing for trial, a panel recommended him to the governor for appointment as a circuit court judge. Because his client was so invisible in the state's case, he often remained silent in Tampa.

Philip Carlton, 49, representing Watts, was the oldest of the defense attorneys and the only one who was never a prosecutor. "A rooster of a man with a ringing baritone voice, Carlton generally argues long after most lawyers quit," Williams wrote. Among his clients was Al Featherston, founder of the Afro Militant Movement. Carlton said he received no fee for defending Featherston, accused of bombing stores and a school, during a seven-week trial. He was convicted. At the Tampa trial started, he had been practicing law for 21 years. "I had no qualms about taking this particular case."

"He was not exciting," Carhart recalled. "Not colorful. He just ground it out [in] meticulous detail. He was never a big name, but he was highly effective. He's a tough dude." Carlton had opposed most of his Tampa defense colleagues when they were prosecutors. "I don't think he had any particular love for any of us," Carhart said.

• • • •

IN CASES WITH MULTIPLE co-defendants, defense lawyers fear a colleague might say his client was blameless because another co-defendant did the crime. This never became an issue in the Tampa case because the former colleagues from Gerstein's office "had a great advantage," Carhart said. "We knew each other, we trusted each other. We had worked together, knew each other's strengths and weaknesses. We were very united, with the exception of Philip," who often had different ideas on how to proceed. "When he was going off the reservation, I would point out to him since I was the last defense attorney to cross-examine the witnesses, that he didn't want to upset me because I could do great harm to his client on my cross-examination."

Katz, Carhart's co-counsel, agreed that "Phil was not a team player. I liked Phil. I had a lot of cases with Phil, as a prosecutor. He was a real Southern gentleman. He had a very big ego, the same way Adorno did, who had one of the biggest egos I've ever dealt with personally. But he didn't let his ego get in way of a case. He wasn't real collaborative. He'd been a sole practitioner most of his career, so he wasn't used to working on a team."

Carlton didn't dispute that analysis. "I do believe I was a bit of a maverick, and my theory of the defense might not be consistent with theirs. They were all excellent lawyers. I believed in strong examination. Some of them didn't believe that some witnesses should be examined to the extent that I did.... I was representing my own client, not with the intention of putting the guilt on any other defendant, but certainly to show the innocence of Officer Watts."

In the Tampa courtroom, the five defendants and their five lawyers couldn't fit at one table, so the bailiff added a second table. Carhart and Kogan grabbed the second, smaller table for them and their two clients, Evans and Del Toro, who were charged with the coverup but not McDuffie's death. Carhart said he and Kogan privately called the distinction between the tables as "the thumpers and non-thumpers." Carhart and Kogan were the cerebral ones. O'Donnell, McWilliams and Carlton were the shouters.

Hovering in the background were the legal fees and the substantial expenses of spending many weeks in Tampa. Marrero's wife, Lourdes, told a News reporter that O'Donnell was charging $25,000 and they needed another $20,000 for accommodations and other expenses. A "Help Marrero" flyer raised about $3,500.

Carlton arranged for Watts to be ruled indigent and not liable for some costs. That meant they received $40 a day for expenses, plus one round-trip air fare between Tampa and Miami. Certain witness fees and depositions were also covered, but not attorney fees.

Carhart told the News his fee was "minimal considering the time involved.... But I guess it's like 'minor' surgery. It's not minor when it's happening to you."

• • • •

THE DEFENSE LAWYERS not only knew each other well, they also knew their opponents. Hank Adorno, 32, and George Yoss, 30, were newcomers in the state attorney's office when their opponents were veteran supervisors.

"When I started in the office," Yoss said, "I interned for Terry McWilliams. The person who hired me, technically, was Ed Carhart. Eddie O'Donnell was still a prosecutor, just about to leave the office. Gerry Kogan was already out, a preeminent defense lawyer at that point. Phil Carlton. I knew all of them. We all knew all of them. I used to go skiing with Terry McWilliams." But he said that didn't affect the atmosphere in the Tampa courtroom. "It was no different than any other case with lawyers on the other side who you knew. No difference whatsoever."

O'Donnell recalled: "I knew them very well. I was one of the people who interviewed Hank Adorno and recommended his hiring, on the recommendation of a police officer. I also interviewed George Yoss and recommended his hiring."

Saltzman, the CBS producer, watched the lawyers in trial video after the verdicts. He was not impressed with the lead prosecutor: "Adorno was young. He was an unsophisticated guy. He had a little bit of the whiny thing."

James Lees, the former officer and prosecutor, notes: "Generally, criminal defense teams are more impressive than prosecution teams. The O.J. Simpson case clearly demonstrated this fact years later. Why? Because the offices of prosecutors are staffed with young lawyers looking to make their marks and acquire skills that can be used to secure lucrative jobs later in life. After a number of years, the vast majority of prosecutors move on to better-paying jobs in the private sector. I myself was a classic example of this pattern, staying in the District Attorney's Office in Pittsburgh for a bit more than six years before moving on to private practice. On the other hand, defense lawyers are already in their lucrative career jobs, and they are almost always better and more skilled than the young people prosecuting the cases."

• • • •

THE OTHER IMPORTANT lawyer in the courtroom — arguably the most important — was Judge Lenore Nesbitt, 47, a rare Miami native. She attended Stephens College, a small, women's institution in Missouri, from which she received an associate's degree in 1952, then a bachelor's from Northwestern in 1954, followed by a law degree from the University of Miami in 1957, graduating first in her class.

Much of her career had been spent in and around courts. For her first two years after law school, she was a research assistant at a state appellate court, followed by two years as a special assistant attorney general, two years as a research assistant in a Miami court, two years as counsel to the State Board of Medical Examiners, then six years in private practice. The governor appointed her a circuit court judge in 1975. Her husband, Joseph Nesbitt, was a judge on the Florida Third District Court of Appeal. She was the mother of two.

The lawyers viewed her as a somber taskmaster who didn't like delays. "Lenore was a no-nonsense judge," Yoss recalled. "She kept everybody's feet to the fire. She wanted to get this done."

Gilder, the black activist watching the trial, was impressed. "The judge certainly has ruled with an iron fist and a velvet glove. It is obvious that she wants to get this case under way and it is obvious while she wants to give everyone concerned an opportunity to exercise their rights, she is not going to stand for any foolishness in her court." *Chapter Notes

Chapter 13
"Hung by Their Thumbs"

For 11 courtroom days, jury selection plodded on, far more than the lawyers or judge anticipated, as it became apparent how much residents on the other side of the state knew about the Miami case. While federal courts and many state courts need to find 12 impartial persons, only six were needed for the McDuffie case. But they weren't easy to find.

A prime example: Annie Reybon, 50, told the court that during the lunch break she'd heard another prospect say that the defendants "should be hung by their thumbs."

Carhart launched into one of his many objections: "I've never seen jurors able to recite details after details as they have done in this case. And how often is it you can hear a [potential] juror say that they should be hung by the thumbs without hearing any testimony. I've come 200 miles and I'm no closer to getting a fair trial."

The questioning droned on. Journalists were bored. "Agonizing tedium," complained Gene Miller in the Miami Herald.

For lawyers, of course, jury selection is crucial to find jurors sympathetic to their clients, or at least neutral. And in this case, that meant the race of the prospect mattered. The prosecution focused on getting black people on the jury, while the defense was determined they shouldn't be allowed on.

Defense attorneys spent an inordinate amount of time on Jo Thomas, a black woman with red hair, a red purse and red high-heeled boots. "You know how you feel," O'Donnell said. "Can you give us a fair shake? We're not going to put you on the polygraph or badger you." She said she could be fair. She stayed on the panel for a while, but the defense did out-of-court research on her. She'd said she'd been the victim of a crime. An investigator found she was a criminal, not a victim. The judge called her back to court. She admitted she was with "the wrong people at the wrong time." She had served nine days in jail.

The defense wanted her off the panel. Adorno argued she was guilty of a mere misdemeanor and should stay. "It is an odd day in a courtroom when a prosecutor wants jail-time folks on a jury," Miller wrote. The defense argued that she had been convicted of a larceny, which state statutes listed as one of the crimes that would disqualify a person from serving on a jury. Nesbitt researched the issue and agreed; Thomas was thrown off for cause.

By the end of the second day, Judge Nesbitt was weary of the slow pace as each defense attorney sought to burrow deep into the past and prejudices of each person. She decided she would do the questioning to learn how much each prospect knew about the case and whether they could put that knowledge aside. Those who remained could then be questioned by the attorneys.

Of the first 72 called, only nine hadn't heard about the case. Some said that wouldn't affect them. But others were like Sarah Arnold: "I don't take the media as gospel truth, but where there's smoke there's fire." The judge dismissed her for cause.

A military man told the judge: "In my mind, I could not give a verdict of guilt. I'm for officers and I think the courts don't uphold them enough."

A cabinet designer, D. Blackston, knew a lot about the case, even the scheduled witnesses. "I would seriously doubt the testimony of Hanlon. He was at one time a defendant." Blackston said he didn't want to serve. "I have 40 people depending on me" in the cabinet shop.

At least he showed up in court. Many didn't. Under defense pressure, the judge investigated and found more than half of the original pool of 400 were excused by local judges, including one who was let off simply because he said he had an important business meeting.

Under state law, only a judge is supposed to release prospective jurors before they get to the courtroom, but in the McDuffie case, some were excused by a court clerk or the clerk's secretary. A total of 176 never showed up: 32 for health reasons, 24 for job-related reasons, another 24 for personal reasons such as "too old," "children at home" or college student.

McWilliams complained that many of those excused were educated, white-collar workers. "Lower income and blue-collar type people have more troubles with the police and would have trouble understanding the inter-politicking" in the police department. Such "inter-politicking" was to be a central part of the defense's theory of the case.

On Wednesday, April 9, in the second week of jury selection, after culling the pool of those who said they couldn't set aside what they knew about the case, Nesbitt gave questioning back to the lawyers. The defense immediately resumed its intense probing with Diane Swank, an unemployed single mother. They wanted to know about her religious beliefs, prejudices, children, her reactions to the sight of blood, the occupations of her mother and father, whether she'd ever ridden a motorcycle, how she felt about the police.

The prosecution didn't question her at all.

After the trial, the National Law Journal said prosecutors made a critical mistake when they waived "their right to conduct their own questioning of all but a few of the prospective jurors.... The defense lawyers took prospective jurors through a lengthy set of questions about pretrial publicity, personal background and attitudes." Yoss told the Journal that they "waived voir dire [jury questioning] for most jurors because the judge asked all our questions for us."

The governor's panel, too, was "surprised" by the prosecution's disinterest in questioning to "ferret out any prejudices against the type of evidence that the State knew it would have to present. It is the State Attorney's position that the Court asked all of the necessary questions and that, as a strategic or tactical maneuver, their actions in this case were not inappropriate. Not a single lawyer-member of this committee agrees with this analysis."

Attorneys often use voir dire to build a personal relationship with a juror, and if they don't feel that relationship developing, they can move to dismiss the person. "You put them at ease," Carhart said. "You're not supposed to 'condition' the jury, but you can certainly establish a relationship" with panelists by dialogues of questions and answers.

Laeser, the veteran prosecutor, viewed such questioning as central to any trial. "I cannot fathom why 'no questions' would ever be the choice of any party to a trial. You get to establish rapport — gauge eye contact, body language, juror interactions — a world of information used in striking jurors." Laeser's strategy was to milk his discussions with prospects as much as possible. "For example, I'll ask every single juror about their feelings about guns. It doesn't have to be a gun case. This [McDuffie] wasn't a gun case. But their feelings about guns tells me a lot about them. How they view the world. Once I do that, then I play them one against the other. 'Well, miss so and so, you're going to be sitting there with this guy who has a safe full of blunderbusses, do you think you can agree?' 'One of your grandchildren found a gun? Tell me how you felt about that?' So I want to build that personal relationship with every single person I can."

In a trial with police defendants, Laeser added, it would be crucial for prosecutors to probe what a person's attitude is toward cops. Some, including at least one who ended up on the McDuffie jury, believed police could do no wrong.

In fact, the jurors noted the prosecutors' lack of questions. In an interview for this book, juror Kenneth Stover said he was puzzled by their silence during jury selection while defense attorneys spent so much time bonding with the panel. He thought prosecutors weren't trying very hard. "It seems like the prosecution didn't want to win."

• • • •

IN THE MIDDLE OF THE second week of jury selection, prosecutors were still battling to get a black person on the jury. They'd sent Phil Edgecombe, a black investigator helping them, down to look in the room where prospects waited. Of the 150 or there at the beginning of selection, perhaps 20 prospective jurors were black.

About 10 had disqualified themselves. "I sway a lot toward guilt," said Olivia Alladice. She knew about the case from newspapers and television.

That didn't surprise Edgecombe, who sat at the prosecution table during most of jury selection. He'd been assigned to do background checks on some of the prospects.

He watched as black prospects, ideal in the prosecution's mind, disqualified themselves. "They said they couldn't do it because their minds were already made up."

Edgecombe knew from his own personal experience and that of his friends and relatives that almost every black person in Florida had at least one negative encounter with police. He believed that the vast majority of black residents in 1980 in Tampa and Miami and many other places thought that white cops mistreated, even brutalized, black people at least occasionally. So when Olivia Alladice said, "I sway a lot toward guilt," she was voicing a commonly held concern.

Edgecombe thought that these black people were simply being honest, while he suspected "white jurors were saying their minds weren't made up, but they were already."

About 10 potential black jurors remained after the first go-round. Each side had 34 challenges. Simple math meant that if the defense wanted to keep black people off the jury, it could.

Years later, O'Donnell was adamant that he had no strategy to reject black potential jurors. "I would be real offended if anybody ever said that."

Still, in the courtroom, he didn't like Nettie Butler, a black woman who arrived with an umbrella. "It is my opinion that they are innocent," she said.

Usually, prosecutors have to knock off such a witness. Not this time. O'Donnell leaped to his feet to object. "I challenge for cause. She has an opinion." Off she went.

After the trial, Carlton, the non-team player, was the lone defense attorney to confess he didn't want black jurors. "A black man has to return to the community where he lives," he told the Washington Post. "I cannot believe a black man could have ignored the repercussions if he had voted for acquittal." [See notes for this chapter for a discussion about what the courts had to say later about selecting jurors based on race.]

While the prosecution remained silent, the defense kept prodding. Carhart invited each prospect to talk about race relations: "We don't always see things in black and white.... You and I could have an argument and it would have nothing to do with race, couldn't we?" He asked them if they belonged to the American Civil Liberties Union or the National Association for the Advancement of Colored People.

Finally, in the middle of the second week, attorneys started using their challenges. The defense quickly knocked off a black railroad machinist born in Jamaica; a black mother of three once booked for assault; a white, bearded 22-year-old motorcyclist; a white, cowboy-booted mechanic with a juvenile record; an unmarried white schoolteacher who lived with her parents; and a former Army nurse. Williams, the News reporter, wrote that the defense's theory was that women tended to make bad jurors in this case because they didn't like the sight of blood.

The state's rejects included a supermarket employee who'd read that McDuffie had been evading police and died when his motorcycle crashed; a communications clerk for the Tampa police department; a banker whose wife was a deputy sheriff; a female ex-flight attendant whose parents' home was once burglarized by a Mexican youth; and a 60ish unionized repairman.

Altogether, the defense booted four motorcyclists who reported bad experiences with police, while the state rejected four who stated friendly feelings toward police.

Angry at the slow pace, Nesbitt kept the process going late into the night. During one session, at 8:58 p.m., after another long day of silence by the prosecution, Carhart apologized to the panel "for the lateness of the hour."

On Tuesday, April 15, in the third week of jury selection, the defense and prosecution were running out of challenges. Four male jurors had been selected. The next two up were women. Adorno quickly accepted them. The defense team huddled. They rejected Josephine Cristiano, a secretary.

Next up was Joseph Tetreault, a retired chief petty officer and maintenance man in a Veterans Administration hospital. In an interview for this book, he said he regarded Reno as "an asshole." Adorno didn't ask him any questions. "The state accepts this panel," he told the judge.

The defense huddled again. Kogan, Del Toro's attorney, challenging the lone woman on the panel, Louise Boyette, a housewife whose son served in Vietnam.

That brought up David Draper, a one-time missionary and the son of a minister.

Both sides accepted him. At 4:40 p.m. on the 11th courtroom day, Nesbitt declared: "We have a jury."

• • • •

THE DEFENSE TEAM, EXCEPT for Carlton, had been working together to manage its challenges. With Marrero facing the most serious charges, the colleagues had been protecting O'Donnell, Marrero's attorney. By the time the panel was selected, O'Donnell was the only one with challenges left. He had three, meaning that this panel was fine with him. Adorno had at least one challenge left.

The jurors were:

THOMAS ROBERT STERNS: A budget analyst in his early 30s for the city of Tampa. He had a degree in accounting and had gotten a speeding ticket in early 1980. Born in Illinois, he grew up in Miami and graduated from Miami Edison High School in 1966, when the school was segregated. He had lived in Tampa for a decade and generally returned to Miami about once a year. He was a Methodist and member of Sertoma Club (a service club like the Lions or Rotary). He was the divorced father of one.

KENNETH STOVER: An engineer for Amoco Oil, in his mid-30s. He had a degree in business management and served previously as a juror on a criminal case. His wife was a secretary for a construction company. They had two dogs and two cats. He served on a Navy destroyer and suffered a shoulder injury. He was discharged with 30 percent disability. "It should be 10 percent. I don't play tennis anymore."

WALTER JULIUS: A retired U.S. Air Force master sergeant who left after "28 years, 13 days," he told the court. That would make him about 50. He was working as a salesperson at J.C. Penney. He grew up in Indiana. In about 1950, he was accused of statutory rape. No attorney asked for details. His son was a postal inspector, and he had grandchildren. He didn't like it when the judge said the jury was to be sequestered. His wife was already upset about his time at the courthouse. "When are you going to get home and go back to work?" she asked him.

JOSEPH TETREAULT: He'd spent 20 years in the Navy and another 20 as "a maintenance engineer" for the VA. He "repairs everything" out there. He was talkative, liked John Wayne movies. "Friendly, gum-chewing, cowboy booted, pot-bellied," the Herald described him. "He keeps a .38 Smith & Wesson in a bedroom drawer and is without expertise on a CB radio. 'I couldn't send an SOS.' When asked how he viewed Marines (McDuffie was one), he said, 'I'm a Navy man – round hat on a square head.' He was arrested once as a juvenile. 'I got caught.'"

DAVID FISHER: An FAA air traffic control computer systems specialist at Tampa International Airport. He was in his 50s, spent four years in the Marines, where he learned air traffic control. An Episcopalian, he had two children, 25 and 27, and his wife did not work outside the home. In court he carried a Reader's Digest book condensation and said he read Joseph Wambaugh police novels. He was a juror in a robbery case that ended before the jury reached a verdict. About 15 years before, he was charged in West Tennessee with "doing 61 in a 60-mile an hour zone." A justice of the peace held court in the back of a Dairy Queen and made him pay a fine on the spot. "It was pretty nasty."

DAVID DRAPER: A market administrator for Stromberg Carlson, manufacturer of carburetors. He was 39, moved to Tampa two years before. Divorced, an Episcopalian, he was the son of a minister of the Reorganized Latter Day Saints church. He had a year of postgraduate study in the history of speech education at Syracuse University. Seven years before, he received three speeding tickets. His 16-year-old son had been recently charged with possession of stolen property. It was resolved without going to court.

• • • •

THE DEFENSE WAS ECSTATIC. Four of the six were government employees. The other two worked for large corporations. Two were career military. Two others had been in the service, one a disabled vet. The defense believed these jurors were accustomed to respecting men in uniform and would be naturally sympathetic to cops working a Sunday night shift in the worst part of town. They were also likely to sympathize with government employees trapped in a big politically charged department, a theme the defense planned to hammer on during the trial.

Kogan said "the prosecutors chose a jury which under ordinary circumstances would be an excellent prosecution jury. They were hard-working citizens of the community — people who were quite frankly the type of jury you would want if you had real criminals on trial. In other words, this type of jury would always be favorable to the testimony of police officers. People who like law enforcement don't like people who take police officers on a wild chase on a motorcycle."

"Old habits die hard," Carhart said of the prosecution's selections. "They picked a law-and-order jury," which naturally sympathized with police. "They understand how difficult their jobs are. They understand the snap decisions that have to be made. They understand dealing with the public can be a real bear. If I were picking a jury in this case, as a prosecutor... I'd be looking for people who had grievances with the police, like hippies." Carhart said the defense went for law-and-order types all along. "And the interesting thing is the prosecution never discerned that. They were scratching their heads at the jurors we were excusing, because they were typical street guys," the type defense attorneys generally want for juries.

Following the verdicts, reporters asked Adorno if he'd do anything differently. Yes, he said. "I'd get a different jury."

"We wanted a black on that jury as badly as they didn't want one," Yoss said. When he realized that wasn't possible, "we tried to get the best six we could." Still, as the selection process went on, "we ended up with six people we wouldn't have ordinarily picked in this case. We had no choice.... I always viewed one of the biggest problems we had in the case was the jury.... When that jury got sworn, we knew that wasn't a great jury for us. Would have been a great jury in any other case." About the defense being ecstatic on the jurors selected, Yoss said, "I don't blame them."

That was the take, too, of Shinhoster, the Tribune reporter: "A very pro-police jury."

Laeser, the longtime Reno prosecutor, said: "With military veterans, they're likely to think, 'Yeah, I had tough times when I was in the service and things like that too.'" For McDuffie, the state needed "little people who think they've been screwed their whole lives.... You know, they screwed them on their taxes, or there was some zoning thing that really upset them, or they gave them a citation for selling beer after 11 or whatever where they think the government oversteps its bounds."

But Laeser acknowledged that there might not be a lot of folks like that in a jury pool for a long trial. Almost half of the original Tampa pool didn't even make it to the courtroom. "If you walk in one day and hear this trial may take as much as two months, every hand goes up. 'Holy smokes!' 'I've got to do this' 'I've got to do that.' 'My daughter's wedding is coming up.' So there's a huge number that get excused for hardship reasons."

That was true in Tampa, and it would have been true if a jury had been selected in Miami, where Laeser practiced for more than three decades. "There was a time when half of my jurors were either Eastern Airlines or National Airlines people [or] worked for the post office. They had the time. They were getting paid for it. It was better than actually slogging to work every day. It was something new and enjoyable. The people at the bottom end cannot do that. The guys working on the roof next door, they can't spend two months doing something else. They're broke. And the executive will walk in with a note from his doctor saying that sitting on wooden chairs will give him hemorrhoids. And he'd like to be excused. And what you're left with are the people who don't have a really good excuse for getting off jury duty."

James Lees, the ex-officer and prosecutor who consults on jury selection, agreed with the critics that it's crucial for trial attorneys to talk to potential jurors. "Perhaps the easiest way to understand jury selection in this case is to ask yourself: If you had a typical crime to prosecute, would you as the prosecutor want a jury of Rush Limbaughs and Bill O'Reillys or would you want a jury of Rachel Maddows and Elizabeth Warrens? Of course, you want the tough law and order jury —in most cases. But NOT in this case." *[Chapter Notes](#)

Chapter 14
"A Time Bomb in the Briefcase"

On Thursday, April 17, with the newly formed jury ready to hear opening arguments, an explosive development sent the case into disarray. The battle raged outside the jurors' hearing, but it was an indication of problems to come.

The drama began at 8 the night before when Carhart was taking the deposition of George Slattery, a polygraph examiner often used by Reno's office. He tested several persons in the McDuffie case, including a City of Miami police officer, Alexander Prince. Carhart asked Slattery what Prince had told him. Slattery stopped the deposition and phoned Adorno. Adorno told him not to answer.

In court the next morning, defense attorneys barraged the judge with objections to Adorno blocking their questions. Adorno gave a lengthy, complicated response.

The issue boiled down to this: Because Judge Nesbitt had insisted in trying the case as quickly as possible, attorneys had been scrambling at night even while working long days in the courtroom to select a jury. Prosecutors were trying to bolster their case. Defense lawyers raced to complete depositions of potential state witnesses. The polygraph operator was one of those. The defense wanted to know whom he'd interviewed. One of those he named was new to the defense: Officer Prince.

Prince, a city cop, had been at the scene along with several other city cops, Adorno explained to the judge. In his first interview, Prince had told Frank that he hadn't seen anything that would help the prosecution, but investigators and prosecutors thought he knew more than what he was saying. While jury selection was going on, a Miami Beach policewoman, Lynn Hackworth, sent a message to Adorno that Prince did know more.

Adorno spoke to Prince and his lawyer. The lawyer said Prince wanted to testify under a grant of immunity. Adorno insisted that Prince first make a sworn statement, then take a lie-detector test. Prince agreed. On Tuesday, as lawyers were using their final juror challenges, Yoss talked to Prince, which led to Slattery meeting with Prince on Tuesday night, Adorno explained.

Like almost all polygraph operators, Slattery used a pre-test interview with the subject to establish what questions would be asked during the polygraph. During that interview, Adorno told the court, Prince "made the statement for the first time that he kicked Arthur McDuffie in the head to get a shot in." As soon as he said that, immunity was no longer a consideration. The polygraph test was not administered. Prince now was pleading the Fifth Amendment.

After Adorno's explanation, the defense erupted with more objections. The lawyers demanded the trial be put on hold until they could question Prince and the polygraph operator in depth. It was quite possible, they argued, that someone not on trial could have struck one of the fatal blows.

"Little did we know that a time bomb in the briefcase of the State of Florida was set to go off just as the curtain was rising," Carlton declared. If an unindicted officer had smashed McDuffie's head, "this is the key to the entire case."

Carhart complained about Adorno blocking an answer in a deposition. "Adorno can't tell the witness that," he told the judge. Carhart said he planned to call Prince as a defense witness.

Judge Nesbitt told everyone to calm down. She ordered prosecutors to turn over Prince's statement to the defense. She said she wouldn't allow any witness to be called if the person planned to plead the Fifth. The trial was to proceed without interruption.

Still, the scenario revealed the state's desperate need to corroborate the three already-immunized witnesses because prosecutors feared these witnesses were about to present big problems when they testified. Instead, Adorno and Yoss uncovered yet another problem: A new bad guy who hit McDuffie "just to get a shot in." And then Adorno tried to hide the revelation from the defense.

In fact, in the sworn statement to Yoss, Prince had said he'd seen an officer strike McDuffie hard in the head with a Kel-Lite or nightstick. He couldn't identify the officer, but he understood what was happening: The cops were dispensing "street justice," which Prince defined as "something that's usually given either verbally or physically to reassure the defendant that he had in fact committed a crime and that even though legally something might not be done toward him, that he was not getting away with it in the eyes of the police officers."

• • • •

DURING A BREAK IN THE lengthy hearing about Prince, juror Tetreault, the ex-chief petty officer, wanted to talk to the judge. He was "mad" because his name was in the newspaper. His wife had seen his name and cried, "Oh my God, what kind of an article is this?" He said he didn't read it himself. "But somebody ought to control the newspapers."

"I don't think I'll make a good juror," he told the judge. She asked him if he could continue to be fair and impartial. His mood shifted instantly. He said he could. "I'm one of the best jurors you've had and probably got. If you want me to stay, judge, I'll stay." *Chapter Notes

Chapter 15
"One-Sided War"

After almost three weeks in Tampa, George Yoss finally made the state's opening statement on Friday, April 18.

At the crucial moment on the night of December 17, he said, "the evidence is going to show that Arthur McDuffie wasn't talking. He wasn't saying anything. He wasn't moving. He wasn't fighting.... He especially wasn't reaching for anybody's gun."

Yoss walked from the podium toward the defense table. "And the evidence is going to show that this man right here, Alex Marrero, declared one-sided war against Arthur McDuffie."

In pointing to Marrero, Yoss accidently touched the shoulder of O'Donnell, Marrero's attorney. Yoss murmured "excuse me." O'Donnell nodded.

"And he stood there over him," Yoss continued, walking back toward the lectern, "with the man handcuffed with his hands behind his back and picked up his nightstick or Kel-Lite and pulled it over his head and struck him, right on the head — not once, not twice, but three times. And the second time he struck him, he struck him so hard blood splattered in excess of four feet away."

Yoss had set up a large green board by the jury box to explain, one by one, the 13 charges against the five defendants. As he talked, he left a small lectern in the center of the well and strolled about. Jury selection had been in Courtroom 2, a fairly small, utilitarian space. Staring with Yoss' opening statement, the trial moved to the larger Courtroom 3, a birch-paneled, windowless room on the third floor, at the end of a long corridor, with a linoleum floor and a judge's bench of varnished beechwood. It held up to 110 spectators. From their standpoint, the jury box was to the right. Beside the jurors, facing the judge, was the prosecution table with three attorneys. On the left wall, facing the jurors, were two defense tables. The "non-thumper" team, Carhart and Kogan, with their clients Evans and Del Toro, sat at the one closest to the judge.

This narrative of the trial is based on the clips of one television station, WTVJ Channel 4 Miami, and six print accounts: The Miami Herald, Miami News, Tampa Tribune, St. Petersburg Times, the Sentinel Star of Orlando and the Associated Press. Their articles generally didn't follow a chronological narrative, but concentrated on the highlights of each day's testimony, and they invariably put the most interesting bits at the top of their stories. The headline in the Herald, for example, was "Prosecutor: McDuffie Yelled 'I Give Up,'" based on the testimony Meier was about to give, a revelation that Yoss made in the middle of his remarks.

But with Yoss' opening argument of almost two hours, the Herald reported that the prosecutor began by "slowly, softly," reading the police reports of the chase, then two follow-up reports about a motorcycle accident, McDuffie's helmet flying off and then the motorcyclist resisting arrest.

"These reports are lies," Yoss told the jurors. "Everything is not true. They made them all up.... The bike was still standing up. There was never an accident. The helmet never was flying off. McDuffie was not injured in any accident." Yoss described the damage done to the motorcycle to make it look like an accident.

The cops at the scene knew the accident was a lie, but "there is no tighter fraternity than the police fraternity. There's a code.... The evidence is going to show these people lived by the code. And Skip Evans was teaching the code. And that is you don't turn in another fellow officer. You don't rat on a cop. But thank God not all police live by that code."

The courtroom was crowded with journalists, black activists, family members and spectators who were just plain curious. People groaned and murmured when Yoss described what the violent blows did to McDuffie's skull. The judge admonished spectators to keep quiet. One of those moaning was Eula Bell McDuffie, Arthur's mother. Someone on the prosecution team noticed her and whispered to a bailiff, who escorted her out. As a potential witness, she was not supposed to be listening to the proceedings.

Yoss described how a mob of "five to seven" officers surrounded McDuffie and pummeled him, and a second row of cop was trying to reach over the first row to get some shots in too. No journalist, lawyer or juror was ever to re-examine that statement, but that was a problematic number. Three ex-officers were on trial for hitting McDuffie. Two immunized witnesses admitted they hit McDuffie. That made five. And then there was Prince, the Miami cop who wanted "to get a shot in." At this point, it wasn't clear whether the jurors would hear about him. But a second row? That implied participants who were neither witnesses nor defendants.

As he went on, Yoss slipped in negative details that he knew the defense would bring out. "He [McDuffie] had no felony past, only traffic violations. He was driving without a license." He also admitted to the jurors that they could expect to hear bad things about the state's immunized witnesses: Veverka had thrown a punch and Hanlon had demonstrated how to break McDuffie's legs and smashed his watch. But at least they were now telling the truth about a brutal, unnecessary beating.

After describing the chase, Yoss concluded, "What happened in the next minute and a half will consume the next six weeks. To us it will seem like an eternity."

These were words that the jurors, to be confined to hotel rooms for the duration, must not have enjoyed hearing. In fact, Yoss overestimated. The trial was to take another four weeks. As it was, when Yoss concluded, the jurors were sent off to their hotel rooms to spend the weekend. It would be Monday before they got to hear the defense's views.

When the jurors left, defense attorneys filed a flurry of motions. Kogan asked once again that Del Toro's charges be thrown out. He said Yoss' argument lasted one hour, 45 minutes. "I timed all reference to my client, Del Toro, and if they exceeded 10 seconds, I'll eat my hat. I can't get a fair trial." *Chapter Notes

Chapter 16
Witch Hunts and Scapegoats

On Monday, April 21, the defense's theme quickly became apparent: The media and the black community pressured a highly politicized police department and state attorney's office to find scapegoats in a rushed, flawed investigation. The cops were really heroes struggling to protect the public in the "Combat Zone." The real culprits were the state's own witnesses.

Four lawyers spoke for an hour each. The fifth, Kogan, made the briefest of opening statements. He said Del Toro blew a tire and was late to the scene. He didn't see anything. He was not involved in a "common scheme," as charged. He hid nothing. He lied about nothing. "There is no evidence against him whatsoever. That's it in a nutshell."

In a booming voice, O'Donnell opened for the defense. He left a yellow legal pad with his notes on a podium in the center of the room and paced right in front of the jury box. He said Marrero was the victim of a "terrible, terrible witch hunt... No crime ever occurred."

O'Donnell was the first — but not the last — defense lawyer to say that the LaFleur wrong-house raid was the reason that they were in this Tampa courtroom. He said police at the LaFleur house "did nothing wrong at all" but came under ferocious "media attack." He told the jury the Miami Herald demanded access to Internal Affairs reports and published them. The newspaper "pushed and prodded" for prosecution.

"Nothing wrong at all" was quite a stretch for the LaFleur affair: The police had raided the wrong house and beaten the occupants. No criminal charges were filed against them, but the PSD did suspend most of them as punishment for their blunders. Of course, Tampa jurors had no way of knowing that.

Because of the LaFleur case, O'Donnell went on, Sheriff Purdy was fired to appease the media. But that wasn't enough, and when the McDuffie case came along, police and prosecutors felt they needed to act quickly — and they did, screwing up the investigation, giving the wrong people immunity, but "the big boys at The Herald were happy."

O'Donnell described how Marrero, who arrived from Cuba at age 7, was an exceptionally dedicated officer working in a dangerous area. One of his friends, a fellow officer, had been killed by a black man he was trying to arrest. Less than a year before, "Marrero came off shift and gave the key to his patrol car to a young officer. At 2 p.m. that same day, the officer was dead and his backup man was left a mental and physical cripple." In another incident, Marrero tried to arrest a man and ended up rolling on a floor of broken bottles. Three times he had been shot at in the Combat Zone.

On the night of the motorcycle chase, Marrero arrived to see "an absolute melee.... a man single-handedly taking on several police officers. He saw a scene totally out of control." Marrero rushed to help. He admitted: "I hit this man. I hit him as hard as I could. I hit him with what I had in my hands [a nightstick]. I hit him all over his body."

Prosecutors ignored what really happened, O'Donnell maintained, and they forced fellow officers to falsely accuse Marrero "to save their own necks." The state charged Marrero with manslaughter, but that wasn't enough. "A black community leader by the name of Don Kelly said, 'Well, all you need to show a murder is a body in the graveyard. Somebody should be charged with murder.' Lo and behold, one day... I get a phone call. 'Bring Alex Marrero down. We're charging him with murder.'" He blamed the second-degree murder charge on the state attorney's office "bending to the whim and the will of the powerful media."

O'Donnell said a state witness would tell jurors that McDuffie resisted, putting up "the most intense" battle he had ever seen. "Officer Charles Veverka will tell you that he threw a punch square to the jaw of Arthur McDuffie and it didn't even shake him. He will tell you that McDuffie began to fight like hell."

This was an extraordinary moment. At the very beginning of the trial, the defense was using the prosecution's lead witness as a key part of its argument. O'Donnell was emphasizing a major weakness in the state's case, the same one that bothered Frank in homicide: If McDuffie started by putting up a battle, then it was a natural defense that the officers were simply trying to subdue him. Prosecutors maintained that at some point McDuffie was subdued, on the ground, and then Marrero's blows became criminal, but their challenge was to sell jurors on when and how that transition took place.

• • • •

MCWILLIAMS DESCRIBED his client, Ira Diggs, as a "sacrificial lamb," a victim of internal politics. Diggs and Bowlin, the Central District commander, had both applied to be director of the PSD, and Bowlin wanted Diggs out of the way. Under pressure from the media, the leaders of the PSD needed to charge officers for McDuffie's murder. Those who conducted this witch hunt, McWilliams said, were promoted: Linda Saunders, who conducted the internal review, was raised from sergeant to commander. Captain Bowlin became Chief Bowlin. And Bobby Jones was made the permanent PSD director.

McWilliams praised Diggs for leading "a life of control and discipline in uniform." He said a tape of the motorcycle chase showed Diggs was "cool-headed and professional" as he had been in Vietnam, where he was wounded six times.

Concerning the McDuffie chase, McWilliams said, Diggs thought the motorcycle had crashed, but then McDuffie resisted ferociously. Diggs tried to grab McDuffie's feet and was knocked back. Diggs "was breathing heavily, looked like he was having a heart attack. He was in severe pain." Diggs ended up going to the hospital.

• • • •

CARLTON SAID ONLY ONE of 90 state witnesses claimed that Michael Watts hit McDuffie and that witness wouldn't "bet his life on it."

Apologizing for getting emotional, Carlton talked about the "thankless job" police perform. "They face the gun. They face the fist. And now they face the jury. They risk their very life to save someone on the street."

Carlton told jurors that city police were also at the scene. "And suddenly you will hear that Alexander Prince has admitted —"

Yoss shouted an objection.

The judge sent the jurors out, then asked what Carlton planned to say.

"I was about to say that Alexander Prince kicked McDuffie in the head."

The judge said Prince had taken the Fifth Amendment. He was not going to be a witness. Adorno said jurors would hear about Prince's statement only if the state called Slattery, the polygraph operator. "And we're not calling Slattery."

Nesbitt ordered Carlton not to say anything about Prince. Still, the jurors had heard that someone, presumably another officer not on trial, had admitted something that the judge didn't want them to hear.

• • • •

SPEAKING FOR HIS CLIENT, Herb Evans, Carhart focused on the immunized witnesses and McDuffie himself. Speaking softly, methodically, he said: "If anyone in this world committed a crime, the two prime candidates for that dishonor are Charles Veverka Jr. and William Hanlon.... Never will those men ever stand trial — for murder, manslaughter, aggravated assault — not now, not ever."

He explained that Veverka was the son of police lieutenant. He was the first to "get religion. The state would have you believe that no deal was cut for Charlie Jr. with his daddy. And then miracle of miracles, Mark Meier admits... perjury, and guess what? He wasn't charged." After these two officers struck deals, "Hanlon couldn't flip fast enough."

The other culprit was Arthur McDuffie, Carhart argued. He "did not give a damn for life on the morning he died. I don't know that he had a death wish or was he seeking to destroy himself."

Carhart said Evans learned from police radio that there had been an accident. When he got to the scene, he saw an officer smash the motorcycle. According to Carhart, Evans yelled at the officer to stop, shouting "Knock it off."

At the scene, Carhart went on, Veverka told Evans that the motorcycle crashed and McDuffie landed on his head. Veverka thought his squad car might have hit the Kawasaki. Hanlon said he slammed into a median and damaged his car trying to avoid the motorcycle. That led to Evans putting in his report that McDuffie had assaulted an officer with a deadly weapon.

Later, Evans went to Jackson Memorial Hospital and heard doctors say McDuffie's head injuries couldn't come from only from an accident. Carhart said Evans related the information to Captain Bowlin, who said he didn't want Evans' "uneducated opinions." Bowlin ordered Evans to "shut his face."

This exchange between Evans and his captain was never substantiated during the trial. Evans didn't testify. Bowlin did, and he gave a completely different account of his conversations with Evans.

Carhart talked about another defendant — Del Toro. He said that Del Toro was not his client, but he advised jurors to pay close attention to that name. Del Toro was late to arrive at the scene because he had a flat tire. Del Toro's name, Carhart predicted, would very rarely be mentioned by the state's witnesses. Clearly, Del Toro was going to be declared not guilty. "And if he's innocent, how many of these other people are innocent?"

James Lees, the ex-prosecutor, noted: "The most crucial things that happen in a trial that sets the course for decision making of jurors are the opening statements. It is here that lawyers get to paint a picture of the story of the case. Jurors listen and will adopt a short story of the case. What story is adopted matters a great deal. During the course of the trial, it will be difficult for the opposing side to dislodge that story.

"In this case, the prosecution spent much of their opening on describing the testimony of immunized witnesses, who were about to come under withering attack. The defense attorneys created the theme of 'rush to judgment' years before the O.J. Simpson case for good reason: It not only fit the facts of this case but it is a winning story. Fundamental fairness is the touchstone for American jurors. People serving on juries will not convict people if they believe there has been something less than a fair investigation… And as far as I can glean from this opening statement, the prosecutor had little in the way of a comeback to this claim by the defense." *Chapter Notes

Chapter 17
"Splattered with Blood"

On Tuesday, April 22, three weeks and a day after the trial began, the first witness, Charles Veverka Jr., strode into court dressed in a dark brown suit and carrying a briefcase stuffed with four volumes of his previous statements.

Under Yoss' questioning, he used a pointer to trace the route of the chase on a large street map set on an easel. Near the end of the chase, he heard three rapid shots. "I slowed down a little bit.... The motorcyclist slowed down. Meier slowed down."

Veverka was the first to reach McDuffie. He jumped out of his squad car and ran toward the motorcyclist, who was seated on the stationary Kawasaki. He saw McDuffie's "right hand coming back to the right handlebar where the accelerator is."

To stop him from escaping, Veverka yanked him off the motorcycle. He said McDuffie swung at him with a closed fist. The fist "brushed against my cheek."

Yoss: "What did you do when his fist grazed your cheek?"

Veverka: "I came back and hit him."

"Did you hit him with your right hand or your left hand?"

"My right hand."

"Did you hit him hard or soft?"

"Hard."

"How hard?"

"As hard as I could."

Veverka said the blow "didn't faze him at all."

Veverka put his arms around McDuffie and pulled him off the motorcycle. "I felt something bump my gun. I don't know if he was trying to get it." Veverka swung his arms down to separate McDuffie from the gun.

Other squad cars pulled up. At least a half-dozen county officers charged at McDuffie. "It appeared to me he was gang-tackled by a football team." McDuffie fell to the pavement, then popped back up. He saw Sergeant Diggs strike McDuffie "in the chest area" with a Kel-Lite or nightstick.

Altogether, Veverka estimated, the cops struck McDuffie 10 to 12 times. He said he saw Del Toro swing at McDuffie with a "closed fist," but wasn't certain whether the blow landed. At this point, Veverka said, he stepped back. "Enough officers were there."

Moments later, Veverka said, the situation changed. Some cops were doing more than was necessary. "I saw him hit in the head." Veverka tried to grab McDuffie by the jacket and pull him away from the group. When he reached for the motorcyclist, he got hit on the hand by William Hanlon's Kel-Lite. He heard Marrero yell: "Easy, one at a time."

Yoss: "Was he moving? Struggling?"

"No sir." He said the hardest blows came from Marrero. "I observed him with either a Kel-Lite or a nightstick holding up with both hands and bringing it down on the top back area of Mr. McDuffie's head twice."

"How hard did he hit him?"

"Uh, extremely hard."

To demonstrate the blows by Marrero, Veverka got down from the witness stand. He clasped his hands together, raised them high above his head and then swung them straight down. Once. Twice. Three times. McDuffie was prone on the pavement. "I was standing four or five feet east of Mr. McDuffie and Mr. Marrero. I got splattered with blood."

"Did he move between the blows?"

"No sir."

"Was he wearing a helmet?"

"No, sir."

"Was he reaching for a gun? Moving in any way?"

"No, sir."

All this action, Veverka estimated, happened in "possibly 30 or 45 seconds" after he arrived. He said he wasn't sure if McDuffie was handcuffed at the time of Marrero's blows.

After the beating, he wanted "to get the area cleaned up as fast as we could and get out of there... I observed for the first time Sergeant Evans on the scene."

"What happened then?"

"I heard, um, Sergeant Evans say something. These words are not exact but as best as I could recall it was, um, the bike needs more damage and go into the car and ride up on it. [Then I] saw a marked police unit on top of the motorcycle."

"Who was driving the car?"

"Officer Hanlon." He said Hanlon used Del Toro's car. Then "Sergeant Evans came over to me and advised me to write the incident as far as Mr. McDuffie's injuries that Mr. McDuffie had hit the curb while turning a corner with the motorcycle. When he hit the curb, he came dislodged from his motorcycle and flown up in the air, his helmet came off."

Veverka said he saw Evans toss the cyclist's keys over his left shoulder, the keys landing on a nearby roof.

At Yoss' request, bailiffs wheeled a dolly into the courtroom with a shape covered by a quilt. The quilt was removed to reveal the orange-and-black Kawasaki 900. The prosecutor asked Veverka if this was the bike McDuffie was riding that night. Veverka opened his briefcase and pulled out a report. He consulted that for a moment, then said yes.

Yoss asked if the bike looked the same as when he pulled McDuffie off. No, Veverka said. There were scratches on the gas tank. The headlight and taillight were broken. The license plate was bent, the front hand brake twisted.

Yoss showed Veverka a white helmet. It was scratched, with dark splotches on it. He identified it as McDuffie's. "The chin strap appeared to be cut off," Veverka said.

Throughout his testimony, defense lawyers kept bouncing up with objections. Carlton's main concern was that the Kawasaki was parked too close to the jurors. He objected to them being able to read the identification tag: "Homicide."

On Evans' orders, Veverka said, he wrote a report that McDuffie had crashed, his helmet flew off and he'd slammed his head on the pavement. After the sergeant went to the hospital, Evans said Veverka needed to change his report, because the injuries to McDuffie's head couldn't have been caused only by an accident: "He told me we had to admit we hit him with nightsticks and Kel-Lites." Veverka rewrote the report to show McDuffie fought with the officers and they had to subdue him. He added charges against McDuffie: battery on a police officer and resisting arrest with violence.

Yoss admitted both accident reports into evidence. Veverka told jurors both were "untrue."

Later, Veverka said, he met Marrero at the Central District station. Marrero said he'd shot at McDuffie. He locked his gun in his car because he hadn't had time to clean it.

On the day McDuffie died, Veverka said, Evans "told me it [the report] had to be rewritten. 'See Sergeant Diggs.' Sergeant Diggs told me he was not one of the first officers on scene. He said he was one of the last on the scene." Veverka rewrote the report again.

Veverka said Evans told him that if he'd been at the scene, he would have stopped the beating by shooting into the air. Veverka said the only way to have stopped the melee was by shooting a police officer. "Well, it's too late now," Evans replied. "We'll just have to stick to our story."

Diggs, the other sergeant at the scene, also told him "to stick to our stories," Veverka testified.

• • • •

VEVERKA'S DIRECT TESTIMONY took most of a day. His cross-examination occupied the next two. The thrust of the defense was that Veverka was a professional liar who would say anything to please the prosecutors and stay out of jail. He admitted he had lied on seven written reports in the McDuffie case: Two incident reports, three arrest reports and two accident reports. Veverka remained calm throughout, answering questions slowly, precisely, without visible annoyance. He had been on the witness stand 200 times before, testifying mostly in drug cases that he worked on during his two-and-a-half years as an undercover narcotics agent.

That experience undercover made fodder for the defense. McWilliams asked Veverka whether he lied during his undercover roles.

"I considered lying on the street part of my job."

"It became a daily thing to lie, right?"

"I wouldn't say daily."...

"You were a professional liar out on the street?"

"I wouldn't say that."

"How long did it take for you to become a professional liar?"

Yoss leaped up: "Don't answer that!" He told the judge that question was out of line. Nesbitt sustained the objection.

McWilliams read to Veverka from his original statement to Yoss in December, when he'd said McDuffie "resisted more than any other person" he had ever confronted. He didn't recall making that statement.

The lawyer wanted to know more about Veverka's stating he saw Diggs hit McDuffie on the chest.

McWilliams: "Do you consider that justifiable force?"

Veverka: "Yes."

McWilliams: "You didn't see anything illegal about that?"

Veverka: "No."

McWilliams: "You never saw Sergeant Diggs strike the subject in the head?"

Veverka: "No, sir."

The lawyer then scored another major point when he asked Veverka, who had dealt with doped-up subjects as an undercover cop, if he thought McDuffie was high that night. "I don't know, but it wouldn't surprise me," Veverka replied.

McWilliams asked Veverka to read his lengthy immunity agreement. It included the state's promise not to prosecute for accessory after the fact, manslaughter, tampering with evidence or perjury.

McWilliams, almost shouting: "Perjury?"

Veverka: "For the Internal Affairs statement."

McWilliams pressed him to explain the lies that he told Sergeant Linda Saunders. "I know I lied to Internal Affairs," Veverka said. "You're asking me if I worried about lying to Internal Affairs. No, I didn't."

Why had Veverka written that Diggs was first on the scene, then that Diggs was one of the last to arrive? Because he was ordered to, Veverka replied. "Just about everything in here is a lie."

There were other scattershot accusations.

"You volunteered for the Combat Zone because you like violence, don't you?"

No, he didn't like violence.

What about the botched investigation? "Did the experienced prosecutors ask you to give them your bloody shirt so they could have it analyzed?" (As with all these questions, the defense knew from the depositions what the answers were.)

No, Veverka said. They didn't ask for his clothes.

When it was Carlton's turn, he asked about his client, Watts. Veverka said he hadn't seen him at the scene.

Carlton: "Didn't you carry a pocketknife in that briefcase the night of December 17? And didn't you cut the chin strap of the motorcyclist's helmet?"

No, he didn't cut the chin strap.

Carlton, the non-team player who liked lengthy cross-examinations, kept burrowing in, seeking details about how Marrero hammered the unresisting McDuffie. This was the kind of tactic that the other four lawyers didn't want to see.

Carhart and O'Donnell objected.

"This is repetitious," Nesbitt decided.

The almost-forgotten fifth defendant, Del Toro, was virtually nonexistent in Veverka's account. Kogan, Del Toro's attorney, questioned him only briefly. He brought out that Veverka never mentioned Del Toro in first three statements to investigators and prosecutors.

Kogan: "Then on January 31, you decided at that time you remembered Officer Del Toro swinging his fist at him."

Veverka: "Yes, sir."

In that belated statement, Veverka said: "I believe I did see him strike at Mr. McDuffie but he might not have made contact."

Kogan brought out that Veverka remembered that just a day before the state charged Del Toro.

• • • •

ON THE SECOND DAY OF Veverka's cross-examination, it was O'Donnell's and Carhart's turn.

O'Donnell: "When you went to Internal Affairs, and swore an oath to God to tell the truth, was that the first time in your life that you had ever knowingly, intentionally and willfully lied under oath?"

Veverka: "That is correct."

O'Donnell shifted to the dried brown spots of what appeared to be blood found inside McDuffie's helmet. "Do you know whether or not Mr. McDuffie was involved in a prior altercation in a bar that evening or during the early morning hours in a bar when struck by a cue?"

Veverka: "I don't know about that, no sir."

O'Donnell: "Have you heard of that?"

Yoss objected. The judge sustained. Throughout the trial, the defense kept dropping occasional suggestions about a possible barroom brawl, without any evidence that McDuffie had been in a bar that night.

O'Donnell moved on to other subjects. "Weren't you calling him a nigger that night?"

Veverka: "I might very well have."

O'Donnell: "Couldn't a fleeing motorcyclist pitch away contraband during a high-speed chase?"

Veverka: "I've had that happen."

Had he heard Sergeant Evans tell Sergeant Saunders to "check out this guy" for drug tests "because he was on something? And no blood test was taken, was it?"

Veverka said he understood that in the hospital McDuffie was given blood transfusions, negating any testing for drugs.

O'Donnell emphasized that Veverka told Yoss that McDuffie had battled ferociously against a half-dozen police officers. "Was this man behaving the way you would have expected an insurance executive to behave?"

Veverka acknowledged that McDuffie's behavior appeared "irrational."

Why was Captain Marshall Frank "brought out of mothballs" to conduct the homicide investigation? Veverka didn't know.

Wasn't Veverka's father, Lieutenant Charles Veverka Sr., a good friend of Frank's? "They know each other," Veverka replied. He also acknowledged that Marrero had told him that he hit McDuffie because the motorcyclist was going for his gun.

"Did McDuffie ever say, 'I give up,' curl up in a fetal position and say he had enough?"

"I don't recall that."

In fact, as O'Donnell well knew, "I give up!" was to be the core testimony of the next witness.

• • • •

AS WITH OTHER WITNESSES, Carhart was the last to cross-examine Veverka. At first, he focused on Evans, his client. Before Evans arrived, hadn't Veverka seen officers "vandalize" McDuffie's motorcycle?

Veverka said he had.

Carhart: "And you didn't arrest them? You didn't intervene? Were you afraid to?"

Veverka: "I didn't care to."

Carhart: "You didn't want to enforce the law? If a bystander had vandalized the motorcycle, you would? You enforce one law for policemen, your friends, and another for ordinary citizens?"

Veverka insisted it was Sergeant Evans who ordered most of the damage.

As McWilliams had done, Carhart asked Veverka to read his lengthy immunity agreement word-for-word. In effect, Carhart said, Veverka had to "stick to the state's story" or his immunity deal would be cancelled, while the state had put his client, Evans, on trial on the allegation that he demanded the squad "stick to the story."

"You have a license to lie for the state, don't you?" Carhart said.

Yoss leaped up and shouted: "I will immunize him right now for any statement he wants to change on anything."

The other defense attorneys shouted objections.

Judge Nesbitt: "Now, Mr. Yoss, that is an improper statement.... And you know it is improper. And in the presence of the jury.... You are admonished. Sit down, Mr. Yoss!"

When Carhart finished his cross-examination and the jury was dismissed, defense attorneys demanded a mistrial based on Yoss' outburst. O'Donnell complained that Yoss interrupted because he knew Veverka was in trouble and he wanted to give the witness time to compose himself. Veverka was "on the ropes," O'Donnell said, "and he did it to cut Mr. Carhart off."

Adorno spoke for Yoss: "He apologizes to the court. But to put it in proper perspective, he was led to it by the defense."

• • • •

AFTER THE TRIAL, CARHART said he believed Yoss' "license to lie" blowup was a key moment in getting jurors to doubt the immunized witnesses. "You walk into a prosecutor's office to get immunity, you can pretty well figure out what they want to hear," said Carhart, whose years as lead prosecutor gave him plenty of experience on how state witnesses behave. When Yoss erupted, Carhart recalled, he "got so angry... that he came at me physically as though he were going to attack me."

No juror cited the "license to lie" exchange after the trial, but the four who talked publicly said they didn't believe the immunized witnesses, and this exchange could well be one of the reasons.

In his three days on the witness stand, Veverka said plenty about Marrero's blows and Evans orchestrating a coverup. But he had little, if anything, to say about the other three defendants. He hadn't seen Watts at all. He considered Diggs' blows "justified" and "not illegal," though he mentioned briefly Diggs had urged him to stick with the fake story. And he hadn't said anything about Del Toro in his first three statements, then remembered only that Del Toro threw a punch that might have missed. In fact, Del Toro wasn't charged with hitting McDuffie, only with being "an accessory after the fact."

On the other hand, the impression Veverka left on the jury was far from impeccable. He'd hit McDuffie as hard as he could, might have called the motorcyclist a nigger, lied in seven reports and been gifted by the state with "a license to lie." All those lies set up a natural defense closing argument: "If he lied so many times before, what's to say he's not lying now?"

What's more, he admitted that McDuffie might have been irrational and high on drugs, helping explain why so many officers were needed to subdue him. And he wouldn't confirm or deny that he'd once said McDuffie "resisted more than any other person" he had ever confronted.

And this was the state's first witness — the prosecution putting its best foot forward, as it were.

James Lees, the ex-prosecutor, commented: "Young prosecutors lack the experience and temperament to hold their emotions in check during trials against experienced defense attorneys who are adept at baiting young prosecutors. Here is another example revealing that the government [made] major blunders in granting immunity far too soon, and now chose to put on the witness stand as their first witness someone who admitted lying repeatedly. First impressions matter, and the government chose a terrible witness to lead off the trial.

"Prosecutors made matters far worse by beginning the direct examination with the traffic stop of McDuffie," Lees went on. "The main fact that would lead jurors to form a story about bad police officers comes from the coverup, and Veverka should have been asked first about all the false reports, why were they created, what was his role in creating them, etc. The coverup should have been Act I, Scene I, but it was not.

"Prosecutor Yoss could not have made a more damaging statement in front of the jurors (who were at that time still creating their initial story about the case) than blurting out, 'I will immunize him right now for any statement he wants to change.' How would jurors actually hear this statement?" Lees wrote. "They would hear a prosecutor saying this witness could continue to change his story as many times as he wished, and the government would never hold him accountable for such behavior. Never....

"Consider that this first witness does not recall Mr. McDuffie ever stating 'I give up.' What Veverka does recall is that he "might very well" have called Mr. McDuffie a nigger. And the second witness called by the government would make McDuffie's statement 'I give up' a major part of his testimony. At that point who — white, black, or green — would give any credence to this type of testimony and evidence?" *Chapter Notes

Chapter 18
"I Give Up!"

The state's second witness, Mark Meir, was lanky and bespectacled. He spoke softly as he described what happened. Near the end of the chase, he, too, heard three shots. He pounded on the side of the witness stand three times to demonstrate.

Prosecutor Stuart Adelstein: "What's the next thing that happened after you heard these three shots?"

Meier: "Mr. McDuffie yelled, 'I give up.'"

The prosecutor asked Meier for more details. He said McDuffie stopped near a freeway entrance ramp. Meier jumped out of his car. "I drew my service revolver, pointed at him, and said, 'Freeze!' He was sitting on his motorcycle. I was standing four or five feet away. That's where I heard 'I give up!'"

Meier said another officer arrived. He came from behind McDuffie, "basically while he was sitting there, not making any aggressive actions." He yanked him off the bike and "pulled off his helmet." He wasn't certain who that officer was.

Other officers flooded the scene. Meier saw "more than three and less than eight" beat McDuffie while he was on the ground. The worst strikes came when Marrero straddled McDuffie, who was "lying on his side, his hands behind his back."

Meier stepped down from the witness stand to demonstrate. He swung his hands like he was swinging a golf club, from one side to the other. He said Marrero hit McDuffie two or three times. Meier said he was four or five feet away.

After Marrero's blows, Meier saw two City of Miami police officers drag McDuffie and place him "between my vehicle and another vehicle." Marrero went over to where McDuffie was sprawled unconscious and struck him on the shins two or three times with a nightstick.

Meier said of Marrero: "I attempted to stop him. I grabbed his arm and told him to cool it. He pulled his arm away and struck [McDuffie] one more time."

The officers discussed faking an accident. Meier said Diggs talked to him about making it look like the motorcycle collided with a squad car, throwing McDuffie into the air with McDuffie landing on his head.

Evans arrived and told Meier he would be a subject for an Internal Review investigation. "I told him I would be a witness," Meier testified, "not the subject, because I didn't hit McDuffie."

When he did talk to Internal Review, he lied.

Adelstein: "Why?"

Meier: "Because you don't hand up. You don't fink on fellow cops."

Around 3 a.m. on December 24, Marrero and Meier saw the early edition of Edna Buchanan's story. They met at the Seaquarium on the Rickenbacker Causeway to talk about it. They agreed in their assessment, Meier testified. "It looked like everyone believed the accident, but not all the injuries were attributable to the accident."

Meier quoted Marrero: "It looks OK. We're covered."

Two days later, on December 26, Meier first lied to the homicide investigators. Then at a second meeting, late that night, he had encountered Veverka in a corridor. "Veverka said he would not go to jail for a murder he did not commit. He told me it would be wise to tell the truth." That's when Meier began cooperating.

When Adelstein was finished with his questioning late that Friday afternoon, Judge Nesbitt adjourned court for the weekend.

• • • •

MEIER AND VEVERKA HAD contradicted each other in a profound way. One had McDuffie fighting ferociously at the beginning and never heard "I give up!" even though he was right next to the motorcyclist. The other said McDuffie surrendered immediately. The jurors could believe one or the other, but certainly not both. In fact, judging from their post-trial comments, they believed neither.

After the trial, much was made of this discrepancy. Ed Bradley said on CBS Reports that this was a "baffling contradiction." In a book on the Miami riots,

Marvin Dunn and Bruce Porter, too, were amazed by the discrepancy: "The jury was left to decide for themselves whether Veverka was lying about the punch in order to make it appear acceptable that he, too, struck McDuffie." That was precisely the point that worried Frank, the homicide investigator.

At the time, daily journalists made little of this. Four print reporters and the first report of WTVJ didn't mention the contradiction at all. The Associated Press and the Sentinel Star of Orlando noted a discrepancy, but only about how Marrero struck McDuffie. Veverka's demonstration was an up-down sledgehammer, while Meier's was a right-to-left golf swing. But neither of those reporters contrasted "I give up" with fighting ferociously.

In the Herald, reporter Gene Miller wrote late in the story that while Meier had seen an immediate surrender, "Veverka was the officer who jerked McDuffie from the motorcycle. He said McDuffie swung at him."

In a Sunday night recap, WTVJ's Frank Lynn mentioned the issue cryptically: "Meier's testimony differed in some detail with that given earlier in the week by... Veverka." Lynn offered no further explanation.

On Monday, Verne Williams in the Miami News noted the contradiction in the middle of a story recapping Meier's testimony:

"Veverka's claim [was] that McDuffie put up a fight. Meier said he didn't see McDuffie throw a punch at anybody or resist in any way."

Still, for many Miami readers who flipped quickly through their newspapers over breakfast, the main impression could well have been the Herald headline: "McDuffie Yelled 'I Give Up' Before Beating, Ex-Cop Says."

• • • •

ON MONDAY, APRIL 28, after jurors sat in their hotel rooms for two days, the defense started cross-examination. Its theme emerged quickly: Meier's testimony kept changing in ways that helped the prosecution.

The prime example was Meier's recollection of "I give up!" He gave several statements to prosecutors and homicide investigators without mentioning it. It was more than a month later that he remembered what McDuffie had said. Under persistent questioning from defense lawyers, Meier kept calmly repeating that he'd simply forgotten about it.

Defense lawyers made him read his earlier statements in which he said McDuffie never said anything during the incident. Conveniently, they challenged, he remembered "I give up!" on February 1. That was the day Meier testified in a hearing in which Marrero was to be charged with second-degree murder.

Shouting angrily, O'Donnell hammered Meier about his memory lapses: "You are telling this jury that for a month and five days after your first statement you didn't remember that McDuffie supposedly said, 'I give up!'" Wasn't that "a new detail" to "sweeten the pot" in working out an immunity agreement, O'Donnell asked?

Meier said he was home when Reno's office called and told him to rush to court for a hearing. It was then he remembered.

"And you are telling me you didn't deliver what Hank Adorno wanted?" O'Donnell bellowed.

Judge Nesbitt sent the jury out and admonished O'Donnell. His shouting was "improper." She said she had never seen him act this way before.

"You will never see me this upset again, your honor," O'Donnell promised.

"Make sure of that," the judge replied.

• • • •

OTHER DEFENSE ATTORNEYS brought out other "improvements" in Meier's memory. In his first statements, he said Marrero struck McDuffie on either "the shoulder or head." He later decided all the blows were to the head. He also admitted he had adopted Adorno's word "straddling" to describe Marrero's stance. He said he used it because was the right word. Carhart pointed out that Meier originally said that Evans wasn't at the scene until after the beating ended. Only in later statements did he claim that Evans arrived while the melee was still going on.

And so it was with Del Toro. Meier mentioned him briefly under direct examination, but only vaguely. On cross-examination, Kogan got him to acknowledge that in a pretrial deposition, Meier didn't even recall whether Del Toro was at the scene.

McWilliams pressed Meier on his first statement, December 26, when he'd said nothing about McWilliam's client, Diggs, discussing how to fake an accident.

McWilliams: "You changed your testimony since that time, December 26?"

Meier: "I added something from my recollection."

McWilliams got Meier to say that he hadn't seen Diggs hit McDuffie: "The first time you saw Sergeant Diggs he was flat on his back with his hands on his chest and you thought he was having a heart attack?"

Meier: "Correct."

Questions about lies kept coming. Meier paused occasionally to sip water from a white plastic cup. He didn't lose his composure.

If Meier lied at first, how could they tell if he was now telling the truth? "Could you tell me, sir," Carlton asked, "is there some way that the gentlemen of this jury or anyone in this courtroom can tell when you mean it and when you don't mean it? Where you swear to tell the truth, the whole truth and nothing but the truth. So help you God. I mean is there little smile on your face or do your ears turn red or — is there some way we can tell when you're telling the truth and when you're not."

Meier: "No sir."

McWilliams: "By the way, are you aware that you're turning red at this moment?"

Meier wasn't sure his face was turning red, but he admitted that his face often flushed when he felt "cornered" or "attacked."

McWilliams wondered if he had a guilty conscience about trying to send fellow officers to prison. "Going to prison for a police officer means death, doesn't it?"

Meier: "I have heard that."

As with Veverka, the defense demanded that Meier read his entire immunity agreement, including: "Immunity from murder, immunity from manslaughter, immunity from aggravated assault."

McWilliams asked why he needed immunity if he did nothing.

"For being an accessory," Meier responded. "I did not commit the murder of Arthur McDuffie. I am guilty of covering it up."

When O'Donnell explored Meier's pathway to cooperation, Meier said the homicide investigators "tricked me." He was in an interview session when Central District's Captain Bowlin played the good cop and Captain Frank, the homicide guy, the bad cop.

Frank convinced him that Sergeant Evans was already talking and admitting there was no accident and McDuffie never resisted. Meier believed him. In fact, Evans had conceded nothing.

O'Donnell listed a few obscenities. Was that what Frank called him? Yes, said Meier, plus some "other than glowing terms."

• • • •

MEIER'S TESTIMONY HAD focused almost exclusively on Marrero. In his early statements to investigators he had said nothing about Evans. It was only in a later statement that he said he saw Evans arrive during the melee, a fact that Carhart brought out on cross-examination. Meier said Diggs participated in the coverup but said nothing to justify Diggs' manslaughter charge. He hadn't seen Watts at the scene at all. He mentioned Del Toro briefly but revealed nothing damaging.

What's more, while his memory had apparently improved over time concerning the defendants, it had remained steadfastly fuzzy in other areas. He never did recall who was the first to touch McDuffie, pulling him off the bike and perhaps yanking off his helmet, even though he testified he was a mere five feet away. The answer, as the jury well knew, was that it was Veverka, the man who first urged Meier to cooperate. As became evident at a later federal trial, the two immunized witnesses had become close friends.

James Lees, the ex-prosecutor, noted: "Major contradictions between the government's first two witnesses, which would have been readily apparent to jurors, is not the way to begin a criminal case," and those contradictions should have been highlighted by the media. "What should have been an important communication to the Miami public, to begin to prepare them for the outcome — that the government's case was in big trouble — never was communicated. For all Miami residents knew, things were going swimmingly for the government, and apparently nothing could have been further from the truth." *Chapter Notes

Chapter 19
"Mad Dog" Takes the Stand

If the tales of the first two state witnesses had been problematic, the state's third immunized witness, William Hanlon, was to prove explosive in different, stunning ways.

Here's how the Herald summed up his day on the witness stand:

"William Francis Hanlon is a squat, mean, reluctant ex-cop.

"He rammed a nightstick into the back of Arthur McDuffie, choked him to the ground with a nightstick, kicked over his motorcycle, suggested breaking his legs, stepped on his glasses, pulled a .38 from an ankle holster and shot at McDuffie's watch and missed, smashed the watch up against a building, threw the watch down a sewer, crawled into a van for a snooze, lifted weights at the gym and then lied to investigators to make himself 'look good.'

"This he testified about Tuesday in the McDuffie trial here."

His testimony began matter-of-factly. He'd damaged a wheel of his cruiser during the chase and arrived to see other officers "struggling" to subdue McDuffie. The motorcyclist was "flailing his arms about and twisting them" as five or six officers struck him with flashlights and nightsticks. "No one was taking him under control."

Hanlon got behind McDuffie and slammed him in his kidneys three times with his nightstick. The blows didn't faze McDuffie. Hanlon then put his nightstick around McDuffie's throat and pulled him down. "After he was on the ground, I cuffed his right hand first. I finally got his other hand and got him handcuffed."

McDuffie was "face down... handcuffs behind his back... doing nothing," Hanlon testified. Marrero "gripped his Kel-Lite in both hands and reared back over the top of his head. Then he came crashing down on the motorcyclist's head — exceedingly hard." Twice again, he struck him, Hanlon said.

Yoss asked him if McDuffie was reaching for anybody's gun. No, Hanlon said.

Yoss handed Hanlon a large, five-cell Kel-Lite and asked him to demonstrate. He stepped off the witness stand, raised the Kel-Lite over his head with both hands and brought it straight down. "He came down like this," Hanlon testified. A spectator in the courtroom gasped. He repeated the motion twice.

After watching Marrero, he walked over to his squad car and examined the bent rim that happened when he rammed a median or curb. Like Del Toro, he'd damaged his car during the chase.

Then he went to look at the Kawasaki. It was standing upright. Its headlight and taillight were smashed. "I kicked it over," Hanlon said.

Evans told him the bike needed more damage to look like it had been in an accident. He asked Hanlon to drive over it. Hanlon jumped in the nearest squad car: Del Toro's. "I drove up on the bike and passed over the front tire. I'm not sure if I made contact."

He saw Evans hand some bullets to Marrero on a nearby sidewalk. "It appeared to be about three." He assumed they were to replace the bullets that Marrero had fired near the end of the chase.

McDuffie was propped up against a squad car. His face was a bloody mess. "I walked over and I, you know, made an off-the-cuff remark, 'If you want to break someone's legs, you could hit him here. You'd probably break them.'" He said he hit McDuffie "lightly" on the knees with his nightstick. "Officer Marrero took the nightstick out of my hands and struck in a similar fashion, a little harder than I did."

As they heard the sirens wailing of the approaching ambulance, someone said, "Cool it!"

As paramedics worked on McDuffie, Hanlon talked to Evans about his damaged car. "Don't worry about it," Evans told him. "We'll make it part of the situation."

Hanlon said he saw Evans throw the Kawasaki keys onto a nearby roof.

Then Hanlon noticed a blue-faced watch with a silver band on a grassy strip. He pulled out a gun from his ankle holster, shot at the watch and missed. He threw the watch against a building, then tossed it into a sewer. He also smashed sunglasses he found on the street.

Yoss asked why he did that.

"I have no explanation," Hanlon replied.

Later from a public phone booth, Hanlon spoke to Evans. "He said we have to make the scene look like an accident." Hanlon said he went back to the scene with officer Eric Seymen. They took a tire iron and scraped the pavement. He wasn't sure if Evans told him specifically to gouge the street. While the pair were at the scene, they talked about the wrong-house raid. "I said this situation is going to make LaFleur look like kindergarten work."

Later, Hanlon said, he went with Marrero and Seymen to Borbon Towing. The place was supposed to be open 24/7, but it was locked. Hanlon stood lookout while the other two squeezed through the fence. They removed part of the oil pan cover that often came off during motorcycle accidents. Two Borbon employees arrived. Seymen told them they had come to check the vehicle identification numbers.

On the way back to the Central District station, they threw the oil pan part in a dumpster. Inside, Hanlon heard Evans order Veverka to rewrite the accident report because "it was not consistent" with McDuffie's injuries.

Marrero was there. "He said, 'Everybody hit him! Everybody hit him!' He was very excited when he said that."

Hanlon said he spoke to Evans about what happened to McDuffie. "I told him Alex had tuned him up. And Sergeant Evans said, 'I know what happened.'"

After his nap and gym workout, Hanlon talked to Internal Review. He lied. So did everyone else, he said. "We were covering up."

On January 4, "trying to make a deal," he'd gone with his lawyer to the state attorney's office. Prosecutors insisted he plead guilty to a felony. He refused. He insisted he hadn't committed any crimes. McDuffie had resisted arrest.

Yoss led him through Judge Nesbitt's dismissing his charges, the offer of immunity and the judge ordering him to testify.

Yoss: "Is it your desire to cooperate with the state of Florida?"

Hanlon: "I would rather not be here."

• • • •

DIRECT EXAMINATION of Hanlon lasted three hours. Cross-examination went on for another nine hours that day as Nesbitt tried to speed up the pace of the trial.

O'Donnell started by asking him why he'd damaged the watch and motorcycle. "Pure vandalism," he replied.

. "What had McDuffie's glasses done to you?" O'Donnell asked. Hanlon didn't know.

Then there were the lies. Even when Hanlon was seeking to cooperate with the prosecutors, he hadn't told the truth. He claimed he saw three City of Miami police officers beat McDuffie. That wasn't true, he told the Tampa jury. He couldn't explain why he lied.

If he lied in two sworn statements, how could jurors know he was telling the truth now? If he admitted to shooting at a watch, how much more was he hiding from them?

Was he aware that his colleagues called him "Mad Dog" behind his back and some thought him insane for some things he'd done on duty? He was unaware of such opinions, he answered, but he insisted his actions that night were not "bizarre."

O'Donnell asked about an incident on November 17, 1979, when some fellow officers were injured and he flew into a rage and broke windows. "Would you characterize that as bizarre?" the lawyer asked.

Hanlon: "I would not use that term. I don't have an explanation."

There was more: He once shot a man in the back. He thought his phone was tapped. He hoped to get rich writing a book about his career.

Then came the exoneration.

McWilliams brought out that both his client, Diggs, and Hanlon had once faced the same charges: manslaughter by excessive force, tampering with evidence and being accessories after the fact.

McWilliams: "You didn't use excessive force, did you?"

Hanlon: "No, at no time."

McWilliams: "You didn't see Sergeant Diggs use excessive force either."

Hanlon: "No, at no time."

• • • •

THE WORK OF ALL SEVEN news reporters examined for this book revealed Hanlon's wild actions. Only Jim Runnels of the Sentinel Star, the Orlando newspaper, contrasted the versions of the first three witnesses. Hanlon said Diggs "never touched" McDuffie, while Veverka saw him use his nightstick to jam the motorcyclist in the chest. Veverka said Hanlon hit him on the wrist with a Kel-Lite. Hanlon said he was not carrying a Kel-Lite that night and didn't hit anybody. And both Hanlon and Veverka disputed Meier, who claimed that McDuffie surrendered at the very beginning.

Only Verne Williams of the Miami News ventured a bit of analysis: "The cross-examination of state witness William Hanlon ... was an event the prosecution will long and sadly remember."

Hanlon may have denied his actions were bizarre, but at the least they were pretty damn weird and many of his statements were lies.

He lied to investigators, he lied to prosecutors. He even at first lied to the polygraph operator.

"Boy, they were terrible witnesses," Yoss said years later of the immunized trio. "These were cops... being forced to testify against fellow police officers. None of them were witnesses because they wanted to be. None of them were standing on a corner as an innocent witness watching some other event. In this instance, all of them, one way or another, was involved in the incident. And either initially lied or at some point lied and then subsequently changed their testimony."

What's more, Yoss said, "They did not want to testify against fellow police officers, on the same squad with them, and had worked with them not only that night but other nights." Was it possible they colored their testimony in ways that kept their immunity agreement but helped the defendants? "I have no doubt. They were forced state witnesses. They were not voluntary do-gooder citizens helping out a prosecution because some cops killed a motorcycle rider. And if we'd had cameras on that corner, all of them would be prosecuted."

One anonymous juror after the trial told a reporter he considered Hanlon a "madman." Juror Draper found Hanlon's immunity deal being "particularly infuriating" because of the acts of "wanton vandalism" he confessed to. When juror Tetreault bought completely the defense's argument that "they put the wrong people on trial," his prime example was Hanlon. The state's immunized trio "were absolutely the bad guys," Tetreault said.

James Lees, the ex-officer and prosecutor, observed: "Officer Hanlon completed the unholy triumvirate of immunized dirty cops. All three had lied, lied and lied. About anything and everything. To everyone, including prosecutors. But yet, for some strange reason, jurors were now being asked to believe the testimony of three lying, dirty, immunized cops whose stories did not even remotely match with each other. Why would anyone ever believe a group of good, decent American citizens would fail to convict people based upon such spectacular evidence?"

Hanlon's testimony had focused on Marrero and Evans. None of the state's first three witnesses had seen Diggs strike what could be considered a deadly blow, though two said he'd tried to cover up the beating. Watts had not been blamed for anything by anyone. As for the almost invisible Del Toro, Hanlon said he'd used his car to drive over the bike, but that was all.

Still, the state's first three witnesses agreed on one major point: Marrero had swung the deadly blows to the head. That unanimity vanished with the next witness. *Chapter Notes

Chapter 20
"You Wouldn't Bet Your Life?"

One of the most revealing moments — perhaps THE moment in the trial — came on Wednesday, April 30, when John "Jerry" Gerant, a 30-year-old City of Miami police officer, testified for the prosecution. He was the first state witness who didn't have an immunity agreement. He didn't need one. He'd hit no one. He didn't lie to investigators.

Prosecutor Adorno asked him who had struck those vicious blows.

"Michael Watts," Gerant said. He climbed down from the witness stand, walked over to the defense tables and pointed at Michael Watts.

Gerant was on the scene for two minutes. He arrived to see the melee underway. He walked past the Kawasaki, upright, on its kickstand, undamaged. He saw "a top of a white helmet" bobbing in the middle of a group of brown-shirted county cops. A sergeant tumbled out of the scrum and fell on the ground. The jurors knew from previous testimony that this was Diggs.

Adorno asked Gerant to identify Diggs in the courtroom. Gerant looked around.

"I don't see him over there." The former sergeant was right there at the defense table, sitting beside his attorney.

Adorno paused for a long moment then moved on. Gerant said he saw McDuffie face up on the pavement, not moving, as the county cops pummeled him. "One at a time," someone shouted. Then he saw Watts slam him over the head with a Kel-Lite, Gerant testified. It was such a vicious blow that he muttered to himself, "Jesus Christ!"

He said he didn't get a "full facial view" of the head-basher. He later identified Watts from a lineup.

Other city officers had arrived, including Sergeant Wayne English. "Wait a minute," one of the county cops shouted. "There are too many witnesses."

Sergeant English looked at the frenzied county cops and asked his city officers, "Why are you guys here? Are you on a call?" Gerant knew what he meant: They shouldn't be standing around seeing such nastiness. "Let's get out of here," English said.

As Gerant left the scene, he paused to look at the Kawasaki 900. "I have one just like it," right down to the same trim and model. He knew it was ultra-fast. "How in the world did they catch him on this thing?" he remembered wondering. Just then a county officer — he didn't know who — smashed the headlight. "It sprayed glass all over me."

Adorno asked him to inspect the motorcycle, sitting on a dolly near the court clerk's desk. Gerant noted the broken headlight, smashed speedometer, broken turn signals, slashed front tire, damaged spark plug and missing dust cover. Gerant said all that damage occurred after he first saw the Kawasaki.

After they left the scene, Gerant, Sergeant English and another city officer went to an all-night Neighbors restaurant on Biscayne Boulevard to discuss what had happened. Gerant told them he wasn't going to lie if anyone asked him. "I had never seen anything like that in my life. I don't know how you can see someone get killed and keep quiet."

• • • •

FOR HIS TWO MINUTES at the scene, Gerant spent almost nine hours on the witness stand. The cross-examination was dominated by the methodical Carlton. Gerant was the only witness to accuse his client, Watts, of doing anything. Thanks to the pretrial depositions, Carlton knew exactly how Gerant would answer his questions.

Carlton spent much of his time on how Gerant came to identify Watts. Gerant acknowledged that he wasn't able to identify anyone in his first interview with Frank. He said the guy who struck the head blows was a really big guy. When he saw photos of Watts in newspapers and on television, Watts looked like the man.

One of Frank's homicide detectives set up a lineup of six or seven. Several were not wearing the PSD brown uniform. He eliminated them. Two were Hispanic. He eliminated them because he was certain that the cop he saw wasn't Hispanic. Another had a receding hairline. The slugger he saw had plenty of hair. That left an officer with a brown PSD shirt and blue jeans. That's the one he picked. It was Watts.

Carlton: "So by a process of elimination you came down to Mr. Watts?"

Gerant: "Well, those combined with other things I came down to Watts."

Carlton: "You wouldn't bet your life it was Watts, would you?"

Gerant: "No, sir."

Carlton: "You could be mistaken?"

Gerant: "I think there is a chance it could be someone else."

The defense attorneys, who had hammered the immunized witnesses repeatedly, dealt gently with Gerant, who said humbly, "I'm doing the best I can."

If he had some doubts about Watts, he had no doubts about Marrero. Under O'Donnell's questioning, he said he saw Marrero walking across the street toward an unmarked police car, with nothing in his hands, at the precise time other officers were striking McDuffie.

He was certain it was Marrero, because he knew Marrero from drinking coffee at a Ranch House with him on the late-night shift.

O'Donnell: "Did you see Alex Marrero walk over to the motorcycle and smash out its headlight like a mad dog?"

Gerant: "No."

O'Donnell: "There is no doubt in your mind today or was there ever that Alex Marrero never struck one blow?"

Gerant: "That I saw, no."

Gerant left the witness stand feeling awful. The defense attorneys "pretty well humiliated me on the stand." He felt the questioning was brutal, "like accusations of molesting my daughter. Everything to discredit me.... Not pretty. They made me play defense, which is not a good way to tell a story."

• • • •

AFTER THE TRIAL, THE jury foreman, David H. Fisher, said the conflicted testimony — the immunized witnesses accusing Marrero, Gerant pointing to Watts — was a key to the acquittals. "You certainly have to take into consideration throwing away two guys who supposedly did the same thing."

The defense viewed inserting Gerant into this trial as a serious prosecution blunder. [For a full discussion of this crucial point, see the post-trial analysis in Chapter 38.]

All seven media reports analyzed for this book contrasted Gerant's testimony with that of the first three witnesses. The Herald and WTVJ emphasized that he had been at the scene only two minutes, implying that he hadn't had time to see in detail what was really happening. The St. Petersburg Times noted, near the end of its story, "Defense attorneys indicated that Gerant's testimony cast 'reasonable doubt' about their clients' alleged action."

Only the small-circulation Miami News attempted to put Gerant's testimony in a perspective that the jurors might share. Under the headline "Cop Confuses Beating Case," which appeared inside the main news section, reporter Williams began: "Miami Police Officer John Gerald Gerant is the first prosecution witness in the Arthur McDuffie case who has not had to admit to lying under oath

— and his candid answers just may have wrecked the prosecution's case."

Williams wrote that Gerant's appearance was a "disaster" that "opened king-sized holes in the prosecution's case."

As it was, many casual readers of the Herald, which had seven times the circulation of the News, may have only glanced at the Herald's headline on the front of the local section: "Watts Smashed McDuffie, Cop Says."

Lees noted: "Jerry Gerant had all the makings of a good first witness for the government. No immunity. Saw what he saw for only two minutes. Was appalled. Maybe could identify one officer, maybe not. But could put a lot of officers into the criminal acts. He was an officer who could and should have been credible with no dog in the fight.

"Instead, he is called only after the unholy triumvirate and was not even adequately prepared by the prosecutors to identify Ira Diggs. The government should have prepared this witness," Lees wrote. "Each time he was asked if he saw a particular officer strike a blow, he could answer, 'During the limited two minutes I was there I was not able to identify your client as one of the many officers beating the crap out of this poor guy.' Where was the preparation and help for this officer from the prosecutors?

"Returning to the media coverage," Lees went on, "the 'Watts Smashed McDuffie' headline is accurate, but what was the takeaway for the jury after all of the questions, both direct and cross? Was the takeaway really that Watts smashed McDuffie, or was it 'Gee, the government does not really seem to have anyone who can say with some degree of certainty who did what at that scene.'" *Chapter Notes

Chapter 21
The Man in the Bulletproof Vest

After a month in the Tampa courthouse, trial participants were settling into a routine in Courtroom 3. About a dozen print and TV reporters were there most days, as well as a handful of black observers representing civil rights organizations. Others dropped by for a few minutes or few hours. Much more regular attenders were the defendants' family members.

Pat Evans, a Miami Beach policewoman very pregnant with her second child, was there sometimes, sitting in a back row, chatting with her husband on breaks. "She had a pleasant smile for everyone, even prosecutors," the News reported.

Diggs' parents were there, too. For a while, they and their son rented an apartment on the outskirts of Tampa. But Diggs was concerned with security. He always wore a bulletproof vest in the courtroom and moved three times during the trial. At one point, he and his parents lived apart for two weeks.

Watts generally stuck to himself. While other defendants chatted or joked among themselves during breaks, he sat at one end of the defense table reading paperbacks. He'd brought six books to Tampa. The first he read was "Carr: Five Years of Rape and Murder." Watts was mentioned in the first chapter as the officer who arrested Robert Carr. The author was Edna Buchanan. By the time the jury went into deliberations, Watts was reading an Alistair MacLean mystery.

O'Donnell and Marrero rented an apartment near the courthouse. O'Donnell was separated, and on some weekends his kids flew in with his girlfriend.

Carlton stayed in a hotel close to the courthouse. He, too, stuck pretty much to himself throughout the proceedings. At one point in the early going, he'd objected when a prosecutor referred to the "defense team."

"We are not a team," Carlton declared.

Prosecutors were a team. Adorno, the lead prosecutor, had turned over much of the questioning of witnesses to Yoss and Adelstein.

For the defense, O'Donnell and McWilliams often became emotional in their cross-examinations, sometimes shouting, while Carlton plodded through long lists of questions. Carhart's attacks tended to be quieter, more thoughtful. And then there was Kogan, attorney for the nearly invisible Del Toro. He was developing a routine that he continued throughout the state's case. When a witness said nothing about his client, he'd stand up when it was his turn for cross and look at the jury: "I just want to refresh your recollection. My name is Gerry Kogan, and I represent Ubaldo Del Toro, and I have no questions." *Chapter Notes

Chapter 22
So Disgusted He Quit

On Thursday, May 1, the fifth eyewitness took the stand: Richard Gotowala, a city police officer for 18 years who was so disgusted by what he saw that he quit that evening.

Under questioning by Stuart Adelstein, Gotowala said he arrived after the melee was over. Seven or eight county cars were already there. The first thing he saw was "a helmet come flying by me, rolling on the ground. I stopped it. I picked it up and put it right back down," he said. It had no strap.

He saw a sergeant, Diggs, moaning and sprawled on the pavement. McDuffie, his hands handcuffed behind his back, lay nearby on the pavement. "His face was bloody." Gotowala walked over to get a closer look at the unconscious man. As he did so, "a hand came by and hit the individual in the mouth." Gotowala was only about a foot away. McDuffie's face looked awful. Gotowala whispered to himself, "Either you are going to be a vegetable or you're going to die."

As he watched, another city officer, Alexander Prince, picked up the limp black figure by his belt and collar and dragged him between two squad cars. "He [McDuffie] started to roll under the car. I was looking at him. I pulled him back to the middle. I saw handcuffs and a bloody face."

While the unconscious motorcyclist lay there, he said he saw Marrero smash McDuffie on the legs with a "blunt instrument."

"He called him a motherfucker as he hit him," Gotowala said. He shouted at Marrero: "Hey! Cut it out!"

He said he stood beside Marrero as he "popped open the cylinder of his gun and said, 'I missed the motherfucker twice.'"

In the courtroom, he pointed to Marrero at the defense table as the man he'd seen smash the legs and talk about his gun.

Gotowala said he also saw someone jump in a county police car and run over the Kawasaki. He wasn't sure who it was. (Hanlon had testified that it was he.) But Gotowala was certain that Diggs had a clear view of the cop damaging the bike.

What he saw that night, Gotowala told the jury, was "the icing on the cake." He'd seen too many bad things. He decided to resign.

Most of the cross-examination came from O'Donnell, who tried to shake the witness' identification of Marrero. He read from Gotowala's sworn statement on Christmas Day about picking out a photograph: "If I'm not mistaken this is the guy who beat him on the leg." But he thought the officer's hair looked different in the photograph.

The man he picked that day was not Marrero, O'Donnell pointed out.

"I didn't pick it out as a positive identity," Gotowala said. He thought that the photo kind of looked like the man who smacked McDuffie's legs, but the hair bothered him. Later, he selected a photo of Marrero.

O'Donnell accused him of changing his testimony "to fit the theory of the prosecution's case." In an early statement, Gotowala said Marrero hit McDuffie in the legs with a Kel-Lite. Later, he said it was a "blunt instrument, like a Kel-Lite."

For Diggs, McWilliams asked: Wasn't Sergeant Diggs "sitting on his ass" most of the time?

Gotowala: "I didn't time him."

McWilliams: "He didn't come over and say, 'Hey, what's going on here,' did he?"

Gotowala: "Maybe he should have."

No reporter was counting, but after the fifth (and last) eyewitness, Marrero and Evans had been mentioned a lot. Several witnesses linked Diggs with the coverup, but no one accused him of striking any unjustified blows that could have killed McDuffie. Watts was already virtually acquitted, since the lone witness against him acknowledged he could have been mistaken, a clear marking for "reasonable doubt." And Del Toro remained almost invisible in the state's case.

James Lees, the ex-officer and prosecutor, commented: "Overall this was a credible witness with evidence to give that went directly to the heart of the government's case against at least one of the defendants. Coupled with the testimony of officer Gerant, the testimony regarding the false police reports, and the evidence related to the damage or lack thereof of the motorcycle (not to mention the evidence of the injuries to McDuffie), the government could have made a solid case against Marrero and a somewhat weaker case against Watts.

"So why not prosecute those two officers first, with no immunity given to anyone? Sequential prosecutions to obtain convictions can obtain cooperation from convicted criminals in exchange for less time in jail; that is a frequent tool of prosecutors. Why not put your best case on against one or two officers, try to obtain a conviction, and then try to deal with the convicted officers to obtain testimony that permits more indictments and hopefully more convictions? Prosecutors, given a choice, would much rather use the testimony of a convicted individual who was involved in the criminal behavior rather than an immunized witness who was also involved in the criminal behavior. But not, apparently, in Janet Reno's office." [More on this point after the trial in Chapter 38, "The Home Run Mistake."]

*Chapter Notes

Chapter 23
"Vague" and "Sketchy" Evidence

Gotowala's testimony had been relatively brief, and Judge Nesbitt decided there was time for a second witness on Thursday. The state called Marshall Frank, the homicide commander. The prosecution needed him to talk about the nearly invisible Del Toro.

Before he took the stand, O'Donnell objected. He told the judge that Frank could not be trusted. "I'll show that he lies and that he lies under oath."

Adorno argued that he didn't want a broad rehashing of the PSD's entire investigation. The state planned to ask Frank only about Del Toro, and he thought it improper for the defense to use his appearance to go off on tangential issues. The judge agreed. Frank was ordered to "restrict his testimony to an interview he had with Del Toro."

Defense attorneys erupted. They insisted they needed to question Frank about the entire case. "I am shocked," McWilliams told the judge, "that the state is afraid to subject this man to cross-examination." The judge didn't budge.

James Lees, the ex-prosecutor: "It is highly unusual and very risky for a judge in a criminal case to restrict cross-examination of a government witness who apparently possesses a great deal of knowledge about the case at issue. It is one thing to rule that a witness may not opine or speculate about what he thinks might have happened (which would be entirely proper judicial rulings), but it is quite another thing for a judge to rule that huge amounts of the witness' participation in and knowledge of an investigation would be off-limits in cross-examination by defense attorneys."

• • • •

JUDGE NESBITT'S RESTRICTING Frank's testimony raises an interesting point, a subtext that would have been completely unknown to the courtroom spectators and journalists: What would have Frank said if asked broader questions about the case?

From his memoir years after the trial, we now know that Frank doubted parts of Veverka's statements, and he thought Del Toro should not have been charged. He was likely confiding these thoughts to his PSD associates during the investigation. Did the defense know what he was thinking?

In an interview for this book, Carhart said he had inside information from the PSD about what investigators thought really happened that night. "One of the officers involved fired a shot — totally against department policy, because you're not supposed to shoot at a moving vehicle for a traffic violation — and McDuffie stopped, got off his motorcycle, and maybe took his helmet off and said, 'What's the big fucking deal? It's only a traffic offense.' And that Veverka came upon McDuffie, became enraged and attacked. And that's what I was told by those in the inner circle. Veverka was certainly one of the brown shirts fighting with McDuffie when Meier came on the scene. And then another police [officer] rolls up and he sees two policemen fighting with a motorcyclist. He joins in, and pretty soon there was a circle of police around McDuffie and they had to wait to get in and engage in the struggle. There were so many policemen."

This was exactly what Frank believed, a scenario that he didn't make public until years later: Veverka initiated the battle. Frank had a sterling reputation for integrity and honesty, and I think it's highly unlikely that he would have leaked anything to the defense. But he was working with teams of county officers and the state attorney's staff. McWilliams was known to be close to many PSD cops. O'Donnell was dating a woman in the state attorney's office. PSD investigators were likely to be friends with friends of the defendants. All that makes it plausible that information was leaked to the defense.

By the time I knew Frank's position, Carhart was dead and I couldn't ask him about the "inner circle" source. He probably wouldn't have answered in any case. I did ask Yoss if he thought someone in the PSD might have leaked to the defense. He didn't respond.

In the Tampa courtroom, it turned out, Frank didn't have much to say about Del Toro. On December 26, he talked to the officer for only 10 or 15 minutes. Del Toro told him about the blown tire and arriving late. "He said he saw just enough force to subdue him and it was perfectly all right," Frank testified.

Still, since other witnesses said Del Toro's squad car was used to drive over the Kawasaki, Frank testified that he found Del Toro's responses "vague and ambiguous." He must have known more, Frank decided, and that's what he told the jury.

Kogan, Del Toro's attorney, finally had something to ask a witness about. Even then his questioning was brief. He got the homicide commander to acknowledge that his interview with Del Toro was "vague." Frank didn't take any notes at the time. He was busy with other matters that night (getting Veverka and Meier to cooperate). Only eight days after did he write a "sketchy" account of what Del Toro told him.

Kogan then ran through other officers at the scene: Did Frank ask Del Toro what Charles Veverka did? Alex Marrero? Kogan named another 11 officers who were at the incident or might have been. Frank hadn't asked Del Toro about any of them.

"You didn't even ask Del Toro if he struck McDuffie, did you?" Kogan asked, knowing the answer from Frank's deposition. He hadn't, Frank said. "And you didn't ask him about his conversations with other officers in the squad room, did you?" No, he hadn't.

Such was the entire state case against Ubaldo "Eddie" Del Toro.

*Chapter Notes

Chapter 24
A "Politicized" Investigation?

The next day, Friday, May 2, the state moved to brief, secondary witnesses.

Omar Molina, a paramedic, testified that he arrived to see a handcuffed black man propped up against a county police car. "He had three or four serious lacerations on his forehead." His eyes were swollen shut, his vital signs "abnormal." He didn't respond to questions. Molina asked for the handcuffs be removed. When an officer did so, McDuffie flailed his arms and tore off a head bandage.

Under cross-examination, Molina admitted that he first assumed that McDuffie was hurt in a traffic accident and that's what he wrote in his report.

McWilliams suggested that McDuffie was still combative when the handcuffs were removed and that's why he was swinging his arms. Molina responded: "Mr. McDuffie was not responsible for any of his movements."

That response brought a chorus of objections from defense attorneys: Molina was improperly making a medical judgment. Judge Nesbitt agreed. She told the jury to disregard Molina's answer.

Next, homicide detective Frank Wesolowski, a 15-year veteran, took the stand to explain how he had set up the lineup in which Gerant identified Watts. At the time, Watts had been suspended. Wesolowski had him put on a brown PSD uniform shirt, but he'd kept on his blue jeans.

Carlton, representing Watts, asked: "Did you ask the others to put on Levis so [Watts] wouldn't stand out?"

Wesolowski: "No, sir."

Carlton: "Would you like to go to jail for years on that lineup identification?"

"Objection!" shouted Yoss. Judge sustained.

Carhart used the detective to drive home the defense's theme of a pressured, politicized investigation. First, he got Wesolowski to acknowledge that the state had slapped Marrero with a second-degree murder charge only after black groups had demanded such a charge on the courthouse steps.

Carhart asked him if he had ever seen a "more politicized investigation and prosecution."

For a minute or more, Wesolowski said nothing.

Carhart: "If you prefer not to answer, I respect that.... I understand you have a job."

Wesolowski: "I don't know that I can answer that."

Said Lees, the ex-prosecutor: "The government's case had deteriorated into a nightmare that a witness was asked about a 'politicized investigation.' It speaks volumes that the question was apparently permitted, an answer was actually given, and no one was held in contempt for raising such an issue in a criminal trial. I will categorically state that such matters are irrelevant in virtually all courtrooms in America and any attorney asking such a question would be reaching for their wallet to pay the contempt fine that was surely coming next."

The next witness was crime lab tech George Turner. He testified he discovered McDuffie's keys beneath an air conditioning duct on the roof. Two previous witnesses, Veverka and Hanlon, had told jurors they'd seen Evans toss the keys on the roof.

Turner's discovery verified details in the testimony of two crucial witnesses—details that had been hotly disputed by the defense. But what was Evans doing? Throwing keys on the roof didn't seem to further a coverup. The act certainly did nothing to embellish the tale of McDuffie being injured in an accident. Tossing away the keys was just a childish response — "pure vandalism," as Hanlon had said about his own actions.

On cross-examination, McWilliams asked Turner about the motorcycle, which was still sitting near the court clerk's desk.

Turner said that during the luncheon recess, he put the ignition key into McDuffie's motorcycle to verify that the keys he found fit the Kawasaki.

"I activated the oil light."

McWilliams asked him to turn on the motorcycle so that the jurors could hear how loud it was. He was seeking to show that it would have been unlikely that Meier could have heard "I give up!" over the roar of the engine.

Turner said the battery was dead.

"Aw, shucks," said McWilliams. *Chapter Notes

Chapter 25
Arthur McDuffie's Last Night

On Monday, May 5, after jurors had spent another weekend in their hotel rooms, the state's case moved on to four witnesses, each with a bit of testimony that prosecutors thought was valuable.

Captain Dale Bowlin, commander of the Central District, was put on mostly to talk about the coverup charges against Evans and Diggs. He told jurors he first learned of the incident when Evans called him at home at 6:01 a.m. and told him a John Doe "had been beaten and might die."

When Bowlin saw Evans later in the morning at district headquarters, Evans said he'd talked to Jackson doctors, who told him the motorcyclist's skull had severe fractures that could not have been caused only by a crash.

Bowlin said Evans told him, "I think they hit him with Kel-Lites."

The captain said he told Evans he didn't want the sergeant to put his own "medical opinion" in the reports because he didn't feel Evans "could read an X-ray."

In fact, that statement dovetailed with what Carhart had maintained in his opening statement.

Evans and Diggs, the two sergeants, both wrote reports that McDuffie had been in an accident. Evans said he based his report on what officers at the scene told him.

Much of Bowlin's testimony focused on Diggs. The sergeant told him he was one of the last to arrive at the scene. He said he was two blocks away when he saw the motorcyclist crash and his helmet fly off.

Bowlin said he told Diggs: "That is a little strange: From two blocks away you see the accident on the other side of the expressway."

Diggs replied he had "a very good view of it." When Bowlin said he doubted that, Diggs backed off a bit and said he assumed it was an accident because he saw the helmet fly off.

"I said, 'No, Ira, you just told me you saw the accident.'" Diggs "just shrugged." The sergeant didn't want to write a report. Bowlin insisted. He warned Diggs of severe consequences. "I said, 'I hope you did your job. I consider this a very serious situation. I'm concerned where many people's careers, or men's careers, are in jeopardy.' And I said I can even foresee where some people will go to jail because of this."

Later, Bowlin told Evans he was suspicious of all the reports he had received about the incident and was particularly "suspicious of Sergeant Diggs'. He [Evans] said he didn't blame me," Bowlin said.

Under cross-examination, Bowlin steadfastly denied that any of his actions were caused by outside pressure, but he conceded that he and three others involved in the McDuffie investigation were promoted, with Bowlin jumping from captain to chief, leaping over the rank of major.

McWilliams tried to get Bowlin to admit that he disliked Diggs because both had applied to be PSD director.

Bowlin: "I would never do anything to put anybody into a homicide to get a job."

McWilliams: "After you suspended him, it eliminated him from the sheriff's race."

Bowlin: "I agree it certainly did not help his chances."

McWilliams suggested that Bowlin felt comfortable transferring the blame from himself to someone else.

"No," Bowlin responded. "I was uncomfortable, too, Mr. McWilliams. I think we were all uncomfortable. And I think we were all ashamed, and I think we were all embarrassed, and I think we still are."

• • • •

MCDUFFIE'S MOTHER, Eula Bell, spent perhaps five minutes on the stand as a "chain of evidence" witness, to explain how the helmet strap and other items had made their way into the courtroom. She explained she went to the hospital to see her comatose son. Then, trying to figure out what happened, she went to the site of the alleged crash. She found there a pair of crushed sunglasses and an officer's marksmanship pin.

Prosecutor: "What else did you find?"
Mrs. McDuffie: "The band of a watch."
"All right. Go on. What else?"
"And a helmet strap."

Most of the defense attorneys wanted the suffering mother off the stand as fast as possible. As usual, Carlton insisted in getting his licks in. For each item she found, he asked her if she was certain the item belonged to her son. "I wasn't there to see [what happened], but I found it there," she responded each time.

Eula Bell was followed by her daughter, Dorothy McDuffie, who testified that she had taken the items her mother found and McDuffie's clothing returned by the hospital. She gave them to the lawyer assisting the family in a lawsuit. The state subpoenaed those items from the lawyer.

• • • •

CAROLYN BATTLE TOOK much more time on the stand. She testified that McDuffie was with her from 5 p.m. Sunday, December 16, until about 1:30 a.m. Monday, minutes before the chase. When she stepped onto the witness stand, it was the first the public had heard of her. All previous news accounts quoted McDuffie's sister as saying Arthur left the house they shared at 5 p.m. and she didn't know what he was doing after that.

Battle, 26, testified that she was a colleague of McDuffie's at the insurance company for three months. McDuffie was a "friend.... There was nothing sexual between us."

She said McDuffie came to her apartment about 5 p.m. that Sunday. They rode together on his Kawasaki to the airport, watched jets take off, then went to Miami Beach at speeds up to 90 mph, got Pepsis at a soda shop, then returned to her apartment.

"We sat and talked and then he took a nap in the bedroom and I stayed in the living room and watched TV. Then I fell asleep on the couch." She awoke about 1:30 a.m., woke McDuffie, saw him put his helmet on and watched as he left on the motorcycle. Her apartment was about two blocks from where the chase started.

Prosecutors called her to rebut repeated defense insinuations of McDuffie being high on drugs. He'd taken no drugs and drank no alcohol that night, she said. Unstated in the courtroom was the awkwardness of her appearance: McDuffie's ex-wife, Frederica, had given many interviews saying she and Arthur planning to remarry. She'd said they would have spent that Sunday night together if she hadn't had to work the night shift at the hospital.

The defense had plenty of questions for Battle. One major one: Why had she waited until March 26, less than a week before jury selection, to tell investigators about McDuffie's last night? Her answer was that no one had asked her, but she had previously told McDuffie's sister.

"I would swear on 10 stacks of Bibles he was at my home," Battle said.

The defense scoffed at the idea that Battle was merely a business associate of McDuffie's. O'Donnell asked if they were conducting "business" on a speeding motorcycle. She said no.

Had she put marijuana residue in McDuffie's jacket pocket? No. Had she come forward only after she'd heard McDuffie was hit that night in the head with a pool cue during a barroom fight? Battle said no.

This question was one of several attempts to raise the possibility of a barroom fight. There was never any evidence to back up the pool cue insinuations.

Battle did get across the message that McDuffie used no drugs that evening, but the defense clearly implied she strained credulity in claiming a nonsexual relationship in which McDuffie just happened to fall asleep in her bedroom by himself after taking her for a thrilling motorcycle ride.

At least one juror didn't believe her story. After the trial, David L. Draper listed questions he felt were not answered the trial. One of them: "Where was he [McDuffie] from 7 p.m. until 1:30 a.m. Dec. 17?"

• • • •

MUCH OF THE NEXT DAY was consumed by two expert witnesses who had examined the Kawasaki 900 and decided its damage was not caused by an accident. One was Edward Whittaker, head of the PSD crime lab for more than two decades. He found puncture holes in the motorcycle's front tire, made by a sharp tool. Two spokes in the front wheel had been cut, and there were nine man-made blows. What's more, he was certain the strap on McDuffie's helmet had been cut off. He draped McDuffie's blue jeans over the motorcycle and said he didn't see any marks on the jeans from an accident.

William Joseph Fogarty, a University of Miami professor who had investigated 3,000 accidents, said flatly that the motorcycle "was not involved in a moving-type accident."

No defense attorney was claiming there had been an accident, but still they battled throughout the day. The defendants' lawyers spent much of the morning trying to keep the helmet and jeans out of evidence. They argued the blood on the pants could improperly inflame the jurors' passions. "I will stipulate that he was not riding the motorcycle naked," Carhart said. The judge rejected his argument.

Ultimately Whittaker backed down a bit under intense cross-examination. "I cannot say if it has or has not been involved in a motorcycle accident."

He did say, however, that the helmet strap, found at the scene by Eula Bell McDuffie, fit McDuffie's helmet perfectly.

Hammering on the defense's politicization theme, O'Donnell brought out that Whittaker, the boss of the crime lab, hadn't done an investigation of his own in years. O'Donnell asked why he got involved in the McDuffie case.

"When I heard a half-dozen, maybe a dozen, officers were involved in a serious incident," Whittaker replied.

O'Donnell asked if Bobby Jones, the acting director, had ordered him to get involved because of the public pressure on the case.

"'Not at all,'" Whittaker replied.

Lees, the ex-prosecutor: "The decision to sneak Mr. McDuffie's mother onto the witness stand under the guise of a chain-of-custody witness was a good move for the prosecution as it would tend to humanize both Mr. McDuffie and the suffering his family endured after his passing. But it was never going to be a linchpin in determining whether the officers were or were not convicted. Much more interesting were the expert witnesses who opined on the motorcycle damage. Why weren't these witnesses called at the beginning to prove the false police reports based upon the damage or lack thereof to the motorcycle?"

• • • •

LINDA SAUNDERS, THE original Internal Affairs investigator in the case, testified how the cops lied to her about what happened that night. Her testimony was crucial in establishing that the defendants had been covering up from the beginning when she first interviewed them at their ends of the shift that night.

The defense hammered on the details. Carhart had plenty of questions for her. Why did Captain Bowlin hold up Evans' use-of-force report for almost a week? She didn't know. Wasn't it true that Bowlin waited until two days after McDuffie died and Edna Buchanan started making phone calls to tell her that he suspected McDuffie was hit with Kel-Lites? Yes, Saunders said.

Carhart: "And Sergeant Evans told you the morning of December 17 Kel-Lites were used, didn't he?"

Saunders: "Yes."

Carhart then sought to establish that Evans had sought to verify the officer's claim about an accident: "To use the vernacular, Sergeant Evans bitched about the fact that the Accident Prevention Bureau refused to come out that night, didn't he?"

Saunders: "Yes, he did."

Carhart asked why Saunders had jumped several ranks in being promoted from sergeant to commander. Was that a reward for her work on the McDuffie case? No, she replied. She was promoted as part of an affirmative action program.

Carhart: "Can you tell me what minority group Captain Bowlin is a member of?" She didn't know.

Left unsaid was Bowlin's demographic: White, non-Hispanic.

Saunders left the witness stand with a bad feeling about where the case was headed. She was taught to make eye contact with jurors when she was testifying. These white males didn't want to make eye contact, she said in an interview for this book. "They were looking away or looking at their hands. They looked bored. *Chapter Notes

Chapter 26
Like Falling Four Stories

The state's last major witness was Ronald Wright, the deputy medical examiner and forensic pathologist. He testified that the main blows against McDuffie's skull were so severe that they were "the equivalent of falling, landing between your eyes from a four-story building."

Yoss: "On what?"

Wright: "On concrete."

Using a plastic model of a human skull, Wright drew lines where three blows had produced a half-dozen fractures to McDuffie's head.

Yoss: "The same six wounds... [were] consistent with being caused with an object such as state exhibit 18, a Kel-Lite." Yoss handed Wright the Kel-Lite.

Wright: "Yes, sir."

He said the blows had almost totally destroyed McDuffie's brain. He said the head injuries were the worst he had seen in 3,600 autopsies.

Under cross-examination, Carhart brought out that Wright hadn't learned about the McDuffie case from the PSD's Internal Review unit or from Captain Bowlin, but from Edna Buchanan.

He also acknowledged that his first autopsy report, after an examination that lasted five hours and 40 minutes, indicated the injuries were caused by a motorcycle accident.

Carhart: "I take it, sir, your expert opinion was that Mr. McDuffie had been involved in a motorcycle accident?"

That was right. "Previously, I had never seen anyone with a skull fracture with that degree of magnitude who had not hit a pole, wall, obstruction," Wright replied.

"You received misinformation from other persons?" Carhart asked. Wright said he had, from the original police reports that classified the injuries as resulting from an accident.

What about drugs in McDuffie's system? By the time of his death, the doctor said, such tests were meaningless because of the blood transfusions he received in the hospital. His body would have also metabolized any drugs over the four days before he died, leaving little or no evidence of drug use.

O'Donnell pressed Wright for alternative interpretations of what caused the blows. "Couldn't the blows have come from a police walkie-talkie or a 2-by-4?"

"Yes."

"How about a boot?" O'Donnell was referring to Prince, the city police officer who'd confessed to the polygraph operator that he'd kicked the prone McDuffie in the head.

Wright said a deep cut in the skin near the right eyebrow could have been caused by a boot. But that wasn't a fracture. The fractures were caused by something much more forceful than a boot.

When it was Carlton's turn, he tried to show that the police weren't responsible for McDuffie's death. "Isn't it correct that McDuffie died because Jackson Memorial Hospital shut off his life support system?"

Wright: "They shut off the life support system after his brain had turned to liquid."

With this last exchange, Carhart confessed later, "I wanted to get under the table. What a kick in the head. You could have heard a pin drop in the courtroom. Let us be honest: There was nothing about McDuffie's death that was decent, honorable or acceptable. There really wasn't. The man suffered terrible injuries." Carhart regarded Wright's testimony as "horrible" from a defense standpoint.

After the Wright fiasco, Carhart said, he again reminded that Carlton could suffer if he wasn't a team player. "I cautioned Philip,

'Please don't go on walks,'" reminding him that since the defense was set up for Carhart to always be the last to cross-examine a witness, "I could do great harm to his client."

Patrick Malone, a veteran trial lawyer of civil cases who wrote the foreword and afterword for this book, though Wright's testimony was a key to this case. "I wondered why the prosecutors called the medical examiner, their strongest witness, last and not first at the trial. It's trial lawyering 101 for a prosecutor (or plaintiff's civil lawyer like me) to start the trial strong, with a witness whom the other side cannot attack, and who can set a tone and a theme for the drama that unfolds after they have left the stand. One of the few things a trial lawyer can exercise total control over is the order of witnesses. In this case, the state's first witnesses bore the stench of their immunity deals and their own admitted bad conduct. The adroit cross-examinations by the far more experienced defense lawyers set up the defense counter-narrative that the prosecutors had immunized the bad guys and unfairly targeted the defendants. Once a story mold is set in a trial, it's hard to break out of it."

James Lees, the ex-officer and prosecutor, offered a similar opinion: "The testimony of the medical examiner makes it clear he needed to be called at the outset of the case, not at the end. Imagine a trial that went something like this: The first witness is a records custodian who introduces the police reports. The next witnesses are the expert witnesses who opine the damage to the motorcycle could not have been caused by a moving-type accident as reported in the police reports. The experts would point out the puncture holes in the tires made by a sharp tool, the cut spokes on the wheel, and man-made blows to the motorcycle. The bloody blue jeans and the helmet with the cut strap would be introduced. Next would come the medical examiner, followed by Gotowala, a witness who didn't need to be immunized."

• • • •

THE STATE'S CASE ENDED with several minor witnesses that it needed to make legal points. Under Florida law, to get convictions on charges of accessory after the fact, the state had to show the defendants were not related. The defense refused to stipulate, and so the prosecutors were forced to call witnesses.

One was Patricia Evans, a Miami Beach police officer who was expecting to give birth in about two weeks. She told Yoss she had been married to Herb Evans for 12 years.

Yoss: "Is your husband related by blood or marriage [to any of the other defendants] as husband or wife, mother or father, brother or sister, grandparent or grandchild?"

"Not to my knowledge," she said.

Carhart, seeking to milk a bit of sympathy for his client by keeping the smiling, very pregnant woman on the witness stand a bit longer, asked how old she was.

"I am 32."

How long had she known Evans?

"Twenty-five years."

"Can you say under oath that he is not related to any of these people?"

"No," she said.

For Del Toro, the other defendant with the accessory after the fact charge, the state called a PSD personnel officer to say Del Toro wasn't related to the others. Sensing an opening, Kogan got the man to discuss Del Toro's excellent conduct record and academic achievements. *Chapter Notes

Chapter 27
"Thank God, It's Over"

On Thursday, May 8, the state rested. The defense responded with a flurry of motions. One of them, alleging "prosecutorial misconduct," stood out for its bizarre twist about the actions of "Mad Dog" Hanlon. When he was on the stand, press reports noted, he admitted he shot at McDuffie's watch and missed, then smashed it against the wall and threw it in a sewer.

Carhart told the judge that hospital records showed McDuffie was wearing a watch when he arrived. He argued prosecutors had misled the jury. "The jury is under the impression that it was McDuffie's watch at the scene. I think that was gross misconduct."

Carhart was deadpanning a profound irony: Hanlon's watch tale was a huge embarrassment for an immunized witness. It clearly didn't help the state's case. And here the defense was shaming prosecutors for revealing this information to jurors, while setting up grounds for a possible appeal.

Adorno told Nesbitt that the state never claimed the watch was McDuffie's. It may have been lost by an officer that night.

Judge Nesbitt: "Whatever the news reporters thought about the watch, I have always thought it was just a watch on the scene. I never believed the state was trying to prove it was Mr. McDuffie's watch." She rejected the "prosecutorial misconduct" motion.

Concerning the standard defense arguments for directed verdicts of acquittal, Judge Nesbitt told defense attorneys that she didn't need to hear them recite all the state's witnesses. She said she realized there were "inconsistencies" in the state's case. "There are many [inconsistencies], but I have a good memory."

She quickly rejected the motions for four of the defendants. But she listened closely to Kogan's argument that the state failed to show that Del Toro was "part of a common scheme with a specific intent to aid" other defendants in avoiding detention by giving false statements. Few of the state's 22 witnesses mentioned him, Kogan argued, and those mentions tended to be innocuous. Frank, the one witness to focus on Del Toro, admitted his recollections were "vague."

Nesbitt agreed. She said she was bothered by a lack of testimony, even about when he arrived at the scene. She concluded there was insufficient evidence for a reasonable jury to convict Del Toro. The state failed to prove Del Toro's actions "excluded every reasonable hypothesis of innocence.... He must, in fact, be entitled to a directed verdict of acquittal at this particular time. He is discharged."

Del Toro broke into a huge smile. He nodded toward the judge. With Kogan beside him, he moved slowly down the defense table, shaking hands with the attorneys and other defendants. Marrero gave him a big hug.

In the corridor outside the courtroom, joined by his wife and father, he stopped to talk to reporters. "Thank God it's over," he said.

"It's a long road for me being a policeman, enforcing the law, to finding yourself on the other side of the bench," Del Toro told the reporters. "And I didn't feel at all comfortable in that position, and I never expected to be in such a position."

Kogan said: "Sometimes when you're involved in a case that has a great deal of political significance, you're not always sure that justice will prevail. However, in this particular case, obviously Judge Nesbitt was unmoved by the political situation and exercised her just discretion."

Del Toro said the ordeal set him back $50,000 in legal fees, lost salary and the expenses of living in Tampa for six weeks. "And there is no price on the suffering." He had faced a maximum of five years of prison. "I would really be facing a death sentence. Send a white policeman to jail, you might as well give him the electric chair. You could give him his own private little room but the moment he gets caught anywhere alone, it would be over. I heard of a trooper who went to jail. I can't remember for what, and he lasted one week."

He certainly had soured on a career in law enforcement. "Now, I look at police work as the dumbest job any intelligent man could take.... I was getting no sleep; I had no social life; I had no time to see my wife. I was called a pig. And for what? To see the people you try to help hurt you or end up being prosecuted."

Now that his case was closed, Del Toro felt he could talk freely about what he had experienced that night. Gene Miller of the Herald tracked him down for a one-on-one interview.

After blowing his right rear tire and bending the rim, Del Toro said, he arrived at the scene to see McDuffie on the ground. He thought he was already handcuffed. McDuffie was clearly injured. "It wouldn't have been a total surprise if some hit [him]. It is stupid but it happens." He was more worried about his vehicle. "I was sure there would be 10 forms to fill out." Evans told him not to worry about it."

He said he didn't see anyone hit McDuffie. As the ambulance approached, he went to his car, popping open the trunk and searching for the jack to change the tire.

When the paramedics were treating McDuffie, he walked over to them. "McDuffie was giving them a hard time as they put an IV syringe in his right arm, pulling off a bandage."

Del Toro "glanced over, he said, and saw someone in his car. He said he didn't give it a second thought," the Herald reported. "Three other witnesses said a cop tried to drive up on the downed motorcycle. Del Toro said he didn't see it. 'I was worried about my car, afraid I was going to catch hell for the damage.'"

That last statement was probably the reason that prosecutors kept pushing him to come clean. His main concern was his car, which Del Toro admitted was parked right by the motorcycle, and yet he hadn't seen someone use it to drive over the motorcycle in an attempt to look like it was damaged in an accident. Why not?

A couple of reporters went looking for Adorno. "I had my day in court," he said, "and lost." He said nothing more.

Years later, Frank, the homicide commander who had been the one witness focused on Del Toro, confessed: "When the indictment was dismissed by the judge, I was all for it, because I felt that was the right thing to do."

Lees commented: "Any experienced prosecutor would have known in advance there was insufficient evidence to charge and convict Del Toro. So why do it? Politics? Appeasement to the black community? Regardless of the motive, this single issue speaks volumes to the incompetence of the prosecution in this case."

• • • •

THE JURORS WERE OUT during the entire Del Toro drama, which happened in the early afternoon. When they returned to the courtroom for the start of the defense case, they saw Del Toro and Kogan were no longer at the defense tables. They were given no explanation.

"That was something I wondered about," Ken Stover said. It occurred to him that the charges might have dismissed because Del Toro was mentioned so rarely, but "it was never discussed by the jurors."

Joseph Tetreault, another juror, said: "We were surprised. We were asking, where the hell is the fifth guy?" He guessed correctly that the judge dismissed the charges because of insufficient evidence. But then "why the hell was he put on trial in the first place?"

Good question. As Yoss described, prosecutors felt a strong need for supporting witnesses because of the problems they foresaw with Veverka and Meier. That's why they immunized Hanlon, even with his "Mad Dog" baggage. Del Toro, with his clean record, would have been a big plus.

After his acquittal, Del Toro revealed that prosecutors approached him three times after his arrest and asked for his cooperation. "They thought I might know something.... They wanted me to tell them what they wanted to hear, not what I knew."

When he refused to cooperate, why not drop the charges before the start of trial? Yoss said he's not certain. Perhaps, as the defense argued in other matters, the answer was political: Reno's office didn't want the black community to think it wasn't aggressive in pursuing as many guilty verdicts as it could. When the judge threw out the charges against Del Toro, the decision was on Nesbitt's shoulders, not Reno's.

The upshot: At least one juror, and probably more, thought that Del Toro's disappearance was a clear indication that the state had a weak case. *Chapter Notes

Chapter 28
"I Don't Remember Anything"

In mid-afternoon, after Del Toro vanished, the defense swung into action, with McWilliams calling five brief witnesses to support his client, Diggs. They included a doctor, who talked about Diggs' right knee that had reportedly been injured in the attack. A PSD officer, Douglas Munday, said McDuffie "shot, in my observation, a birdie" at him near the beginning of the chase.

Ex-officer Francis Mungavin, riding in a squad car with Watts, said he arrived to see Diggs on his back, moaning in pain. He helped him for three minutes, his back to "the struggle." He said he saw McDuffie kicking but no one hitting McDuffie with Kel-Lites or nightsticks. He said Watts was carrying a three-cell Kel-Lite only six inches long that night. "It was the same as mine." Gerant had testified that he saw Watts hit McDuffie with a nightstick or large Kel-Lite, which would have at least five batteries.

The next morning, jurors entered the courtroom to see the usually half-full spectator seats virtually empty. Gone were the Tampa television reporters and many others who usually occupied the front rows.

McWilliams announced he was calling his client, Ira Diggs. For the first time, a defendant was walking toward the witness stand, a truly dramatic event in any criminal trial, and the reporting corps seemed to be boycotting. "We all wondered what was happening," recalled juror Stover.

A disaster was happening. At 7:38 a.m., about an hour and a half before court started, a 600-foot freighter crashed into the Sunshine Skyway Bridge, about a 30-minute drive from the courthouse. A central span of the bridge collapsed, sending a Greyhound bus and at least four cars plunging into Tampa Bay. More than 30 died.

The Miami print reporters — Gene Miller of the Herald and Verne Williams of the News — raced to the crash site, as did all the television journalists. The two local print reporters — Shinhoster of the Tampa Tribune and Marcia Slacum of the St. Petersburg Times — stayed in the courtroom, along with some wire service reporters.

For jurors, the mysterious disappearances highlighted their isolation. Tetreault was angry. Jurors were not allowed to watch television news, and they received copies of the local newspapers only after bailiffs had clipped out stories that they thought they shouldn't see. "Mainly we were looking at sports." Juror Stover too was upset: "I wish we had known what the newspapers were saying."

Trying to focus on the day's proceedings, they saw Diggs sit stiffly on the witness stand. He looked directly at McWilliams when his lawyer asked a question, then swiveled self-consciously toward the jurors to give his answer.

Diggs said he arrived late at the scene. As he neared, he saw "a white object flying in the air. I assumed it was a helmet." He arrived to see McDuffie "punching, swinging and kicking at all the officers." With a flashlight in his hand, he ran toward the scrum. "When I got over to him, he was kicking at everybody and no one could grab him.... His right foot was very close to me. I tried to catch the foot in between my arms.... I was closing in when a blow landed just above my knee," resulting in "severe, shooting pain."

He fell to the pavement, where he remained for a couple of minutes. "I don't remember anything except getting kicked and going to the ground."

McWilliams: "Did you ever get a chance to hit McDuffie?"

Diggs: "No, I did not."

"Did you use any force, like grabbing his leg, that you would consider unreasonable?"

"No, I did not."

He added that he didn't see Marrero hit McDuffie. When Diggs managed to get up, McDuffie was already handcuffed, his face bloody, sprawled on the street. Diggs said he called fire rescue.

Later that morning, he testified, he talked to Sergeant Saunders in Internal Review. He testified that he "assumed" there had been an accident, and that's what he told Saunders. McWilliams asked him if he thought there had really been an accident. "No, not positively," Diggs responded. He added that Evans, his co-defendant, never asked him to write a false report.

McWilliams probably felt it necessary to put Diggs on the witness stand because he had signed a blatantly false use-of-force report. To avoid a cover-up conviction, he had to come up with some explanation. In the first report he filed, he'd stated: "The subject's motorcycle hit the curb upon attempting to turn. The subject had no chin strap on his helmet, which flew off during the accident. The subject landed on his head and was bleeding profusely as officers arrived." A struggle with officers followed. "The subject continued to fight violently, kicking and punching. Officer Marrero, using a night stick, struck the subject all over the body. The subject went for Officer Marrero's gun twice, and the officer and subject fell to the ground.... The subject had evident head injuries, but it is unknown if these occurred during the accident or the fight."

During the state's case, Bowlin, the central district commander, said he'd challenged Diggs' report about seeing the crash, since he was supposedly two blocks away at the time. He said Diggs told him his report was accurate.

Diggs told the jurors that Bowlin had it out for him because both applied to be PSD director. Now, Diggs testified, he wasn't certain there had been an accident. He said he'd been pressured by Bowlin and others to write the use-of-force report. Before doing so, he said, he talked to three others at the scene: Hanlon and Veverka (both later given immunity) and Marrero (a co-defendant). Both Veverka and Hanlon insisted there had been an accident, he said.

One memory he was certain of: When the paramedics arrived, McDuffie struggled with them. Diggs said he warned the motorcyclist: "If you don't quit fighting, we're just going to leave you here to die."

At the end of McWilliams' direct examination, Judge Nesbitt adjourned court for the weekend.

• • • •

ON MONDAY, MAY 12, with the trial expected to be done by the end of the week, Shinhoster of the Tampa Tribune published an analysis that no other reporter attempted. In the midst of a summary of the trial to date, after talking about the testimony against Marrero and Evans, she wrote: "Some court observers feel that the cases against two of the other defendants may not be enough to warrant a conviction of manslaughter from the all-male jury."

Using "court observers" is a traditional crutch of trial reporters. In this case she may have meant representatives of civil rights groups who regularly attended the sessions, and perhaps other reporters.

Her story went on: "Testimony that Michael Watts and Ira Diggs delivered skull-fracturing blows to the head of McDuffie has been minimal. Both men are charged with manslaughter, manslaughter by unnecessary killing and aggravated battery.

"Only one witness has said that he saw Watts straddle the body of McDuffie and strike him in the head. And that witness' identification of Watts was shaky."

Another witness said he saw Diggs hit McDuffie with a nightstick, but that was in the chest, not the head. "Others said they saw Diggs lying on the ground, suffering from a kick to the knee."

She went on with an even-handed sentence that strained to be impartial, stating that the testimony of two immunized witnesses,

Veverka and Meier, "though riddled with inconsistencies, could prove damaging to the four men on trial."

• • • •

ON MONDAY IN THE COURTROOM, Yoss questioned Digg's theory that Bowlin was out to get him. Diggs was 32, a sergeant for three years. "Do you really think you had a shot at the director's job?"

Diggs responded quickly: "As good a shot as anyone else did."

Yoss pestered him about why he'd written a false report, starting with his claim that he saw the helmet "flying off."

Yoss: "Was anybody inside the helmet?"

Diggs: "Not to my knowledge, I don't think anyone was in it."

Diggs said he wrote what others told him and what his supervisors wanted. His first report didn't include Watts. Lieutenant Donald Arney ordered him to rewrite it and insert Watts. Diggs said he hadn't seen Watts at the scene. Diggs submitted a handwritten report, which was typed up by a secretary. The typed version differed from the original because a sentence was changed to include Watts' name.

Nesbitt ruled that Diggs' written notes and typed reports could be introduced into evidence, but with Watts' name edited out.

• • • •

A SECOND WITNESS THAT day took the stand with all sorts of precautions. George Slattery was the polygraph operator who interviewed Prince, the City of Miami police officer, during jury selection. Since Prince had pleaded the Fifth Amendment and the judge decided he shouldn't be called as a witness, she ruled that the defense could call Slattery. But lie detector tests weren't admissible in court, so Slattery couldn't say he was a polygraph operator. (In fact, Prince never completed the polygraph.) It also couldn't be brought out that Prince was pleading the Fifth.

Without preamble, McWilliams asked Slattery about a conversation he had with officer Alexander Prince.

"He told me he kicked Mr. McDuffie in the head, while wearing a boot, in the area of the left ear. And he also told me he dragged Mr. McDuffie between two police cars and dropped Mr. McDuffie from a height of six inches and Mr. McDuffie's head hit the ground."

Why had Prince kicked McDuffie?

"He said he wanted to get a lick in, too."

On cross-examination, Adorno asked Slattery to demonstrate how Prince had re-enacted the kick during their interview. Slattery stepped from the witness stand and kicked the court clerk's desk with considerable force.

"A vicious blow," Adorno said sarcastically.

"No editorializing," the judge warned.

"Did it dent your desk? Leave a mark on it?" Adorno asked.

"No" said Slattery.

If jurors were counting, they'd now heard about three persons not on trial who admitted to hitting McDuffie. Veverka testified he'd struck him as hard as he could with his fist. Hanlon had jabbed McDuffie in the kidneys with a nightstick and pulled him down with a chokehold. And now there was Prince, with no explanation to the jurors about why he wasn't standing trial. The medical examiner thought none of those blows killed McDuffie, but with each man the defense was adding to its theme that the wrong people were on trial.

*Chapter Notes

Chapter 29
"I Felt A Hand on My Gun"

An anecdote from Marrero's defense attorney, Ed O'Donnell: One night he ended up in the same Tampa restaurant as Hank Adorno. "Hank had met a pretty girl. He went out with her. And we were getting toward the end of the state's case. And Hank said to me, 'You better tell your client to take the stand. I'm cross-examining him.' And I said, 'You know, Hank, I will.' We're not mad at each other. I like Hank. He likes me. But I did go home that night and tell Alex. I think that motivated him a little more."

Marrero was charged with second-degree murder, which in Florida meant "evincing a depraved mind regardless of human life, although without any premeditated design." As the prosecutors had boasted to the media when they slapped the charge on him, the maximum penalty was life imprisonment. No lawyer expected any reasonable judge to impose that kind of sentence on an ex-cop, but with the huge public pressure on this case, the defense team was no longer sure what reasonable meant.

Certainly, Marrero was feeling an immense weight as he took the witness stand. He was wearing a beige suit and a dark tie. He and O'Donnell had been preparing for this moment for weeks.

To get him comfortable in the witness box and to personalize him to the jury, O'Donnell started by asking about his personal life. He was born in Havana, the son of a military man. He came to Miami at the age of 7. In high school, he stood out as a left-handed power hitter on the Miami Springs baseball team. He signed a contract with the St. Louis Cardinals, but a compound shoulder fracture ended his sports hopes.

Marrero said he became interested in a police career when still a child: He met an officer at the site of his sister's murder. Her husband had just killed her and her two children, and the police sought out Marrero as next of kin because he was "the only one they could get hold of."

He'd been with the PSD for four years, two of them in the Central District. He testified that he had gone to the hospital four times with injuries suffered on duty. He said he'd been shot at five times but never shot back. Four times, he said, he'd requested transfers out of the district. The requests were ignored.

On the night of December 17, Marrero testified, he was in an unmarked police car prowling the streets of Liberty City looking for burglars. He joined the chase and reached the place where the motorcycle stopped just in time to see Veverka smash McDuffie in the head with a Kel-Lite.

This was a major variance with Veverka's testimony: that he had hit McDuffie as hard as he could, but with his fist, not a heavy five-battery Kel-Lite. McDuffie continued to battle after the Veverka blow, Marrero testified. Hanlon then choked the motorcyclist with his nightstick, bringing him down the pavement. Still, McDuffie was doing "a typical karate kick," one of which hit Diggs in the knee. Diggs collapsed.

It was then that Marrero jumped into the fight. He said he was carrying a nightstick. He said he no longer owned a Kel-Lite: He'd given his away to a female officer.

As he tried to subdue McDuffie, he testified, he felt McDuffie reaching for his gun.

O'Donnell handed Marrero a nightstick so he could demonstrate.

Marrero: "I grabbed McDuffie. I didn't touch him. I grabbed him."

O'Donnell, standing right beside him: "You could feel it."

Marrero, with a nightstick in his hand: "I could feel it, pulling away from me, pulling my gun away from me."

O'Donnell: "What did you do?"

Marrero: "I said something to myself."

O'Donnell: "What's that?"

Marrero: "I felt a hand on my gun, and I said, 'Oh, shit!' And I went back like that, and — "

O'Donnell described for the court reporter what Marrero was doing: "A snapping motion with the right hand and the right hip pivoting back and the left hand coming forward with the nightstick."

Marrero was standing beside the witness stand. "And I struck the man in the area around here." With the nightstick in his left hand, he moved it toward the right side of O'Donnell's face. With both men standing, he showed his left hand with the nightstick motioning toward striking the right side of O'Donnell's face.

Marrero said he slammed McDuffie again, once in the shoulder, then in the face, between the forehead and mouth. McDuffie collapsed to the pavement, Marrero said, and he stayed down. The fight was over.

Sitting back in the witness stand, he said all the action was over in about 45 seconds. He estimated that he hit McDuffie at least three times, but less than six. McDuffie was not handcuffed when they fought, and he certainly wasn't down on the pavement.

Marrero said he felt "excruciating pain" during the fight. He said he had to go to his first aid kit afterward and apply bandages to his knee and elbows.

Everything he did, Marrero said, was legal and justified. When McDuffie got a grip on his gun, "Right then, it was just him and I."

If he to do it again, "I would do it the same way.... I feel bad a man is dead," but "I felt that everything I did personally was the right thing to do."

O'Donnell asked Marrero if he'd shot at McDuffie during the chase that night, as state witnesses insisted. Gotowala, the city cop who quit the night of the incident, had testified that Marrero exclaimed, "I missed the motherfucker twice." Both Veverka and Meier said they heard three shots.

Not true, Marrero said. He had an explanation for witnesses who saw Evans giving him bullets. After subduing McDuffie, he said, he walked up to Sergeant Evans. "I told him, 'I'm worried. I lost a speed loader,'" a device for loading bullets into his revolver quickly. "Sergeant Evans had a smile on his face, and he said, 'Here you go, dumbbell.'" Evans gave him "a cracked and scratched up" speed loader. Marrero removed the bullets and put them in his pocket.

Later that morning, Marrero testified, he told Veverka, "Hell, if I would have shot at him, I wouldn't have missed." Marrero said he'd scored 299 out of 300 in target practice. In fact, he had an outstanding marksmanship pin, which he lost that night. (It was found hours later by Eula Bell McDuffie.)

Later, Marrero said, he went with Hanlon and officer Eric Seymen to a yard where the Kawasaki had been towed. The place was closed. "It was supposed to be open 24 hours." They entered between a chain-link fence and a wall. Tow-truck employees returned just then, he said, and showed them the cycle.

This coincided with Hanlon's testimony, but Marrero said it wasn't true that they had removed a part from the cycle and thrown it in a dumpster, as Hanlon alleged. Marrero said they just went to get the Kawasaki's vehicle identification number.

Back in the Central District squad room waiting to give statements to Saunders of Internal Review, Marrero said he heard Hanlon say that he only handcuffed the motorcyclist. He didn't hit him. Marrero said he shouted at Hanlon: "You hit the man, you lying bastard. Why are you scared? You know it's justified."

O'Donnell: "Alex, who was the first to go to Internal Review and give a statement under oath?"

Marrero: "Myself."

When O'Donnell was done, Carhart had some questions: "Have you ever at any time, under any circumstances, and for any reason ever denied that you were at the scene of Arthur McDuffie's arrest?"

"No, sir."

"Have you ever at any time or for any reason in any form, whether under oath or not, ever denied that you hit Arthur McDuffie?"

"No, sir."

• • • •

AS PROMISED IN THE restaurant, Adorno did the cross-examination.

Why hadn't Marrero informed Sergeants Evans and Diggs about Veverka hitting McDuffie with a Kel-Lite? Why wasn't that in any report? "I didn't have any reason to say what others did."

Adorno asked if he used his left hand to swing the nightstick with such force. Marrero said he had. Wasn't he considered to be a left-handed power hitter in baseball? Yes, said Marrero.

Had he ever seen an officer use unnecessary force? "No, never," he said emphatically. "I think officers should have used more force to avoid getting killed." He added McDuffie committed six felonies that night.

Adorno then ventured down a road of citing bad behavior of his own witness, Hanlon. Wasn't there a time when he and Hanlon were on a call, and there was a fight that made Hanlon so angry that he knocked out every window in a house? Yes, said Marrero.

Adorno didn't go into details for jurors, but this was a call in Liberty City in which a man knocked Evans unconscious with a heavy wooden statue. Marrero had eventually subdued the man, who was 6 foot 3 and weighed 220 pounds.

Had Marrero arrested Hanlon for knocking out the house's windows?

Hanlon might have had his reasons, Marrero responded. "Somebody might need air."

Adorno kept pressuring. He insisted that Marrero reenact the way he'd hit McDuffie, with Adorno playing the motorcyclist.

As Marrero raised his nightstick high above Adorno's head and started to bring it down, Judge Nesbitt shouted: "Don't!"

Marrero mumbled something to the judge, perhaps an apology. The laughter of spectators drowned out his words.

Another time, Adorno tried to get Marrero to slip. "All right, as you grabbed your Kel-Lite, jumped out of your car and ran to the struggle, did you —"

"Sir," Marrero interrupted, "I didn't have a Kel-Lite."

Adorno apologized and moved on to the reports written by his co-defendants, Diggs and Evans. Marrero said they wrote exactly what he told them: McDuffie was resisting arrest and went for his gun, and that's why he hit him.

The prosecutor returned to Marrero's visit to the tow yard, which Marrero claimed was to get the motorcycle's vehicle identification number. Adorno played a police radio call of a dispatcher reading the VIN number to the squad at 2:08 a.m., a half hour before Adorno visited the yard.

"Hear that!" Adorno shouted. "Every officer on the scene already knew that VIN number!"

Carhart used that to make a point when it was his turn: "Know what the dispatcher did at 2:08 a.m.?" he asked the jury. "They gave her the bike's tag number, she punched it into the computer and it gave her the VIN number from the registration." Carhart paused for emphasis. "And suppose the tag had been switched? You don't need the real number on that motorcycle? That's basic police work." Carhart, Gerstein's onetime chief assistant, had just shown that he knew more about police procedures than did Reno's chief assistant.

• • • •

WHEN MARRERO STEPPED down from the witness stand, it was almost 7 p.m. The defense attorneys announced they were resting their cases. Evans and Watts had chosen not to testify. *Chapter Notes

Chapter 30
"It's All or Nothing, Judge"

The state put on one rebuttal witness: Carol Haas, a nurse in the emergency room of Cedars of Lebanon Hospital. She treated Diggs when he came in with an injured knee about 3 a.m., an hour after the incident. Diggs had testified that he left the ER in a wheelchair.

Not true, said Haas. He "walked normally" as he left. She watched him go down the hallway on a closed-circuit TV monitor. He never used a wheelchair.

Haas testified that she had seen his chart. He had put a series of Xs through the part that said "injured when suspect kicked him." She asked him how he was injured. "He said he injured his leg wrestling with a suspect. I asked him why it was changed. He said it was because of insurance purposes."

No explanation was given to jurors, but a county cop was eligible for workers' comp if he fell chasing a suspect but was not necessarily paid if he was injured by a suspect during a disputed use of force.

••••

ON WEDNESDAY, MAY 14, with closing arguments scheduled the next day, the lawyers held a lengthy session about what instructions the judge should give the jurors, who were locked in the jury room with newspapers taped over the windows.

Defense lawyers showed how confident they were when the issue of "lesser charges" came up. Jurors are often given the choice of finding a defendant guilty of a lesser crime, such as convicting a person of aggravated battery when they're charged with manslaughter. But for this trial, both the defense and prosecution agreed that conviction must be based on the original charges filed by the state attorney's office.

"It's all or nothing, judge," McWilliams said. His client, Diggs, "did nothing wrong. He wants no lesser includeds, not even a parking ticket."

James Lees commented: "The decision to forgo any lesser included offenses was a smart one as it eliminated one way for jurors to compromise."

The rest of the day, the lawyers spent preparing final arguments. Each defense attorney was to have two and a half hours, the prosecution four. The four defense attorneys were to go first, the prosecution in the middle, and then the defense would get a final say. Defense attorneys could choose to split their allotted time between the two sessions any way they wanted.

• • • •

ON THURSDAY, MCWILLIAMS led off for the defense, using all his allotted time to defend Diggs. He'd leave it up to other attorneys to respond to Adorno.

He portrayed Diggs as a dedicated officer who "stops violence, fights crime, catches crooks and protects citizens." He played a tape of the radio calls made during the frenetic chase of McDuffie through the streets, a chase that endangered the lives of the officers.

He showed the jurors a whiteboard with the names of the major witnesses. He cited the problems with each, erasing each name when he was done. Veverka was a "weasel." Meier was "more of a social worker than crime stopper, the most pliable." Hanlon was "mad dog crazy man."

He blamed Captain Bowlin for the charges against Diggs. And it was "Bowlin's brigade" that benefited by getting promotions, while Diggs and the others were offered up as "sacrificial lambs" to please the politicians and media.

McWilliams also blamed McDuffie. "He was a mad man taking on the world." He fought fiercely, perhaps because he was high on drugs. "He kept committing those felonies... battery on a police officer.... And the McDuffie family interest is money, money," referring to the multimillion-dollar lawsuit against the county, the PSD and defendants.

McWilliams walked close to the jury box to show his pig tie clasp. He wore it proudly, he said, to support the police and to defy all those who used "pig" as an insult.

As he summed up, he was on the verge of tears, his voice rising as he proclaimed that Diggs was innocent. "He's a cop. He's not a crook. He didn't kill anybody. This was justifiable use of force. He didn't cover anything up. All he did was go out there and fight crime and protect the citizens...."

"Don't make a mistake and bury your mistake in a prison like Raiford," the name of the state's central penitentiary. "Don't send him to prison for some political nonsense going on back in Miami."

• • • •

O'DONNELL MADE A STRATEGIC gamble. With his client, Marrero, facing the most serious charge, he chose to spend a mere 10 minutes or so in the opening round, leaving himself more than two hours to speak after the prosecution presented its case.

He warned jurors to be wary of the prosecutors. "They will wave those [morgue] photographs of McDuffie like a red flag to get you to act like a crazed bull and charge to the verdict they want."

O'Donnell declared that the case was flawed from the outset, as pressured police leaders led "the most slipshod, vile investigation probably in the annals of criminal justice."

Carlton, the defense's non-team player, accentuated that distinction by asking Watts to sit in a chair in front of the defense table.

He told the jurors they should consider his case alone, ignoring the charges against the other defendants.

He decried the state's tactics of giving "impenetrable, steel-vault immunity" to three ex-cops, and he said McDuffie was responsible for his own death: "This man who risked the lives of each of these defendants and other police officers created his own destiny."

Carlton could be long-winded in the courtroom, as reporters and colleagues pointed out, but he had one main, simple point to make. Of all the state's witnesses, only one said anything against his client, and that identification was wobbly. The lawyer sat in the witness stand as he mimicked Gerant's hesitation: "I am not sure.... I could be mistaken.... I wouldn't bet my life on it."

Speaking last for the defense, Carhart told the jury that the state's first two witnesses, Veverka and Meier, were the ones who had the motive to cover up: They were the first two officers on the scene of the incident, and they were the first two to get to the state attorney's office for the immunity deals.

He said their testimony over time kept changing to help the state. "See how the testimony improved in the case, just like good wine. He says, 'I think' in December, 'I believe' in January and 'I know for sure' in May."

Carhart belittled Meier taking more than a month to remember "I give up!" He challenged the state to start the Kawasaki, still resting near the court clerk's desk. "After they do that, I want to hear the state argue to you that those words could have been heard by Mark Meier."

Carhart knew he could be confident in issuing the challenge: A PSD tech had said the battery was dead.

All Evans did, Carhart went on, was write what he was told by those who saw what happened, and that included the false statements by the state's witnesses. Why blame Evans for writing there was an accident when the paramedic, the hospital and the medical examiner all thought at first there was an accident?

"And there is not a hint from the witness stand that anyone came up and said, 'No motorcycle accident, Herb. We just beat up the guy. Help us cover it up.'"

How could the state accuse Evans of a cover-up when he "called the Accident Prevention Bureau to the scene to investigate within minutes after he arrived there himself," awoke Bowlin after doctors told him McDuffie's injuries were life-threatening and "called the Metro Internal Affairs section before dawn to alert them to a serious use-of-force incident?"

While Evans acted promptly, Carhart argued, "why did he [Bowlin] hold up Evans' use-of-force report for eight days, hoping it would blow over? Why didn't the crime lab go to the scene until December 26? Why did the lady [McDuffie's mother] have to do her own crime scene investigation?"

Carhart, too, bashed McDuffie. "There is a war out there: Who is going to control the streets? For reasons I know not why, Arthur McDuffie joined that war." He said the motorcyclist "made a gesture" before leading police on a long chase. "Is this a man who is a good, law-abiding citizen?"

Speaking softly, he said he didn't know McDuffie personally. He didn't know if he was a good or bad person. His death was a "tragedy," but McDuffie "attacked the peace and dignity of the community. He set himself against the law."

Yet the state insisted on going after the dedicated police officers who chased McDuffie down. Evans "was offered an opportunity on December 25 to hand up his men. Just as he wouldn't cover up for his men, he wouldn't hand them up to save his own skin and testify falsely."

Carhart said the case was "Alice in Wonderland. Except it is Herbert in Wonderland. It is like the emperor with no clothes, walking nude. They are pretending they have a case," he said, nodding toward the prosecutors. "I say they are stark naked. They have no case. This is insanity. What is this man doing in a courtroom for seven weeks?...

"McDuffie's death is a tragedy. I submit it is not the only tragedy. This investigation is a tragedy. The prosecution of Herb Evans is a tragedy."

Despite Carhart's eloquence, James Lees, the former prosecutor, believes closing arguments "are generally overrated. More important is the good opening statement that permits jurors to know and adopt a certain story about the case and then during the trial have that story supported by the facts, while facts that do not jibe with the adopted story are easily rejected by jurors. Psychologists call this "belief perseverance." The vast majority of jurors have indeed made up their minds before closing arguments. Lawyers' egos will never permit them to admit this, but the main purpose of closing arguments is to provide the majority of the jurors (who hopefully are on your side by this point) with some language and analogies to use to bring over the few minority jurors in order to obtain a verdict." *Chapter Notes

Chapter 31
Cops Used "Street Justice"

Speaking from a lectern in the center of the courtroom, Adorno said the defendants used "street justice" to punish Arthur McDuffie when they should have let him have his day in court. They forgot their duty as police officers and lost all self-control. McDuffie had been speeding. He'd broken the law, but he shouldn't have been treated like a rabid dog. "When you think about what is alleged to have happened, if it happened, it destroys the criminal justice system in Dade County."

He used a whiteboard to list the four defendants and the 13 charges against them.

The officers wanted to teach McDuffie a lesson. They hadn't expected to kill him. "They expected him to live and to file a complaint. And it would have been 15 to one. And who would have believed McDuffie? He would have walked into the state attorney's office and we would have laughed in his face.... And asked, 'Who are you, some ass who rode 110 miles an hour?'"

Instead he died, and there was a coverup. How do prosecutors "uncover a coverup?"

He wrote COVERUP and below it NIXON in eight-inch-high capital letters on the whiteboard.

(Later, Lees questioned the wisdom of this: 'Rule No. 1 in jury arguments: Don't use examples from politics because everyone has his own opinions about politics. If you were a devout Richard Nixon fan — and even in 1980 there still were plenty — you might not like the government lawyer using Richard Nixon as an example of similar conduct to police officers who allegedly beat an innocent man to death.")

To break open a coverup, Adorno said, "you have to get one of the members, somebody to break the code.... How did we find out about President Nixon? Was that not a coverup? Didn't John Dean have to come forward? You got to have someone come forward and when they do, you've got to promise them something."

And that's what happened with Veverka and Meier. Without them, "we never would have uncovered the cover-up." It was "their duty when they see evil, when they hear it, when they hear it spoken, they're supposed to go out and do something about it. And that includes when it's one of their own."

Adorno granted that there were problems with the immunized witnesses.

"They got a free ride, no doubt about it. But we know somebody beat McDuffie, causing his death."

Perhaps sensing that the jurors might be bothered by witnesses who admitted to lying under oath, he acknowledged the immunized witnesses were no longer fit to be cops. He said the PSD was right in firing all of them – both defendants and immunized witnesses – months before.

Almost screaming, he said "They have no business being police officers. They are despicable. They lied under oath." He singled out Hanlon for special scorn: "I agree he is bad. He was also a police officer. He was one of them," he said, waving toward the defense tables.

Still, Adorno begged that the immunized witnesses not be ignored. They were there. They saw what happened. "You got to have someone come forward and when they do, you've got to promise them something. If they never came forward and were not immunized, we would not be here. Arthur McDuffie would be buried. Every one of these gentlemen would be home," Adorno said, pointing to the defendants.

Adorno mocked the core of the defense's claim that eight to 10 officers couldn't get the 148-pound McDuffie under control without resorting to deadly blows. He said the fight was obviously "unfair."

He lambasted Marrero and Diggs for claiming that the slender McDuffie was "a wild man... able to jump buildings... the Incredible Hulk," whereas the truth was that he was on the pavement, "totally incapacitated, bleeding, handcuffed, defenseless," when he was beaten to death.

Adorno ran through the defendants.

Marrero hit McDuffie out of "ill-will, hatred and spite." These words were used to support the state's claim that this was second-degree murder. Adorno said Marrero's muscular shoulders were as big as his thighs. He said Marrero was well aware that he could justify using enough force to kill a man if the man was reaching for his gun.

"Somebody beat that man's brains out. Hanlon told Sergeant Herb Evans that Alex Marrero 'tuned him up.' What was Skip Evans' response? 'I know.'...

"Veverka tells you that Marrero was loading bullets in his revolver and said, 'I missed the fucker twice.' Hanlon saw Sergeant Evans hand the bullets to Marrero to load his gun."

As for Watts, Adorno argued, Gerant saw Watts hit the cyclist in the head at a different time that Marrero hit him. Gerant identified Watts, and he should be believed, Adorno argued, ignoring Gerant's admission that he might be mistaken.

As for Diggs, he wanted Veverka's report changed so that he was among the last to arrive, not among the first. And yet he claimed to have seen the motorcycle crash and McDuffie fly through the air. And then Diggs conveniently fell to the ground and couldn't do anything. Diggs "sat on his ass," Adorno charged, with "his eyes closed and cotton in ears," unable to see or hear the beating and hear the blows that shattered motorcycle headlight and taillight, "while his men acted as judge, jury and executioners....

"Only Diggs could have stopped what was going on out there," Adorno argued. It could only have been Diggs who said, "Easy, one at a time" and "there are too many witnesses."

In fact, Veverka said it was Marrero who exclaimed, "Easy, one at a time."

For Evans, Adorno recited the testimony of the bike needing more damage and Evans tossing the keys on the roof. He disputed an accusation that he failed to let the jury see a voluntary statement Evans made on Christmas Day. "The law won't allow me to let it into evidence," Adorno declared.

Carhart leaped up and objected. He said that comment was deliberately misleading. Nesbitt sent the jury out.

The usually soft-spoken Carhart shouted: "He says the law won't let him, and I say he's a liar. And I say it to his face."

Adorno shouted back. The judge sighed. "Mr. Adorno, that was an improper statement," she said. "I am going to tell the jury."

As when he stated that "somebody beat that man's brains out," Adorno used the "somebody" accusation again, this time about the Kawasaki: "We know somebody vandalized that bike." And also about the blows to the head: "Somebody beat [McDuffie's] brains out. Somebody went too far. Somebody used unnecessary force."

But the question was who. Adorno's "somebody" theme fit in with Carhart's post-trial question: "The real question was who did what?"

Adorno had disparaging words for McDuffie as well, perhaps understanding that he was speaking to a law-and-order jury. "Here are officers sworn to uphold the law, all trained like Ira Diggs, proud to be police officers, and… some ass riding a bike at 110 miles an hour, putting everybody's life in danger. You are going to have to figure it out yourself. You are going to have to do the best you can in a difficult situation and come out and reach the verdict you feel is just in this particular case. I submit to you that verdict is guilty.... but I will await your final judgment."

• • • •

ADORNO'S ARGUMENT CONSUMED four hours. That left time for some defense rebuttal on Friday afternoon. Carlton repeated that there was only one witness against Watts, and this witness admitted he could be mistaken.

O'Donnell, who had two hours left for his remarks, focused on the politics and the immunized cops. He said the only reason Marrero was charged was "to get the mob off their backs. They did that once many years ago. They even had a trial, too. Then they hung him on Mount Calvary. They crucified him."

If the prosecution had gone over the top by comparing the cops' coverup with Nixon's Watergate, the defense certainly topped that by likening Marrero to Jesus on the cross.

O'Donnell hammered on the immunized witnesses' lies. One had been revealed just a few days before, when Hanlon's attorney notified prosecutors that Hanlon "wants to change his testimony." He claimed on the witness stand he hadn't talked to Veverka or Meier, but the defense had found phone records that Hanlon talked with Veverka for 23 minutes shortly after Hanlon met with prosecutors. Now, he remembered the call but didn't recall what the two talked about. "But this is also the man who remembers exactly how many bullets he saw Sergeant Evans give Alex Marrero," shouted O'Donnell. "It was three, of course, because he knew other witnesses said they heard three shots."

To show how bad the investigation was, he said the state had a firearms expert who was willing to testify that Marrero's police-issued Smith & Wesson revolver matched a casing found at the scene. "Then they learned from us that he never carried that gun," but preferred his own stainless-steel .38 with special stocks.

"I am not going to let Alex be half-truthed into Raiford," O'Donnell said, again mentioning the state's main penitentiary. "Alex is innocent. I don't know if I have proved it. But I feel there is at least an overwhelming reasonable doubt in this case."

With that, the judge adjourned court for the day. Carhart was to have the last word on Saturday morning, then the case would go to the jury.

*<u>ChapterNotes</u>

Chapter 32
"I Have a Gut Feeling"

On the morning of Saturday, May 17, Carhart gave the final defense argument, summarizing the themes that he and his colleagues had been emphasizing all along.

He insisted the investigation was flawed: first almost nonexistent, then rushed to meet the howling protests. "It is a shame that a 3,000-man, how-many-million-dollar department [needed] a phone call from a newspaper reporter to make them give a damn." Then they screwed up the investigation. "The state flunked the test. They do not have a case. The emperor is naked."

The immunized witnesses could not be trusted. He returned to Hanlon's late admission that he erred earlier in the trial when he denied conversations with other immunized witnesses. He now admitted he'd talked to Veverka but couldn't remember what they'd said. "You saw a liar in living color."

He returned to his tragedy theme: "Let Arthur McDuffie rest. His death was a tragedy. Take the politicians off the exploitation of the man. Do not commit a [another] tragedy. Find Herb Evans not guilty."

And finally: "The only thing I fear is mob psychology. We spent three weeks selecting a jury. I don't think we picked a mob."

When Carhart concluded, the judge read the lengthy jury instructions. One was key, and Carhart's final argument was likely aimed at that instruction. Nesbitt told the jurors they should use special caution in weighing immunized witnesses. "You should consider whether the testimony may be colored in such a way [as] to further the witness's own interest, for a witness who realized that he may procure his own freedom by incriminating another has a motive to falsify."

• • • •

SHORTLY AFTER 11:30, the six jurors entered the jury room, which had two tables, more than a dozen aluminum chairs, a watercooler, a coffeemaker, and a two-pound can of Luby Lee coffee. A note to the janitor was on the wall: "Do Not Throw Cups Away Please. The Jury." In the room with them were the trial's 84 exhibits, including McDuffie's 640-pound Kawasaki 900 motorcycle, the scuffed white helmet and the plastic skull that Wright had drawn lines on.

Reporters waited in the corridor outside the courtroom. Only Shinhoster of the Tribune had ventured to suggest in print that one or two defendants might be acquitted. But as the wait began on Saturday morning, those who sat through the trial daily speculated among themselves.

Slacum of the St. Petersburg Times had been hearing a common mantra for days among the civil rights observers and some reporters: "I have a gut feeling they're all guilty, but..."

"Scarcely a day passed," Slacum wrote later, "that some courtroom spectators did not utter those words. The statement usually ended with doubt about whether the former... officers would be convicted.... When Adorno rested his case, both black and white spectators who had a 'gut feeling' admitted that the prosecutors failed to show that the officers were positively guilty of the charges against them."

Williams of the Miami News heard speculation that at least some were likely to walk. "In the hours before the verdict, reporters speculated," he wrote later. "The newsmen agreed that one or two defendants might walk away from manslaughter charges. The cases against Michael Watts and Sergeant Ira Diggs appeared weak. The case against Sergeant Herb Evans Jr.... was up in the air. Only on Alex Marrero... was there general agreement on a conviction. 'But never on second-degree murder, only manslaughter,' said a TV newsman, summing up the general view."

Meanwhile, the defense team was warned by a bailiff that Judge Nesbitt had ordered the defendants to be immediately taken into custody if there were guilty verdicts. Carhart was outraged: "These were men who had dedicated their lives to law enforcement. Surely, they could be allowed to turn themselves in later, if they needed to start prison sentences."

After two hours and 44 minutes of deliberations, the jury sent the judge a note: They had reached verdicts. No one was expecting such speed. Evans' wife, the pregnant police officer, was out shopping. Adorno was at the airport to pick up his wife.

"You never know what a jury is going to do," O'Donnell said in an interview. "But as certain as I could be, I thought he [his client, Marrero] was going to be acquitted. And that verdict came down very, very fast. No questions, nothing. I told Alex, 'This is awfully good.'" The judge wanted to wait. "Lenore is so nice: 'Oh, let's wait for Mr. Adorno.' I was really pissed. Their fate has already been decided.... Yoss was there. Why do we have to wait? Come on. Let's read the verdict."

His colleague, Carlton, was more cautious: "I'm naturally a paranoid individual when it comes to trials." He felt good about how he had handled Gerant, the only witness against Watts, but "I never predict how a trial will go.... I didn't expect a verdict to be that quick. Not at all."

Finally, the judge passed the 13 forms to the court clerk. Adorno rushed in just as she started to read:

"We the jurors at Tampa Hillsborough County the 17th day of May 1980 as to the defendant Michael Watts, as to manslaughter charged with count two of the information: not guilty. So say we all, David H. Fisher foreman."

Carlton, Watts' lawyer, calmly made a note on a legal pad. Behind the defense table stood a uniformed officer.

The clerk followed methodically with other charges against Watts: not guilty of manslaughter by unnecessary killing, not guilty of aggravated battery, each time reading out the details, including the foreman's name.

On it went: Diggs not guilty of two counts of manslaughter, not guilty of aggravated battery, tampering with evidence and accessory after the fact. Diggs brought his right hand to his mouth, choking back sobs, as McWilliams put his left hand on Diggs' shoulder.

Marrero not guilty of second-degree murder, not guilty of manslaughter and not guilty of tampering with evidence. Marrero bowed his head and rested it on his folded hands as O'Donnell rubbed his neck and back.

And finally, Evans not guilty of tampering with evidence and accessory after the fact. Evans stared down at the table. It took the clerk 13 minutes to read the verdicts on all charges.

The stunned prosecutors sat in their chairs. Reporters rushed to the defense table.

Diggs, still wearing his bulletproof vest, said: "I thought it was a joke when it started, and I don't think it should have ever gotten this far in the first place."

"The truth came out," Marrero said. "We have to live with it, and if people can't live with the truth, then what are they going to live with?... Thank God this country still has people who are honest and can base their opinion on the truth."

Evans told reporters: "This would not have happened if the investigation had gone forward internally and if necessary over to the state attorney's office immediately the day or the day after it happened. But since it was delayed for eight days and nothing — not until the press got a hold of it that this was blown up out of proportion. That's why we were here, and that's why we were charged."

Adorno and Yoss went off to a room to call Reno. They struggled to remember the best number to call. Finally, Adorno reached her: "No dice. Sorry, boss." Reporters asked him if he would do anything differently if he had it to do over. "I wish I had picked six other people."

"We were terribly depressed," Yoss recalled. Even with the problematic witnesses, he and Adorno had held out hope for some guilty verdicts. "We thought we had enough evidence. They [the jurors] had to believe, based on the injuries, on the coverup, they had to believe at least to some degree. We thought we proved our case. We were terribly disappointed with the verdict."

The clerk finished reading the verdicts at 2:36 p.m. The Associated Press put out a bulletin on its teletypes at 2:42 p.m.: All acquitted on all charges.

On WTVJ, Frank Lynn went live from outside the courthouse: "It took two weeks to find a jury here. It took four weeks to hear all the arguments and the evidence, but it took the jury less than three hours to reach the verdict."

Eula Bell McDuffie was shown waving her hands and shouting in agony: "They're guilty! They're guilty! They're guilty! They're all guilty and they'll be guilty from now on and God knows it."

After giving an impromptu press conference, the defense group gathered at a hotel bar. On the television set, a newsman announced their acquittals. They cheered. Diggs was still wearing his bulletproof vest. His mother, Wanda, leaned over and hugged him. "Heads snapped up when pictures of McDuffie's smashed and bleeding head ended the newscast," the Sentinel Star reported. A lawyer gave a toast: "Here's to change of venue!" *Chapter Notes

Chapter 33
"The Fires Are Going To Start"

On Saturday, May 17, 1980, when the Associated Press issued its news bulletin at 2:42 p.m., Bobby Jones, PSD director, and Ken Harms, chief of Miami police, were on a raised platform addressing a group of about 80 in African Square Park in the heart of Liberty City.

They were talking and listening to concerns about how to battle crime in their area. "We were really working hard to do something in the community," recalled Clarence Dickson, a Miami major who was the highest-ranking black officer in the city. The meeting had been scheduled well before anyone knew when the jury might be deliberating, and even now, they weren't expecting quick verdicts.

Harms: "The mood was fine. They were asking me questions. You know, we'd like more policemen in the neighborhood. There's a lot of crime."

Lonnie Lawrence, head of the PSD's Public Affairs Bureau: "We were sort of wrapping it up when I got a call that everybody had been found not guilty. It sort of stunned me."

Lawrence whispered to Jones, "We need to get out of here right now." They went to Jones' car. Lawrence told him: "All those guys have been found not guilty."

Jones responded: "You've got to be shitting me."

As the top brass departed, the news spread through the crowd. A black man, Otis Denkins, was angry Jones had left the stage without commenting on the verdicts. "With all that has happened with the Cubans and the Haitians, we did not need that," he told a reporter. "People are going to react.... There are going to be some horrible repercussions."

Two miles away, WEDR, a disco FM station popular with young black listeners, was receiving angry phone calls. By 3:45 p.m., several hundred were gathered around the station, which was about two miles from African Square. Civic leaders were huddling. Something had to be done quickly to give people a way to vent anger peacefully. They planned a demonstration at 8 p.m. at the Criminal Justice Building, where Reno's office was located. The announcers of WEDR and of WMBM, the black-oriented AM station, urged listeners to join the protest.

Other young black residents gathered at a public housing project. A 19-year-old complained about what he'd seen on television: "We had watched the trial every night. All those pictures and descriptions explaining how they beat the man to death, and they found those guys guilty of nothing? Not nothing? That's like saying the man didn't die."

Tom Petersen, Reno's chief administrative assistant, said the Tampa prosecutors had been warning top brass in the state attorney's office that there were problems with the trial: "The word around here was that an acquittal was a distinct possibility. What I can't understand is why the cops had no contingency plans. The verdict came down about 2 p.m. on a hot Saturday afternoon. No rain. The start of a weekend. It couldn't have come at a more inopportune time."

Around 5 p.m., on Northwest 62nd Street by the large Liberty Square housing project, the first rocks and bottles were hurled at cars driven by whites. Police cars attempted to block traffic. Shortly after 6 p.m., a mob on that street beat a white homeless man. Bloodied, he was rescued by a PSD sergeant, who asked for backup, which apparently caused a squad car to leave its post blocking traffic from moving down the street.

That meant there was nothing to stop a cream-colored 1969 Dodge Dart from going down 62nd Street. Michael Kulp, 18, was driving. Someone threw a chunk of concrete through the windshield. The car crashed. A crowd began beating Kulp and his brother, Jeffrey, 22. When Herald reporter Earni Young arrived, she saw the bodies of two young white men in the middle of the street. A black man in an old pale-green Cadillac ran over the bodies.

"The crowd cheered and yelled," Young reported. "There were children no more than 5 or 6 years old standing in the doorways, watching.... There was a lot of drinking."

Dunn, the FIU professor, had been at his home in Coconut Grove when he heard about the verdicts. "I just sat stunned for a while." He had a shot of bourbon, and then another, before a wire-service reporter called and asked if he'd heard about whites being attacked on 62nd Street. Dunn jumped in his car and raced to the area. By this time, officers had closed off the street.

Dunn talked his way through the barricades. "Hundreds of people were in the streets, most of them coming out of the Liberty Square housing project. Men were still beating the Kulp brothers.... with hundreds of people watching, including myself, with nobody intervening, including myself."

Maybe 20 or 30 young men were doing the beating. "I don't think anybody was over 30," Dunn said. "I'll never forget that one of the things I heard was 'We're going to get those Uncle Tom niggers next. Those black leaders haven't done anything for us.' And I thought: They're talking about me." Dunn drove to a Miami police command post set up in a nearby fire station. "I told them: They're killing people up on 62nd Street. You all need to do something about that."

Major Dickson heard Dunn's plea. He summoned a team that jumped in a police wagon and a squad car. "We came flying around the corner and we saw the bodies," said Arnold Gibbs, a black officer. "The crowd took off, hundreds of them.... We started taking shots right away. Bullets were bouncing on the sidewalk right in front of us, hitting the truck." One of the bodies had a rose stuck in its mouth. They grabbed the Kulp brothers and raced to Jackson Memorial. Jeffrey Kulp died several days later. Astonishingly, Michael survived, but spent months in the hospital.

Stierheim, the county manager, was having dinner at the Key Biscayne Hotel, attending some annual event with a large crowd, when he received a phone call about the riot. He left the dinner — "I hadn't had a bite, really" — and raced to the Central District station.

"I would direct officers to set up a certain intersection," recalled Bowlin, the PSD commander, "and I would say, 'Stop the citizens from going in there. Let's seal this area off where the violence is taking place.' And they would come back on the radio and say, 'I'm not staying here. I'm being shot at. I'm pulling out of here. You get somebody else in here.' I mean, just open defiance on the air. And looking back on it, I can't blame them. We were totally overwhelmed by the anger and the number of people.... We weren't ready for it."

Well before 8 p.m., about a thousand people gathered four miles south of African Square Park at the Justice Building, which housed the criminal courts as well as the state attorney's offices. Most were young and black, but there were also older folks, some with children, plus some white protesters. They carried signs like "Reno Must Go" and "Justice, justice, justice."

Soon, the crowd grew to 3,000. Some sang "We Shall Overcome." Others chanted "Reno! Reno! Reno!" They demanded her resignation. Others waved placards: "America is a Damn Lie." "All-White Is Not Impartial." "Where is Justice for the Black Man in America?"

Many in the audience were "working black people: schoolteachers, postmen, the guy who paints your house," said Major Dickson. "I was out there among the crowd. It was looking pretty good, pretty peaceful. An angry rally yes, but peaceful." At first.

When a minister was asked to lead a prayer, some in the crowd yelled: "We are tired of praying!" The pastor prayed for God to give blacks a direction, but he was shouted down: "Reno must go!" and "No white police in black neighborhoods!"

Police, both city and county, circulated in the crowd. A county squad car moved slowly through the throng toward the nearby PSD headquarters. Some people roared that the car ran over the foot of a black girl. The crowd erupted.

An unoccupied PSD car was overturned. Some kids set another car on fire. Then came more fires. Men smashed windows in the Justice Building. Rocks shattered the glass doors. Men started a fire in the lobby. Others moved toward PSD headquarters a block away and broke through those glass doors, too.

Older people and those with families left the scene.

Carlton, the defense attorney, arrived back in Miami that evening and went to an Italian restaurant for dinner a few blocks from the justice center. When he left the restaurant, "I could hear the sound of people rioting in the distance.... I was sad in a way, because it didn't reflect well on the judicial system. I understood the feeling of people, on the emotions and the racial issues," but as the attorney as one of the acquitted officers, he certainly didn't feel any responsibility. "I was just doing my job."

When Marshall Frank, the homicide commander, received a phone call at home that the PSD headquarters was under siege, he tried to get to the building. A black guy waved him away: "Get out of here!"

Frank showed his badge. The man shook his head. "You don't want to go in there." He didn't have a police radio with him, but he knew that the Herald monitored all police communications. Edna Buchanan met him in the parking garage and led him to the elevator to go to the fifth-floor newsroom.

In Frank's memoir, he wrote: "Alone now, we looked at each other with a dire expression, knowing local people were out there being killed, that this was going to be a sad and momentous day in the annals of Dade County. I don't know what really came over me when I ignored the crisis of the moment and pressed closer to Edna, wrapping her in my arms and kissing her. We were both stunned. For a few moments, we stared at each other, thoughts raging, until the door slid open.... Then I felt a pang of guilt. After all, my guys were out there in harm's way, and here I was making out with the queen of media."

Buchanan's memoir relates: "I was scared; everything was out of control. It was all coming down around us. We boarded the slow and creaky elevator to the newsroom and simultaneously stepped into each other's arms, hugging tight through the rest of the ride."

Later, Frank learned that about that time, rioters broke the glass doors of the PSD headquarters. On the floors above were the communications division, crime lab, central records — the core of the department's operations. The lobby desk was manned by "a rookie black female named Betty Johnson and Clarence Balanky, an old-salt drunkometer technician.... Frightened beyond words, [they] pulled their revolvers and pointed straight ahead." The crowd saw them and retreated.

At 9:25 p.m., police launched a counterattack with 90 officers and forced the mob away from the Justice Building and then the PSD headquarters.

Near the spot where the Kulp brothers were attacked, three young white men returning from a fishing trip were dragged from their cars. Benny Higdon, 21, a baker; Robert Owens 15; and Charles Barreca, 15, were slammed with rocks, boards, bottles and a metal newspaper rack. The crowd kept an ambulance from reaching the victims. All three died.

Sgt. Wayne English, a city officer who had arrived at the McDuffie beating as it was ending, and Sgt. Ray Jaffie drove a police van to the scene and loaded up the bodies. The two teenagers were already dead. Higdon died two hours later.

About 9:30 p.m. Bertha Rogers, 55, was driving past the Scott housing project when her car was struck by rocks. When she stopped, men poured gasoline on her and set her afire. She died.

Fires were breaking out in stores everywhere. Looters dragged merchandise through broken windows. Despite pleas from store owners, county fire officials said they could not send out trucks without armed escorts.

Terry Williams, a News reporter, saw looters leaving the stores with arms filled with merchandise. Some stuffed goods into their car trunks. They left with TVs, stereos, jewelry, clothes. Some were selling: A fifth of liquor for $2, Converse sneakers for $3, four tires for $30.

Ferre, the mayor of Miami, and John McMullan, executive editor of the Herald, were in the air overhead in a Knight-Ridder Newspapers plane, returning from a symposium at Princeton University to discuss community issues. McMullan had invited Ferre along, and when the rioting broke out, they rushed back.

"As we flew into Miami," Ferre recalled, "you could see the plumes of smoke coming out in five or six different places."

At 12:05 a.m. a mutilated man was found on a street corner. Shirtless, he had been stabbed, beaten and ran over several times, perhaps with his own car. The face was an unrecognizable pulp. The corpse had no eyes. It took several days for the body to be identified as Chabilall Jagarnauth, 22, a graphic artist from Guyana, father of a newborn.

Mildred Penton, 65, was returning from Flagler Dog Track with her husband and daughter when a crowd threw rocks at their car. Like the other white victims that night, they hadn't heard about the Tampa verdicts or the Miami rioting. She was struck on the head with a brick. She died five weeks later.

About 3 a.m., Emilio Muñoz, 66, a Cuban butcher, was ambushed by a crowd. Trying to get away, he smashed his car into a wall.

The crowd threw rocks at him and poked him with sticks, then set his car on fire with him inside. Police did not retrieve his body until the next morning, about the time his wife and son were in Mariel harbor in Cuba waiting for a boat to take them to the United States.

Stierheim, the county manager, recalled getting on the roof of the police station and watching the fires raging in Liberty City. "Of course, we'd sent the fire trucks in," but after those first trucks were fired upon, that stopped. "It was a terrible situation," he said in an interview for this book. "It's a little emotional for me now after all these years, but I was crying. I had tears coming down my face. This is your town, and it's going up in smoke."

Annie Love, head of the tenants' association at the Scott housing project, called Stierheim, "begging me to send in the police. She said there are 13-, 14-year-old boys walking around with .357 Magnums stuck in their belts. I felt a little helpless, because I couldn't send them in. We made the decision to cordon off the area with the help of the National Guard, but what happened inside is all the looting, they broke the store windows.... There were as many women going into the stores as men — and kids!" Shooting looters? "You can't do that. Wow — you talk about having a problem. Shooting because they're looting a 7-Eleven? Wow. That give me heartburn just thinking about it."

Harms said: "We had officers quitting during the course of the riots. We've had them walk out of roll call. 'I'm resigning my position. You can't pay me enough to do it.' And they'd check their gear just like that. It was a very difficult time.'"

Harms ordered his men not to shoot looters. "You are only allowed to use deadly force if your life or the life of another is in jeopardy. You don't want a police officer to shoot a little 7-year-old in the back."

All eight white residents who died were attacked on Saturday night, Bruce Porter and Marvin Dunn noted in "The Miami Riot of

1980." The 10 black deaths occurred starting early on Sunday morning.

Shortly after 3 a.m. Sunday, Elijah Aaron, 43, father of five, an irrigation system worker, was shot dead by a PSD officer who said Aaron had pointed a gun at him while looting a tire store.

Abram Philips, 21, was shot and killed by a Miami police sergeant who said Philips fired four shots at him. The police report said Philips had a .357 Magnum that had been stolen from a North Miami policeman.

About 4 a.m., Kenneth China, 22, was killed near his Brownsville apartment by a "stray bullet," according to police reports. At 4:05 a.m., Michael Scott, 17, a student, was killed by security guard at Jet Food Market. The guard said Scott had been looting the store.

On Sunday morning, as 500 National Guardsmen started to form a perimeter to curtain off the rioting area, looting in Liberty City resumed at about 10 a.m.

The Community Relations Board, a quasi-governmental agency created in 1963 to ease tensions between racial and ethnic groups, met that afternoon for four hours. Black leaders demanded Reno's resignation. She refused. "I am as bitterly disappointed as I can tell you," she told the board. "I opposed the decision that this case be transferred out of this county as vigorously as I knew how.... I assigned my four best prosecutors to this case, and I have never worked so hard in any case."

In New York City, Tom Petersen, Reno's top administrative assistant, was walking through Harlem that Sunday morning, seeing people "sitting on the stoops reading the New York Daily News with the cover being the riots in Miami." Reno had sent him up before the verdicts to explore vocational programs for minority youth that she wanted to institute in Miami." Even before the riots broke out, "Janet was very much attuned to and supportive of programs for indigent black youth."

After four hours at the Community Relations Board, County Commissioner Ruth Shack groaned, "Dark is coming in, and we're still here bullshitting." As the meeting ended, Georgia Ayers, a retired black social worker, urged the black residents present to go to the streets and tell people to stay inside their homes. "If you don't, a lot of our young people are going to get killed."

At 6:15 p.m., in the Larchmont Gardens public housing project, Andre Dawson, a 14-year-black youth, ran to get his sister at a store and bring her home because of the curfew. He was shot twice in the head by a white man in a blue pickup truck.

Not far away, Eugene Brown, 44, a construction worker, was waiting in his car while his wife and children went into a convenience store to buy orange juice. He was shot and killed by a white man in a blue truck.

About this time, Thomas Reese, 35, a truck driver, was drinking beer in a crowd watching a fire burning in a grocery store. Boys were throwing rocks at cars. They hit a truck, which stopped. The white driver opened fire. Reese was shot in the back and was killed.

About 8 p.m., in a predominantly Haitian neighborhood, a minister, LaFontant Bien-Aime, 39, was driving with his 13-year-old son. He was shot and killed by a police officer, Karl Robbins, who claimed the minister tried to run him over while the officer was chasing looters away from a furniture store. Bien-Aime's family said he'd been on his way to teach his regular Sunday evening church service a block away. The state attorney's office found no evidence the pastor had been in the furniture store. Later, a grand jury decided not to indict the officer.

By midnight Sunday, 3,000 National Guardsmen were in the area. The rioting was pretty much over.

The carnage was overwhelming. Dunn and Porter's research showed 417 persons were treated at nine local hospitals during the rioting. The vast majority on Saturday night were white. After that, the majority were black. An ER director said many of these injuries were cuts from glass or other lacerations, perhaps suffered during looting.

About 200 stores were burned, looted or damaged. Dunn and Porter reported. The burned stores were almost all white-owned, but "where black stores had merchandise worth stealing, and where they were left unguarded, they fell with everybody else."

Who rioted? Or more accurately, who was caught in the riots? They were by and large not the thuggish criminal element that many civic leaders blamed. Dunn and Porter examined 855 arrests and found only 32 percent of those people had been arrested before, a marked contrast to other riots. (In Watts and Newark, that figure was more than 70 percent.) The PSD noted that the city of Miami arrests included curfew violations.

"The statistics do seem strongly to disprove the riffraff theory, that the riot was the work of criminals." Dunn and Porter wrote. "It may have been criminals who started it, and it may have been criminals who did the hard-core killing, beating and burning and who opened up many of the stores to looting. But the figures suggest that the good people of the ghetto joined the rioting in large numbers, and that a sizable proportion of them were willing to commit criminal acts and expose themselves to arrest." *Chapter Notes

Chapter 34
"Shudder When You Say Justice"

What really happened in that courtroom that caused such devastation? Let's step back and take a deep look, peeling back layers to examine the question from many viewpoints.

Let's begin with the shock at the verdicts, as expressed by editorial writers who were reflecting the astonishment of the general public that had been reading the same trial stories that the editorialists saw. These writers crafted their first opinion pieces before seeing most juror interviews and the reporter analyses.

At the Miami News, it appeared that the editors had not been paying close attention to their own reporter's articles, which several times had pointed out prosecutors' problems. "We were stunned into disbelief" on learning the news, wrote Louis Salome, editorial page editor.

The main News editorial was headlined "The system let us down."

"Shudder, even weep when you say justice. There is a criminal justice system in this country, but the irony is that sometimes it wars on itself. Sometimes the system wins, justice loses and those who should be punished go free. In our opinion, this is one of those times....

"It was simply numbing, impossible to comprehend that an all-white jury in Tampa found four white Dade County police officers innocent of all 13 charges.... The jury deliberated less than three hours before returning its decision, after hearing testimony for about a month, which makes it reasonable to wonder whether it deliberated much at all.

"As outrageous as that finding is, the street reaction in Dade County is just as outrageous...."

The editorial cartoon in the News showed six white guys, labeled Tampa McDuffie jury, smiling as they used Kel-Lites and nightsticks to pummel a blind woman of justice, the scales falling out of her hand as she was pushed down to the ground.

The Herald's editorial on Monday, entitled "Miami Is Now on Trial," was adamant: "The jury in Tampa mocked justice. For reasons unknown, the system went awry. Those six white jurors said by acquitting them that none of the policemen who took Mr. McDuffie's life did anything wrong."

On the Herald's front page that Monday, columnist Joe Oglesby blamed the change of venue: "The move to Tampa may have been legally perfect, but I think it was a social travesty.... A jury I once served on took two hours to decide a simple slip-and-fall case. Although only money was involved, we wanted to be damned sure we did it right.

"It seems obvious now, with 20/20 hindsight vision, that a Miami jury might not have given such short shrift to so important a case. We have to live here; the Tampa jurors don't."

Oglesby, who had covered courts for the Herald, added a thought not mentioned by any of the reporters covering the Tampa trial or by any Miami editorial writers: "It is a recognizable lawyers' tenet that cops are more difficult to convict that anyone else. We all want to believe cops. And there is the almost impenetrable in-the-line-of-duty defense."

Oglesby went on: "Some courageous cops... broke the code and testified against their law-enforcement colleagues. Because the McDuffie case seemed so outrageously wrong, few people expected complete exoneration.

"The man's skull was cracked five times, some of the blows delivered while he was handcuffed and motionless. There was evidence of phony police reports and a deliberate attempt to inflict and disguise the damage on McDuffie's motorcycle....

"Yet Tampa's jury rejected all charges," Oglesby went on, "even the coverup and evidence-tampering charges. What extraordinarily talented jurors, to be able to dig through a mountain of evidence so swiftly." *Chapter Notes

Chapter 35
No, the Jurors Weren't Rednecks

Of those who attended the trial, the most incisive post-verdict analysis came from Verne Williams of the Miami News:

"How could the jury acquit the cops?

"If the cops didn't beat Arthur McDuffie to death (and then cover it up), who did?

"Those are the first questions a newsman hears back in Miami" after seven weeks in Tampa. "No, the jury was not composed of idiots and rednecks. The foreman was an FAA data-systems expert. There were an engineer, salesman, a former Navy petty officer, a disabled veteran, a marketing executive....

"What went wrong with this case of policemen going berserk, of 'street justice' carried too far, a case that seemed so clear to the layman from a reading of newspapers and watching of television?

"What went wrong was that the case crumbled. Not like a house of cards, all at once. More like a big three-story frame hotel caught in a hurricane. First the windows, then pieces of the roof, then the porches washing away.

"Inside, the occupants — the prosecution — ran around frantically boarding things up."

One example: The surprise revelation that Prince had kicked McDuffie in the head. Jurors heard about it from the polygraph operator but were given no explanation of why he wasn't a defendant.

"The defense attorneys, four of Miami's best, blew feathers off three of the key prosecution witnesses like expert marksmen at a pigeon shoot."

He went through the problems with the three immunized witnesses. "All had to admit to the jury they had first lied, then switched their stories after they got immunity. And their stories clashed in important respects. On cross-examination this was sometimes devastating to the credibility of the prosecution case."

Williams singled out Hanlon as "a disaster for the state." He first told prosecutors City of Miami officers struck McDuffie, then on the witness stand admitted that wasn't true. His "credibility [was] in tatters," wrote Williams. He also described the fiasco with Gerant, who named Watts while the others pointed to Marrero.

Ultimately, Williams wrote, "the truth and the lies were inextricably tangled." He blamed the rushed investigation and immunizing cops without the "usual precaution" of polygraphing them.

Then there was this: "A defense attorney remarked after the verdict that one big break for the defense was being able to take depositions, or question, some witnesses without Adorno present. 'He would have blocked us,' the attorney said." In fact, in quite a few depositions, the prosecution team was represented by its junior member, Stuart Adelstein, 29.

"Whatever happened," Williams' analysis concluded, "it's clear the prosecution never got the shutters on and the roof nailed down before the hurricane struck."

• • • •

THE ST. PETE TIMES analysis by Slacum led with her courtroom observers frequently saying, "I've got a gut feeling they're all guilty, but..." While editorial writers in Miami found the verdicts "impossible to comprehend," she laid out a clear roadmap of why the ex-cops were acquitted, starting with an excellent summation of the state's problems: "A crime had allegedly been committed by police officers, and the only eyewitnesses were police officers. Defense attorneys sang one song throughout the trial: 'The state attorney's office did a slipshod investigation because they did not take enough time.'"

Slacum found Adorno on Sunday. He was "shocked and stunned" by the violence of the riots. "He did not expect all four men to be acquitted, but Sunday, looking back at the case, he said that even if he had six months to three years to work on it, the verdicts still would have read not guilty."

Adorno added: "I think the Public Safety Department... did a hell of a job under pressure and tension," supporting a main defense point about the pressure investigators felt. "There were a great number of officers who I believe saw what happened but would not admit seeing things."

Slacum praised the "excellent job" by defense attorneys in making the immunized witnesses "look like liars. By the time defense attorneys finished their cross-examinations, it was plausible that the witnesses could have been responsible for McDuffie's death."

She then went through the defendants, starting with this remarkable sentence: "If Michael Watts had been found guilty of manslaughter... he certainly would have been railroaded. Only one witness said Watts hit McDuffie and that witness was not certain if his identification was correct."

"Prosecutors said Ira Diggs... saw McDuffie beaten and did nothing about it. One witness said Diggs hit McDuffie, but several witnesses said the sergeant was on the ground in pain the whole time...."

"Herbert Evans was not present when McDuffie was beaten. Prosecutors said he wrote false police reports.... Witnesses, however, said Evans did not deliberately falsify reports, but merely relied on what police officers had told him...."

"Marrero saved himself. He testified like a man with nothing to hide. He admitted hitting McDuffie. He said he was justified. As a police officer going to the rescue of fellow officers, he said he would do it again. Prosecutors failed to shake Marrero's cool, calm appearance."

Two black civil rights activists who sat through virtually the whole trial were quoted in other stories.

Ray Fauntroy, head of the Dade chapter of the Southern Leadership Christian Conference, said, "What you had was poor prosecution and inexperience that lost a case that should have been won hands down." He was left with "the indelible impression that the law stinks."

Bob Gilder, a Tampa resident and member of the advisory committee of U.S. Commission on Civil Rights, added, "I prayed to the Lord that I would be proven wrong as it related to my previous statement of Tampa being the home of the whitewash." McDuffie wasn't given a jury of his peers. Those jurors were peers of the defendants, the attorneys and the judge, he said.

The other newspaper reporters who sat through the trial daily didn't write analyses. Gene Miller of the Herald did his follow-up through interviews with the trial attorneys assessing what could have been done differently. More on that in a moment.

Shinhoster of the Tampa Tribune didn't do an analysis because she rushed to Miami to cover the riots. When I interviewed her, she agreed with Slacum about a "gut feeling" that the ex-cops were headed for acquittals. "There was a sense that the defense lawyers were very good. They flipped this thing so McDuffie looked like the bad guy, drugged up, some of the stereotypes of black males," while the real McDuffie was a white-collar insurance man whose worst errors were an unpaid traffic ticket and a suspended license.

"Plus these were police officers in Florida. Police officers must have reasons to do what they did. That's the way most citizens, including the jurors, were inclined to feel. It was a very pro-police jury," Shinhoster said. Still, after sitting through all the testimony, her main takeaway was this: "The brutality was awful. His head cracked like an eggshell.... I think my general sense was that the cops were bad," including the ones given immunity. *Chapter Notes

Chapter 36
"Notoriously Difficult to Prove"

What follows are the concluding comments of James Lees, the former police officer and prosecutor who has spent decades since as a trial lawyer and organizer of focus groups. He reviewed all the chapters of this book up through the verdicts and made his comments without looking at any of the other post-trial analyses.

"Both the investigation and prosecution were very poor. For the life of me, I do not understand why immunities were handed out like candy so early. If this exact same case were presented to one hundred different juries, each comprised of different makeups — including young and old, male and female, black and white — the verdicts would be the same the vast majority of the time.

"Reasonable doubt means just that: Do you have a reasonable doubt that arises about who did what, who is telling the truth and who is not, who is guilty and who is not? Based upon the first three witnesses alone, this case was heading for not-guilty verdicts on the express train, and the lack of experience in young prosecutors matched against experienced defense attorneys simply made the train have even less stops in the way to its final destination.

"As for the riots and civil unrest, the surest way to cause such unrest is to have the public misinformed about what is happening in a trial so that when the verdict is rendered vast numbers of people are shocked and surprised. Had the public during this trial read and seen media accounts as to how badly the prosecution was doing, how effective the cross-examinations of the defense attorneys were, the public would not have been surprised at the verdict. But surprise leads to shock, shock leads to anger and frustration, and all of you know the rest of the story.

"I do leave you with one thought: There are only two times your country requires you to do something for the privilege of living in this country. One is military duty in the time of war, and one is jury duty. It is the singular thing that separates our nation from many of those countries in which we fight our wars. I would rather have a group of reasonable American citizens deciding my fate any day rather than having it decided by a Saddam Hussein or a Kim Jong-un. The right to trial by jury is one of the most precious gifts given to us by our Founding Fathers. Yet what is the No. 1 reaction of most Americans when asked to perform that duty? 'Why are you bothering me?... I don't have time for this.'

"Sometimes the system does not work, but most of the time the blame lies not with the jurors but with the people responsible for bringing the case to the jurors. It is far too easy and too simplistic in this case to blame the jurors, and frankly I think to do so is dead wrong. 'They're guilty,' as Mrs. McDuffie shouted after the verdicts were read. 'They're all guilty.' All we need to figure out is who is 'they.'"

• • • •

IN THE MONTHS AFTER the trial, criticisms of the prosecution flowed in. The eight-person Governor's Dade County Citizens Committee lambasted Reno's office on a wide variety of fronts. It was chaired by Irvin J. Block, 53, a onetime state prosecutor and former president of the Dade County Bar Association. The panel included several other prominent lawyers, such as William Meadows, a former U.S. Attorney for the Southern District of Florida.

The panel criticized Reno's staff for not using the grand jury and not battling harder against change of venue. It lambasted Adorno for not questioning potential jurors. The committee gave Reno a backhanded compliment, saying her office wasn't racist, but added that she sometimes showed "insensitivity to the black community." It criticized her tardiness in handling of the LaFleur wrong-house raid and insisted she ignored her "duty" when she didn't bring charges against Shockley, the Hialeah officer who killed the black man urinating by the warehouse. The report expressed deep concerns about the case of the state trooper who pleaded guilty to molesting the 11-year-old black girl. "We question whether the same type of callous and indifferent inquiry would have taken place if this had been an 11-year-old white female."

The report's damning conclusion: "The State Attorney appears to have aligned herself on the side of the police even when such alignment is insupportable."

• • • •

ANOTHER TOUGH ANALYSIS came from the National Law Journal, in a July article by Tamara Levin, who reported that the McDuffie defense attorneys "and other local lawyers who followed" the case "say the prosecutors severely hampered themselves by making key tactical mistakes."

She mentioned the rush to indict, questionable immunity deals, not using a grand jury, not asking questions of jurors and putting on contradictory witnesses. "Lawyers familiar with the McDuffie investigation say that its handling reflects badly on Reno. They say she was in a double bind. First, she is known more for her administrative skills than her trial ability. She had not tried a case since taking office. Second, her predecessor, Richard Gerstein, who held the job for more than 20 years, had a practice of trying the most important cases himself as a means of signaling his commitment to them. So while few lawyers thought she should have been in the courtroom herself, her absence was taken by some as a sign that she was not giving the case top priority."

Reno responded: "I didn't try this case because to properly prepare it would have required three months away from my other duties. Hank Adorno is my top assistant."

• • • •

ON WEDNESDAY, AUGUST 27, 1980, CBS Reports showed an hour-long documentary: "Miami: The Trial That Sparked the Riots," produced by Harvard law professor Eric Saltzman and hosted by 60 Minutes veteran Ed Bradley.

Bradley was shown walking down a burned-out block: "Last May America was stunned when this community, the Liberty City area of Miami, exploded.... Today there is no more volatile issue in America's black ghettos than police violence — and our criminal justice system's response to it."

Bradley went on: "In Miami's newspaper and television reports, the McDuffie case seems open and shut, but inside the courtroom it is a different story. Police brutality cases are notoriously difficult to prove. Because there are no civilian witnesses to the beating, the state's testimony will have to come from officers who watched or even committed the same crimes the defendants are charged with."

On camera, Adorno told Bradley: "None of the officers who testified in this particular case are what you would call willing... witnesses. I think it's quite obvious that I had to draw out from them every bit of evidence that in any way incriminated their fellow officers. And I think that's natural."

The show went through the contradictions between Veverka's and Meier's testimonies, then how Gerant "jolted" the trial by pointing to Watts and vindicating Marrero.

Bradley: "At this point in the trial, the main problem with the prosecution's case is their own witnesses are contradicting each other."

Adorno: "Any time you're trying a case based only upon eyewitness recollection of an event, you're always going to have three people looking at the event seeing different things. And that's what I had to get across to the jury. It doesn't mean it didn't happen. It means they're looking at it from different angles. That their recollections of the event are different.... [Keep] in mind they just had an eight [minute] chase at 100 miles per hour. Your adrenalin is pumping. And everything happened in a minute and a half. And this wasn't something that happened in slow motion and stop action. it's something that happened with a lot of people being involved. Anywhere from five to 10 people all being involved in a gang fight, a gang tackle."

CBS tore apart Hanlon, including the "pure vandalism" of smashing the motorcycle and making the off-handed remark: "I had a nightstick with me. I said if you wanted to break somebody's legs, you could hit here."

Carhart: "That was the most chilling thing I have ever heard a witness testify to in a courtroom.... I find that an incredible thought process."

Bradley: "A grant of immunity can be necessary, but it can backfire. With Veverka, Meier and Hanlon, it was especially dangerous because they were all part of the cover-up. And Hanlon and Veverka were accused by the defense of striking the blows that killed McDuffie."

Ed Bradley in conclusion: "The acquittals in the McDuffie case reflect not so much what happened to McDuffie as they do the evidence the prosecution presented in the courtroom. On that evidence, the jurors were not convinced of guilt beyond a reasonable doubt. But understanding what happened in the McDuffie case makes it no less disturbing. One black man in Miami told me we felt we always could find justice in the courtroom, but if we can't get some kind of redress there, where do we turn?"

Saltzman, the producer, did most of the research for the show, then Bradley flew in to do the on-camera interviews. Saltzman's takeaways: "I had enough courtroom and academic experience to know how a trial works. My conclusion: It was unfair to tag the jury as racist." He agreed with the defense that the state "immunized some [who] were worse than the guys they put on trial. That's never palpable to a jury." *Chapter Notes

Chapter 37
Jurors: Bring "Dirty Laundry" to Tampa?

Even decades after the trial, jurors are still stung by the accusations, widespread in 1980, that they were racists who ignored the facts in order to protect brutal white police officers.

That racist tinge was the first thing Kenneth Stover mentioned to me when I reached him by phone. "That 'all-white male' — that just amazed me."

A Navy vet who worked as an engineer for Amoco Oil, he said no one discussed race in the jury room. The jurors had only one desire: "Everybody wanted to do a good job."

After almost four decades, he was fuzzy on details of specific witnesses, but he remained adamant about the overall picture. "There was way too much doubt."

When they entered the jury room, he thought, "we should convict someone of something," but as the six men discussed specifics, there wasn't enough for any guilty verdicts. "I couldn't do it. There wasn't the evidence. I think the prosecutors could have done a better job."

Starting with the prosecutors' silence during jury selection, Stover felt that Reno's assistants appeared indifferent. "It seems like the prosecution didn't want to win. They didn't put on the evidence that's going to make us convict."

He had no idea how accurately the news media portrayed the case. Jurors weren't allowed to see courtroom stories during the trial and he didn't make any effort to look at them afterward, in part because he was angry because he felt the media had exposed him and his wife to danger by publishing the names and addresses of the jurors.

In fact, the six print accounts I examined listed jurors' names and occupations, but not addresses, though in those days finding an address was often as simple as opening a phone book. After Miami exploded, at least two jurors were threatened at work. A sheriff's deputy in a squad car remained outside the Stover house for days.

The deaths of 18 in Miami weighed "heavy on your heart and the hurt that I have," he said. "People were dying maybe because of something that I decided. It had a huge effect on me." Still, he's certain the jurors reached just verdicts.

• • • •

STOVER SEEMED A QUIET, thoughtful guy, unlike Joseph Tetreault, the 20-year chief petty officer who then spent another 20 years working as a maintenance engineer for the Veterans Administration. He didn't like the press then, even asking the judge at one point to order the newspapers not to print his name. A day after the verdicts, he refused to talk about the trial. He told a Tribune reporter he was furious his name was in the newspaper. "We're getting out of the house. Just getting the hell out of here." His wife, Betty, was also angry at the press. "You wouldn't be happy until someone comes out and shoots us," she told a reporter. "You're trying to get us killed."

Decades later, his views hadn't changed. When I contacted him by phone, he said he didn't want to be interviewed. "No! Don't you come looking for me. I said no to 60 Minutes. I don't need this stuff."

He then talked for 40 minutes. He said he tried to get out of the trial, telling the court that his brother was a deputy sheriff in New Hampshire, but the judge kept him on, despite his protestations. "She was very stern."

He was pissed about the trial from the start. "They should have left it in Miami. Why bring it to Tampa? They sequestered us for 30 or 31 days. It messed up my life. I was fortunately on paid leave, but I couldn't go home, not even on weekends."

The bailiff took them to the hotel each night, took them to dinner and then in the morning back to the courthouse. That was their lives for a month. He got to know his colleagues quite well.

"I tell you what: I didn't like the way they tried the case." He meant the prosecutors, whom he regarded as "stupid bastards." They "overreacted" in bringing the charges. He thought the defense lawyers were far better: "The money is very good. That's why they stopped being prosecutors."

About McDuffie: "He was really stupid." At the start of the chase, he gave an officer "an Italian salute": flipping the finger. "What was he doing?"

When they started deliberating, one juror had an idea. Tetreault couldn't remember his name, but he was "one of the smartest guys I've ever met. [He] made a list of all the charges and all the defendants." This was probably Fisher, the foreman. The jurors went down the list, one by one, and each told how he felt about the charges. "It was pretty quick." On each charge, each juror said he was not convinced that there was guilt beyond a reasonable doubt. He didn't recall any protracted arguing. Later, some commentators criticized the jurors for not taking more time to deliberate. "But who says how much time a jury is supposed to take?"

He summed up the McDuffie case this way: "They brought their dirty laundry to Tampa — but they forgot to bring the goddamn soap. We don't need that shit."

Twice he repeated that dirty laundry phrase, perhaps indicating that it has become his mantra when explaining the trial to friends and neighbors over the years.

He agreed completely with the defense's argument that the immunized witnesses were the real guilty parties: "They put the wrong people on trial." Those testifying for the state "were absolutely the bad guys."

After decades, he didn't recall names, but he was especially turned off by one of the ex-cop witnesses who was wearing "big jump boots, an ex-paratrooper." This was probably "Mad Dog" Hanlon.

Tetreault also detested Janet Reno: "She was an asshole." When he learned in 1992 that Clinton had appointed Reno attorney general, "I said to myself, 'Well this guy should have been strung up.'" Tetreault, a Vietnam vet, suspected Clinton was "smoking dope with the Russians."

Again, he reiterated: "They put the wrong guys on trial. ... They had a sergeant there. He wasn't even at the scene. He was back in the sheriff's headquarters." This was Evans.

After the trial, "I was threatened" at the VA where he worked. A groundskeeper told him: "One of the guys was looking for you." Tetreault meant a black man. At their house, his wife drove off a newspaper reporter who knocked on their door. "Look, you son of a bitch," she told the reporter. "I hope you rot in hell."

The riots were "probably in the newspaper for three or four days," he said. He viewed the rioters a "a bunch of assholes. Stupid, stupid destroying their own area, their own pharmacies."

His summation of his trial experience: "The whole thing was a mess. A goddamn waste of time. A bad experience. The jury was just doing its job."

From a prosecution standpoint, Tetreault would have been among the worst in the world to put on a jury chosen to ponder the guilt of white officers accused of killing a black man.

He was the second-to-last person added to the jury. Near the end of selection, when defense attorneys had few challenges left, they eliminated a female candidate. "That brought up Joseph Tetreault," the Miami News reported. "Adorno liked him. 'The state accepts this panel.'"

The prosecution still had challenges left. After the trial, Adorno admitted that he wished he had made different juror choices. "There was no way I could have gotten a black or a woman on the jury.... But I could have gotten a different six."

• • • •

RIGHT AFTER THE VERDICTS, most jurors refused to speak to reporters who tried to talk to them at the courthouse. The next day, after the riots exploded in Miami and they saw themselves being blamed on television as racists who caused the deaths of 18 people, most jurors didn't respond to phone calls or knocks on their doors. The exception was David H. Fisher, the jury foreman. He gave a brief interview on Saturday to the Herald and at least one television station. On Sunday and Monday, he talked to several more reporters.

Unlike Tetreault, Fisher came across as measured and thoughtful. He was a Federal Aviation Administration employee who worked at Tampa International Airport as a computer specialist for air traffic control. After the verdicts, Fisher told reporters, a woman called his office and passed along a message: "Tell him he's a dead man." He too had a sheriff's deputy guarding his house.

He told reporters that the verdicts didn't mean everyone was innocent. "We're not saying, 'Hey, there was nothing wrong.' Something was wrong. But it doesn't necessarily mean pin it on somebody in the courtroom."

Fisher insisted the jury wasn't racially biased, "but the black community won't look at it this way." Still, he had lingering questions about white officers working in black neighborhoods. At some point, jurors were shown photos of officers working in the Central District. "They are telling us this is a predominantly black district. Yet I don't recall ever seeing a black officer... in the pictures shown. I don't know whether there are any. It looks to me like there should be."

His statements showed that he, too, bought the defense's arguments completely. He found Carhart and O'Donnell to be "very good" for the defense, while he viewed Adorno as "a little abrasive. I was not impressed." He believed prosecutors were spurred by pressure from the Miami Herald. "They were so eager to nail somebody they grabbed the first people they could and some of the culprits are still up there." He blamed the PSD for a "mishandled" and "improper investigation.... If the investigation had been handled properly from Day One, the verdict might have been different. When there are a lot of doubts, you have to go in favor of the defendant... especially where it's that serious. We're not talking about somebody charged with a traffic violation...."

"The defense said nothing wrong happened. I don't agree. I think it was mishandled. It just appeared that individuals [PSD leaders] overreacted. Why did it take an article in the newspaper a week or two later to get them to do something? According to the testimony I heard, they sat on the reports." Indeed, as Frank said years later, that's exactly what happened.

"The guys who looked the guiltiest, they got immunity." He didn't think it right to send one person to prison while another was just as guilty but was given immunity.

Unlike Tetreault's recollection years later, Fisher said at the time that the jury wasn't unanimous at first. There was a "lot of soul searching. Several of us were pretty emotionally choked up over the thing.... Obviously, we changed some minds. We all had reservations. I don't think any one person, any one day, any one piece of evidence or testimony convinced us. There was some shouting and some anger. We did what we felt was right with what they gave us....You've got to be beyond a reasonable doubt."

He said the jurors had the toughest time deciding on the Marrero charges. The easiest one was Watts, the officer identified only by one witness, who wasn't certain he'd picked the right man.

The Herald asked him: "Did the jury believe Marrero when he testified McDuffie twice grabbed for his gun?"

Fisher: "Well, I don't know whether McDuffie did or didn't go for his gun. But you certainly have to take into consideration throwing away two guys who supposedly did the same thing."

This is a key: Fisher didn't automatically buy Marrero's convenient description of McDuffie grabbing for the gun, but with Gerant saying Watts struck the deadly blows and others saying it was Marrero, two stood accused of doing "the same thing."

He refused to tell how many ballots the jurors took.

What about the media? When he got home for the first time in weeks, Fisher saw a stack of newspapers. He said his wife "saved me all the Tampa Tribunes, and I read them last night and this morning, and I would really have to say they're pretty objective."

Still, in another interview, Fisher told the Tribune that the media didn't present the "full picture" that the jurors were getting. What was the full picture? "Fisher said he and the other jurors simply could not believe the testimony of the… officers who spoke against the four defendants…. 'You have to weigh the credibility of these guys.' One juror described… Hanlon… as a 'madman.'"

In a particularly revealing statement, Fisher showed how he, a federal government employee, imagined himself caught in a situation like the defendants, who had been Dade County employees: They have "a felony rap against them, lost their jobs and I guess are dead broke. If someone arrested me tomorrow for something I didn't know anything about, I'd probably be broke the rest of my life to get out of it." In the jury box, his natural sympathies leaned toward the defendants.

Of the riots, he said: "Unfortunately, I would guess I would have to say it was expected. But not to that magnitude. Obviously, I expected it [the black community] to react unfavorably, but not quite that violently. It is a tragedy…. We feel bad enough about the whole thing," but "I wasn't there to appease anyone."

As did many legal and police leaders later, he questioned the timing of the release of the verdict. "In hindsight, it would obviously have been better to wait until Monday rather than Saturday. Years ago, my father had a business. He paid his people on Monday, didn't pay them on Friday or Saturday. And he never had to have them get drunk [on Saturday]."

A Tribune reporter asked: If he had it to do over, would the deaths and turmoil cause him to change his mind? "Not about the decision. But I would like to go back about eight weeks, I would have done whatever I could to get off the jury in the first place."

The Herald interview with Fisher ended with this: "Should Arthur McDuffie's death have been left, wrongly classified, a traffic death? 'Well, I'm sure the people killed in the riot would have thought so.'"

• • • •

THREE DAYS AFTER THE verdicts, juror David Draper wrote a letter to Governor Bob Graham, who forwarded it to a federal grand jury. Eventually it became public when filed in a federal court case.

Draper, 39, a market administrator for Stromberg Carlson, a manufacturer of carburetors, echoed the sentiments of foreman Fisher: "We did not say with our verdict that no crime was committed: only that in accordance with the testimony, evidence and the instructions of the court that these men do not lose the presumption of innocence. That, sir, is the foundation of justice."

Draper, who had studied the history of speech education as a post-graduate at Syracuse University, was also stung by accusations that the jurors were racists: "Since the undeniable tragic events in Miami after our verdict were fueled in part by a perception that 'Florida justice is racist.' I invite you to consider the following:

"In my opinion, brutal violence was done to Arthur McDuffie in the early morning hours of 17 December 1979. Two men not brought to trial have admitted to committing such acts. One of them [Prince] has to my knowledge not even been arrested; the second was granted immunity to testify for the state."

This could have been either Veverka or Hanlon, both of whom admitted to hitting McDuffie, but not in the head.

"Prince's action [a kick to McDuffie's head] was apparently a gratuitous act and, of all the blows described in any manner to us during the trial, seems most likely to coincide with the 10-inch fracture in Arthur McDuffie's skull. Except for the suspect testimony of Veverka and William Hanlon, there is no clear evidence that the blows struck by Alex Marrero were responsible for Arthur McDuffie's death."

In fact, Wright, who did the autopsy, testified a kick to the head could not have caused McDuffie's severe skull fractures. Marrero himself testified he smashed McDuffie in the face as hard as he could with his nightstick.

Draper wrote that granting immunity to Hanlon was "particularly infuriating in light of his own sworn testimony that he committed at least three acts of wanton vandalism at the scene with no explanation."

The virtually nonexistent case against Del Toro was "merely the most blatant example of the carelessness of the state attorney's office in preparing this case. The case against Herbert Evans Jr. is almost nonexistent. It depends almost entirely on the uncorroborated testimony of the state's immunized witnesses. The case against Michael Watts is based on an extremely weak identification by Miami police officer John Gerant.... The charges against Sergeant Ira Diggs with respect to battery or manslaughter are totally unsupported by the evidence.

"The charges against Alex Marrero included second-degree murder. That charge was added to the information in the case without any additional evidence to support it. It is indefensible — as is the effrontery of the state to assume that a jury could support it with a 'guilty' verdict.

"I can no longer remain silent. In the place of one man dead, we now have many. The state must bring proper charges against Prince, the role of acting Sergeant Eric Seymen must be investigated, the role of Miami officer Richard Gotowala bears study and the present validity of immunity for Veverka, Mark Meier and Hanlon stands in doubt in view of numerous material differences in their various sworn statements."

This paragraph and some of those that followed show how deeply Draper distrusted the state's evidence. Seymen had been at the scene and later went with Hanlon and Marrero to the tow yard to look at the Kawasaki. Prosecutors felt there wasn't enough to charge him, but the PSD fired him. The Gotowala mention was particularly odd. He was the City of Miami officer so distraught over what he'd seen that he resigned from the force the night of the incident. No witness or defense attorney accused Gotowala of any illegal activity.

Draper went on: "Look now to the competence of Janet Reno and her staff; to the ambitions and image of the Public Safety Department hierarchs; to the practices and policies of District Two in selecting and monitoring the behavior of its officers. Look now also to the realities of the Combat Zone."

Attached to his letter was a list of 57 questions that "must be answered by any further inquiries into the case."

He wanted to know what insurance company employed McDuffie. His income? Where was he from 7 p.m. until 1:30 a.m. Dec. 17? Those were the hours that Carolyn Battle said she was with McDuffie.

Draper's last questions revealed how profoundly he distrusted every state witness, as he wondered whether the Kawasaki 900 displayed in the courtroom was "the same one that Arthur McDuffie was riding on December 17?" Crime techs, Veverka and accident experts all said that's what he was on that night. *Chapter Notes

Chapter 38
The "Home Run" Mistake

Starting shortly after the trial, the defense lawyers pounded prosecutors for their errors. Many of those same views were expressed to me much later and appear throughout this book: The rushed investigation, not using the grand jury, questionable immunity deals, the selection of a law-and-order jury.

But Carhart began offering a new one, one that he was to remain adamant on for the rest of his life: The state committed a major error by putting a big group on trial. (Originally, it was to be six, with Hanlon.)

He told the Herald shortly after the verdicts that Reno's office failed because they tried to do too much. The gist of his argument: Prosecutors tried for a home run to improve the state attorney office's image after the wrong-house criticisms "when a Pete Rose scratch single" might have won the game.

His argument: Del Toro and Evans should never have been charged. Put Marrero on trial by himself. Put on the witness stand cops not involved in the beating. That would have been Meier, who saw Marrero strike the blows, and perhaps Gotowala, the city officer, who arrived after the cracks to the skull but saw Marrero slam McDuffie in the legs. Then put Wright on to discuss the "cracked like an eggshell" skull, a blow so severe that McDuffie's head must have been on the ground or leaning against a wall. "Marrero would have been in trouble," Carhart told the St. Petersburg Times.

"I do think the state made a serious judgmental error when they charged Mr. Marrero and Mr. Watts in the same case," Carhart told CBS. "I think their contention was that the same act was done twice, two different times by two different people. The evidence was not there, in my opinion, to support that theory."

Adorno told CBS he disagreed: "It was just a matter of explaining to the jury that the Watts thing came at the beginning before Marrero ever got there. And the Marrero beating occurred later on. Gerant positively said, 'I know for a fact it wasn't Marerro.' Of course, the defense took advantage of that. I'm accusing two different people of doing the same thing, you've got to remember. I've only got Marrero as hitting Mr. McDuffie three times in the head. I only had Watts as hitting him one time. That's four blows. I have six blows."

To me, Carhart emphasized that trying Marrero by himself would eliminate all the "who did what" confusion. If Marrero was convicted, then prosecutors could then go after others.

Marvin Dunn, the black activist-author-professor, liked the idea of separate trials for a different reason: By trying the defendants together, their lawyers pooled their challenges to keep black people off the jury. A single defense lawyer, with perhaps one-fifth as many challenges, might not have been able to reject all black jurors.

Yoss' response: "If we charged one person, you don't think Edna Buchanan and Miller and everyone else in the world would have been writing stories about how we let everyone else go?" Also, multiple trials would have meant Veverka and Meier giving multiple depositions, with the defense searching for minute discrepancies.

What's more, Yoss went on, if trying a single defendant would have been such a good idea for the prosecution, why did the defense file pretrial motions demanding separate trials? They argued to the judge that they were worried that one defendant might claim on the witness stand that he was innocent because another defendant did the crime. Lawyers were also concerned about "the spill-over effect" — one very guilty defendant could unfairly taint others who might be innocent. In fact, many prosecutors believe that it's to the government's advantage to try a group together, precisely because the whole group gets tainted with the actions.

Nesbitt rejected that argument. In a 12-page ruling, she concluded: "Since only one homicide is charged, only one crime has been committed.... All of the criminal activities with which the defendants are charged relate to and are logically and intimately connected."

The issue of separate versus group trials of police keeps arising. In the case of Freddie Gray, a black Baltimore man who died in a police van in 2015, prosecutors decided to try the officers separately. End result: Three acquittals and one mistrial, which was never retried. So there may be no simple answer.

Still, in researching this book, any time I mentioned to lawyers and journalists the problem of three witnesses pointing to Marrero and another identifying Watts, they wondered why prosecutors let that occur.

Yoss' comeback was that a Marrero-alone trial wouldn't have made any difference. Since defense lawyers received all the state's research materials, they knew what Gerant's testimony would be. If the state hadn't put Gerant on the witness stand, O'Donnell certainly would have — for his statements blaming Watts and for saying it couldn't have been Marrero. And so, Yoss maintained, that'd be right back where they were in the Tampa situation.

Or maybe not. The defense putting Gerant on the stand would have been different than the prosecution doing so. That distinction of who calls a witness is at the core of "Sponsorship Strategy," a groundbreaking book by two veteran criminal trial attorneys.

Robert H. Klonoff and Paul L. Colby wrote that, if one side calls a witness, jurors view that side as sponsoring the witness. "Put another way, the jury views each attorney in the case not as a neutral arbiter, but as a 'hired gun' with one task to perform: to win the case for his client. Therefore... the jury assumes that everything an advocate says and does is calculated to reflect his client's case in its best possible light."

When the state put Gerant on the witness stand to say that Marrero couldn't have done the deadly blows, the jury believed that prosecutors were sponsoring – endorsing – those statements. If the situation was flipped for a Marrero-only trial, and the defense called Gerant, jurors would naturally be suspicious about an officer who looked like he was helping a fellow cop. In that situation, the state, not the defense, would gleefully point out that Gerant "wouldn't bet his life on it."

"Sponsorship Strategy" was published a decade after the Tampa trial. Until then, the commonly held theory was that one side was better off revealing negative information about its own case. The book shows in many specific examples that that the old theory is wrong: If one side brings out the disgraceful XXX, that's sponsorship and the other side can hammer away on what's wrong with XXX.

In the Tampa trial, this idea of "owning" a witness was catastrophic when it came to Hanlon, who admitted to many acts of "pure vandalism." Carhart said if the state hadn't put Hanlon on the stand, the defense would have – to show his damage to the bike, if nothing else. But in that case, the defense would be sponsors of his horrendous conduct, and the state could properly look askance at his bizarre behavior.

Still, Reno's office would have faced a problem if Marrero had stood trial alone. That meant Michael Watts would be ignored, at least at first. Watts was the original bad boy of the defendants, the lead subject of a 1979 front-page story in the Herald on the worst police brutality cases. He was there that night. Yet Gerant's identification was likely mistaken, since Marrero confessed to slamming McDuffie in the head. Other than Gerant, no witness said anything about what Watts did that night.

Even so, the commanders of the Central District viewed him as a bad boy and wanted him included. That's why a lieutenant ordered Diggs to insert Watts into his report, even though Diggs had no memory of him being there.

Yoss was right: The Herald and other media would have likely screamed if Marrero was brought to trial and Watts left on the sidelines, even temporarily. *Chapter Notes

Chapter 39
Veverka on Trial

If critics thought that the legal battles involving the McDuffie case had been odd up until this point, they certainly became even odder with the federal investigation, which began the day after the Tampa verdicts, as rioters still roamed through Miami's black neighborhoods.

Atlee Wampler, the acting U.S. attorney in Miami, told reporters his office would seek civil rights indictments against the four acquitted officers and planned to start presenting evidence to a grand jury on Wednesday, May 21, four days after the Tampa verdicts. At a press conference, federal officials made it clear they wanted to dissipate the black rage that was destroying the city. The feds' investigation, said Arthur Nehrbass, special agent in charge of the Miami FBI office, "in effect, guarantees a second look at the killing of McDuffie to assure that justice is done."

On July 28, after two months of hearing testimony and examining evidence, a federal grand jury issued an indictment — not against any of the six officers originally charged, but against Charles Veverka, the first cop to be granted immunity.

He was charged with four counts: "(1) knowing that an offense had been committed against the U.S., received, relieved, comforted and assisted offenders by preparing a false report; (2) conspired to submit false reports; (3) conspired to injure, oppress, threaten and intimidate Arthur McDuffie, a citizen of the U.S. in the free exercise of Constitutional right; and (4) while acting under color of the laws, did willfully file false criminal charges against Arthur McDuffie, a citizen of the U.S. and willfully deprived him of his Constitutional right."

He faced a maximum of 26 years in prison, the media reported.

The charges were based on a 46-page statement he gave Dade prosecutors on December 26, the first day of his cooperation. Fed prosecutors maintained that the state's grant of immunity did not retroactively cover that statement. Veverka's lawyers objected. U.S. District Judge William Hoeveler rejected their claim.

Denis Dean, one of Veverka's lawyers, told reporters that the indictment "doesn't make a lot of sense to me. The whole thing will have a stifling effect on police officers coming forward to testify or give evidence of possible wrongdoing by other officers."

Veverka was angry. "There is no way," he told reporters, "they could indict me without my statements. There wouldn't even be a McDuffie case if I hadn't told the truth. And because I told the truth, I'm the one getting screwed."

Dean said federal prosecutors twice approached Veverka about pleading guilty to lesser charges in return for his testimony against others. It appeared that the feds wanted his cooperation without offering him immunity, which had been such a stumbling block in the minds of Tampa jurors. "He was the easiest one to go after," Dean told me, because Veverka's own statements could be used against him. "There wasn't a whole lot of work for them to do," while building a federal case against Marrero would take "more months." So the cooperating witness was now the bad guy.

Laeser, the Dade prosecutor, believed giving Veverka immunity was a mistake to begin with and was even more convinced after Veverka proved to be a terrible witness in Tampa. He thought the federal case "was essentially just a payback. You screwed us. Here's a chance to make your life exciting."

Samuel Smargon, a federal prosecutor, told reporters: "We were not bound by the immunity given in state court. The investigation reached a point where the evidence was sufficient to indict Veverka." He said Veverka was charged first "because the evidence developed against him first." More indictments could be expected, Smargon said.

Miami's black leaders applauded the feds. "It's just the beginning," said Bill Perry of the NAACP. Black lawyer H.T. Smith said the indictment of Reno's star witness was "another indication of the incompetence and bungling of the case" by her office.

The Herald and News covered the case matter-of-factly, including Veverka's astonishment and reaction from the Miami black community. But a month before the trial, Marvin Dunn, the FIU professor and black activist, inserted a perceptive analytical note when he urged caution in a column in the New York Times headlined: "Why Miami Blacks Might Riot Again."

Before the Tampa trial, Dunn had been a hard-charger, a leader in the campaign to get Marrero's charges ramped up to second-degree murder. Since then, he'd seen the bloodshed in the riots and apparently was listening to lawyers as he warned that the complexities of federal law meant black expectations of a conviction might be dashed again: "The difficulty in obtaining indictments and convictions in federal court is rooted in federal prosecutors' need to show not that McDuffie was murdered, which is a violation of state law for which the officers have been acquitted, but that the officers involved specifically intended to violate Mr. McDuffie's civil rights. To do that would be a very difficult task. However, many Miami blacks believe that Mr. McDuffie's death is itself sufficient grounds for construction of a strong federal case. It is not. The death is almost irrelevant to federal civil rights charges.

"Attorneys for the defendants, if there is a trial," Dunn went on, "likely would argue that nothing has come to light in this extremely sensitive case that would suggest specific intent to violate Mr. McDuffie's rights. The former officers might advance the argument that their intent was merely to stop him for a traffic violation after a high-speed chase that threatened their lives and public safety. After stopping him, they could submit, their intent was to subdue Mr. McDuffie, whom they have contended strenuously resisted arrest. In prosecuting the officers, Florida found it very difficult to disprove that he had resisted arrest."

The reason for that difficulty was Veverka himself. The state's lead witness had insisted that McDuffie had forcefully resisted.

"Given this approach," Dunn went on in the Times, "the federal jury might be left to conclude that the killing was at best accidental and at worst criminal negligence, neither of which, however reprehensible, are federal offenses. If the defendants were found not guilty of civil rights violations, Miami might well be hit by another race riot."

Then he took a dig at the Miami media: "As in the first McDuffie case, the Miami public remains basically uninformed about the legal complexities, and expectations are as high as they were last May, if not higher. For Miami blacks, there is an urgent need to nip great expectations in the bud before another tragedy occurs."

Judge Hoeveler struggled to find a location for the trial. Miami was quickly ruled out. He chose Atlanta, but racial tensions there were running high because of stories about the murders or disappearances of 15 children, and city leaders begged for the trial to go elsewhere. The judge looked to New Orleans, but after four black residents were killed in a police shootout, the mayor said his city didn't want it. Next came San Antonio. The city's black leaders objected, but Hoeveler decided to take a stand in the city of the Alamo.

Certainly, emotions were running high in Miami. Before he left for San Antonio, Dean, Veverka's attorney, said he was told by a black activist: "If he's found not guilty, I hope your car is the first one to burn." Veverka's father, the PSD lieutenant, came with his son to Texas. The mother wasn't well enough to travel. "His mom was dying of cancer at the time," Dean recalled. "A sad situation. Saying goodbye, she said to me: 'Please take care of my boy.'"

On Sunday, December 7, the day before proceedings began, Herald staff writer Mary Voboril, a veteran court reporter, previewed the trial. Unlike the Tampa stories, her reporting cautioned readers not to expect too much and included a quote from Dunn: "Unfortunately, a lot of people expect the federal government to be successful. That expectation is just very unrealistic. These charges are very hard to prove in court, and I don't think there's a snowball's chance in hell that they are going to get [Veverka] on civil rights charges."

The Herald, News, Tampa Tribune and St. Petersburg Times sent reporters to San Antonio. The News sent a veteran reporter, Heather Dewar. The Tribune and Times sent Shinhoster and Slacum, the veterans of the Tampa trial.

The case did not start well for the defense, as Hoeveler ruled that Veverka's attorneys could not tell the jury about Veverka receiving immunity in the state case and could make no accusations of unfairness against the federal government.

Forty were called for jury duty, including two black potential jurors. Some had heard about the case from local media. One black prospective juror told the judge, "If I had come forward as a witness and helped the case and then the government came around and used that against me, I would be very unhappy."

Another prospect said that he was concerned about "a moral law.... You make this promise to this man that he would be immunized, and then the federal government comes down says, 'We are not going to; we are superior.'"

Those opinionated people were left off the final jury panel, which included one black woman, five Mexican-Americans and six non-Hispanic whites. Six were male, six female. They included a part-time receptionist, a medical center technician, a Motorola sales manager, a restaurant worker and three homemakers.

In his opening statement, prosecutor Smargon charged that Veverka conspired with other officers to make the beating look like a motorcycle accident by preparing at least seven documents "that are false and untrue," including two accident reports and two arrest complaint affidavits.

Defense attorney Douglas Hartman said Veverka committed "the heinous crime of following orders" and "had nothing, absolutely nothing, to do with the death of Arthur McDuffie." He was the youngest member of the squad and ordered by three superiors to write the false reports — to "do the dirty work." Hartman called Marrero "the murderer" and said Evans was "another main character" in covering up the beating.

Mark Meier was the first prosecution witness. He had first refused to testify before the federal grand jury, then was given immunity and agreed to cooperate. Meier said he was one of the first to arrive on the scene, stepping out of his police car, drawing his gun and ordering the motorcyclist to freeze. "An officer in a county uniform came up and grabbed him off the back of the motorcycle." Veverka later told him he was that officer.

While Veverka had told investigators that he hit McDuffie as hard as he could, Meier testified that he never saw Veverka swing at the motorcyclist. He added he himself didn't touch McDuffie.

He called police chases "enjoyable, exciting and fun" for cops, and the beating that followed "was not really so unusual.... Hitting a subject that gave you all the trouble that Mr. McDuffie gave you can be as described as, maybe, a tensions release. Teaching him a lesson. If you put a little hurt on somebody who has led you on an eight-and-a-half-minute chase like that, you're going to say, 'Hey look, sucker, don't run again. The next time a police officer turns on his red light, you stop.'"

He described Marrero straddling McDuffie and striking him, as well as the interchange between Hanlon and Marrero about the best way to break someone's legs. When Marrero hit McDuffie on the shins, "I grabbed his arm and told him to cool it." Meier "cleared the scene as quickly as possible" after McDuffie was taken to the hospital. "I didn't want to get involved in any of the paperwork. As the first officer on the scene, that would normally be my responsibility."

On cross-examination, he acknowledged that Veverka caused him to come forward and tell investigators what he knew: "I don't know what I would have done if Veverka had not gotten me to tell the truth that night.... I did not want to be the first person to flip."

When Hartman asked him if the beating was unusual, he replied, "The initial blows, no. The later blows, yes."

None of the print accounts mentioned Meier's famous quote "I give up!" from the Tampa trial. It was such an astonishing phrase that the reporters certainly would have used it if he'd said it. But that quote came with a lot of baggage, as the Tampa defense attorneys hammered him on why it had taken him more than a month to recall this key fact. Perhaps neither side in San Antonio wanted to go down that road again: The prosecution thinking it might damage Meier's credibility; the defense not wanting to dispute Veverka's account that McDuffie had initially resisted arrest.

Outside the courtroom, Veverka told Dewar that he and Meier hadn't known each other before the incident, but since then they'd become friends. "I don't blame him," he said about Meier testifying for the prosecution. "We've been through a lot together. He has to do what he has to do." Meier said he was amazed Veverka had been charged. "The whole thing is a crock."

To disprove the defense's claim that Veverka was the first to come forward, prosecutors called Richard Gotowala, the city police officer, to testify that he had talked to investigators on Christmas, a day before Veverka. Wright, who did the autopsy, was put on to say that he first learned about the case from Edna Buchanan, but on cross-examination, he acknowledged Veverka had helped him by describing Marrero's vicious blows. That description assisted him in concluding, in his second autopsy report, that McDuffie's death was caused by blows to the head.

Metro Homicide Sergeant Frank Wesolowski, called by the government to introduce Veverka's December 26 statement to homicide, was asked by the defense who was the first officer to come forward.

"To my knowledge, it was Charles Veverka Jr.," Wesolowski said.

Yoss took the stand to testify about Veverka giving him a statement. At the prosecutors' request, Yoss read the entire 46-page report to the jurors, which included Veverka saying he "grabbed him in a bear hug, just so he wouldn't get away till some other officers came up. It seemed like a very long time, but it was a very short time."

About Marrero striking McDuffie, Veverka stated: "The blood splattered on my uniform, and I was at least four or five feet away. I turned my back after that. I understand there was a third blow, but I didn't see it." He stated he wrote and rewrote the false reports three times on Evans' orders, including the "totally false" accident report.

Under cross-examination, Dean asked Yoss if there ever had been any criminal charges filed against Veverka in state court. Prosecutor Smargon objected. The judge sustained. Twice Dean tried to ask whether Veverka had done anything to impede the investigation. Both times, the prosecution objected. Twice the judge sustained.

Outside the courtroom, Yoss told reporters it was "very unlikely" that officers would have been charged without Veverka's cooperation.

Dewar wrote in the Miami News: "Government prosecutors have tried to convince the jury that the McDuffie coverup would have unraveled if Veverka had never come forward. But Yoss said, 'The coverup was not falling apart when Charles Veverka came in.'"

The defense called Veverka as its only witness. He said he followed the orders of superiors in writing the reports, which he admitted were false. Veverka testified that he'd spent Christmas with his son while thinking McDuffie's daughters would never spend another Christmas with their father.

Dewar: "His voice was calm and even, but Charles Veverka's hands shook and his eyes filled with tears."

Prosecutor Brian McDonald asked him if he had read the "Obedience to Unlawful Orders" section of the PSD rules: "No employee shall obey an order that is contrary to law or ordinance."

McDonald: "You understood that on the night of December 17?"

Veverka said he hadn't read the rule and didn't remember thinking about it.

In motions outside the jury's hearing, prosecutor McDonald asked the judge to instruct jurors that "an order to prepare false official documents and file false criminal charges would be an illegal order, and if the defendant knew the order was illegal, or should have known it was illegal, then obedience to such an order is not a valid defense."

Hoeveler agreed.

Defense attorney Dean complained: "Our defenses are being slowly whittled away, one by one."

Hoeveler added that the defense could not in summation suggest the guilt of other officers. "The fact that some others could have been included in this indictment or should have been included even before this defendant — and I think that might be the case here — is not relevant."

Dean said his defense was reduced to "basic fair play and sympathy."

In closing arguments, McDonald said: "The Christmas story is nice, but what affected him was McDuffie's death. Mr. McDuffie died, and Mr. Veverka knew his name was all over the reports. The fact that he finally came forward is not an excuse for the fact that he did the wrong thing for nine days.... If he was ordered, that order was illegal and he knew it was illegal."

Dean summarized his defense by saying: "Charles Veverka did not violate any civil rights of Arthur McDuffie, and those who did are not sitting here." He said people's civil rights are abridged by injuring them or by killing them, not by paperwork. "I think Veverka is guilty of only one thing. He is guilty of breaking the code of silence that says you don't 'hand up' another officer. The death of Arthur McDuffie is a tragedy," he said borrowing Carhart's phrase. "There is no question about that. I submit to you that the prosecution of Charles Veverka is another tragedy....

"I am not asking you to commend or applaud Charles Veverka. But don't let the tragedy of Arthur McDuffie be compounded by the conviction of Charles Veverka.... [He] is very unhappy being here. There are some officers who won't have anything to do with him, but Chuck Veverka has a clear conscience. He knows what he did was right.... Do you have the feeling that things are backwards in this trial?"

Because the judge had restricted the defense from mentioning so many things, Dean recalled in an interview, "In my closing argument, I got real close to the line."

The jury deliberated for two hours on the afternoon of Monday, December 15, then returned to their homes. They talked all the next day. And the next, until shortly before 6 p.m., the foreman sent the judge a note: "Hopelessly deadlocked at 11 to 1. Further debate would be fruitless. Suggestions?"

"God, it's absolutely shattering," the judge said. The next morning, he read the jurors an instruction known as the Modified Allen Charge, emphasizing the importance of the case, of the time and expense in trying it, and asking them to try again to reach a unanimous verdict.

On Wednesday, December 17, the anniversary of McDuffie's beating, the jurors deliberated for another five hours. At 3 p.m., they agreed on the verdicts: Not guilty on all four charges.

The jury foreman, Pat McNamara, 36, the Motorola sales manager, talked to reporters: "I would find it hard to believe that justice was done if we convicted Chuck Veverka and all the others were still out on the streets." He said the jury "was appalled by accounts of the savage beating.... But we could not in good conscience bring a guilty verdict."

He acknowledged "sympathy played a part in my decision.... The overwhelming factor of positive evidence was the defendant's confession, because it was made without an attorney and in as truthful a manner as he could muster. Mr. Meier's testimony only helped because it pointed out that Mr. Veverka acted differently."

He said that the word "willful" in the indictment was key, coupled with the jury instruction that ordered jurors to convict the defendant only if they were sure he had a "specific intent" to do something he knew, or should have known, was wrong. This was precisely the point that Dunn had warned about in his New York Times column.

"We were aware that obedience to an illegal order wasn't a defense. But we were still troubled by his intent. There were none of us who could have said definitely that he didn't intend to participate in the cover-up, but we had a reasonable doubt."

Prosecutor Brian McDonald: "People just don't like to convict police officers."

Black leaders in Miami were dismayed. T. Willard Fair of the Greater Miami Urban League called the trial "a farce." Eula Bell McDuffie, the motorcyclist's mother, begged for calm in the streets.

For the afternoon Miami News, one front page headline stated "Feds: McDuffie case isn't over yet." More indictments were still possible, prosecutors said. Another front-page story revealed that Veverka had a contract with a Hollywood producer to do a movie about his life. The article said the ex-cop "may make a cool million dollars on the Arthur McDuffie case."

That evening, police put up roadblocks to keep unsuspecting white drivers out of some black areas. Several dozen police officers stood by if needed. They saw only isolated incidents of rock throwing.

There were no more McDuffie trials. The Veverka movie was never made. *Chapter Notes

Chapter 40
"When in Doubt, Shoot the Black Guy"

In the four decades since the McDuffie case, America has continued to wrestle with how to deal with police misconduct, sometimes with anger erupting into riots.

In several cases, white officers have been convicted for killing unarmed black men, usually with videos from officers' bodycams or spectators' cellphones. Even so, it remains extremely rare that an officer is charged, much less convicted, for killing someone while on duty.

Philip Stinson, who heads the Police Integrity Research Group at Bowling Green State University, says that roughly 1,000 people in America are killed by police officers each year. (That compares with 20 U.S. soldiers killed in combat in Afghanistan in 2019.)

That's a very rough estimate. Here's the take of James Lees: "Accurate statistics on the number of people killed each year by police officers is exceedingly difficult to come by because of the lack of transparency by many police agencies throughout America."

For civilians killed by police officers, Lees cited a Washington Post database that tracks police "shootings" rather than overall civilian fatalities caused by police officers. For 2019, the data base showed 1,004 people shot and killed by police officers in America, 12 more than the year before.

"It's almost impossible to glean from the data how many of these shootings were legitimate police actions and how many might be characterized as criminal/excessive force," Lees wrote. "The reality is that the overwhelming number of civilian deaths caused by police officers most likely are legitimate police actions necessitated by the behavior of the civilians (pointing a gun at an officer for example), but clearly there are cases in which officers far exceed the boundaries of established force when dealing with civilians, and statistics do seem to show that black civilians are the victims of such excessive force much more often that are white civilians."

A Bowling Green study, examining criminal proceedings from 2005 through June 24, 2019, found that 104 nonfederal sworn law enforcement officers were charged with murder or manslaughter involving an on-duty shooting. With roughly 1,000 killings a year, that means 14,000 deaths over the timespan of the study – making 104 charges in police killings fewer than 1 percent of total deaths.

Of those 104, only 22 — about one in five — were convicted of murder or manslaughter. Another 13 were convicted of lesser crimes, such as official misconduct, reckless discharge of a firearm, or federal deprivation of civil rights.

In 40 cases, nonblack officers were charged with killing black people. Nineteen were convicted, 21 acquitted. About half, in other words. But prosecutors know how difficult it is to convict police officers, and they tend to indict cops only when the evidence seems overwhelming.

One case that didn't make it to trial: Darren Wilson, a white police officer in Ferguson, Missouri, who shot and killed Michael Brown, an unarmed black teenager, in 2014. The case went to a grand jury. It didn't indict. Rioting and demonstrations went on for weeks.

A lengthy federal investigation found that Ferguson police "routinely violate the Fourth Amendment in stopping people without reasonable suspicion, arresting them without probable cause, and using unreasonable force against them," but it found no reason to charge Wilson with violating Brown's civil rights. Contrary to some eyewitnesses, federal investigators concluded that the evidence and most credible witnesses said Brown was moving toward the officer and "Wilson fired at Brown in what appeared to be self-defense."

The bar for proving police misconduct is high: As Stinson describes it: "A cop is justified in using deadly force if the officer has a reasonable fear of an imminent threat to serious bodily jury or death against an officer or someone else. The legal test requires that a reasonable police officer would have perceived the threat." Because so many people sympathize with the officers sworn to protect them, a great many jurors are likely to give an officer wide latitude in what is "reasonable fear."

Still, the Ferguson anger prompted a nationwide push to have police wear bodycams. Those videos, plus the increasing use of bystanders recording on their phones, have led to some notable convictions.

In 2018, a jury found Chicago officer Jason Van Dyke guilty of second-degree murder in the fatal shooting of 17-year-old Laquan McDonald. Police investigators first decided that the shooting was justified, based on officers' statements that McDonald had lunged at them with a knife. Then video emerged that showed the teenager walking away from police when he was shot. A judge acquitted three other officers charged with covering up the shooting.

That same year, in the Dallas area, officer Roy Oliver was found guilty of killing Jordan Edwards as he fired five times at a speeding car. Oliver said he believed the car was heading toward his partner and might kill him. A bodycam showed the car moving away from the officers, and Oliver's partner testified that he didn't think his life was in danger.

In each case, video was the overwhelming factor. "There's a lot of truth to the idea of 'no video, no justice,'" said John Fullinwider, co-founder of Mothers Against Police Brutality.

Yet not even damning video can guarantee a conviction. In 2015, Michael Slager, a white officer in South Carolina, shot an unarmed black motorist, Walter Scott. Video showed Scott running away when he was shot eight times. A trial in state court ended with a hung jury. Slager pleaded guilty in federal court to violating Scott's civil rights.

In Miami, after McDuffie, there were more police killings that led to riots. Sometimes the riot happened after the shooting, sometimes after the acquittal. The state attorney's solution: Stop indicting cops. For more than a quarter century, no on-duty police officer in Miami-Dade County was charged with a shooting, though there were a number of incidents that might have led to prosecutions.

Then came an astonishing case, with video, in North Miami in July 2016. The incident started when an autistic man, Arnaldo Rios Soto, walked away from a group home for the developmentally disabled. Charles Kinsey, a behavioral therapist, went after him. Police received a phone call that a man was trying to kill himself. Squad cars raced to the scene. With guns drawn, officers confronted the pair, who were in the middle of the street.

Rios Soto was sitting down, playing with a silver toy truck. He appeared a bit confused by all the police attention. Kinsey, a large black man, was well aware of the many cases of police shooting unarmed black men. He saw the cops and their guns. He knew he was in trouble. He sat down in the center of the street. He raised both hands in the air. He shouted that Rios Soto was not a threat. "All he has is a toy truck." A spectator recorded the incident on a cellphone.

The officers closest to the pair saw what was happening. One said on police radio that the guy was holding a toy. Jonathan Aledda, a SWAT team member armed with a M4 rifle, was 50 yards away. He fired three times. Two shots missed. The other hit Kinsey in the leg.

The Herald ran an editorial headlined: "Police officers' unwritten rule? When in doubt, shoot the black guy."

No riot broke out after the shooting. Prosecutors did not rush to judgment. After long deliberation, they decided this was such an outrageous case that they had to go ahead. In April 2017, nine months after the incident, the Miami-Dade state attorney's office filed charges against Aledda, the first time since 1989 that an officer in the county had been indicted for an on-duty shooting. Prosecutors said Aledda acted recklessly.

Flash back to 1980 for a moment, to all those critics who believed the McDuffie trial should have been held in Miami because they were certain a jury would convict the cops. That assumed that Miami is different from all the other places where police convictions are rare.

For two years, the trial was postponed. Finally, in March 2019, a jury was seated. Aledda took the stand. "I believed it was a hostage situation." He thought Rios Soto was about to shoot Kinsey. "It appeared he [Kinsey] was screaming for mercy or for help or something. In my mind, the white male had a gun." He said he didn't hear the radio report about the toy truck. He said he was shooting at Rios Soto. He hit Kinsey by accident.

The trial ended in a hung jury. Five of the six jurors told a reporter they voted to acquit.

A second trial was held in June 2019. During his testimony, Aledda said, "I'm sorry for what happened to him. It was a big mistake."

The jury acquitted Aledda on two felony counts of attempted manslaughter. He was convicted of a misdemeanor charge of culpable negligence.

Local television mentioned the Aledda verdicts only in brief reports. The lone print journalist, David Ovalle from the Herald, wrote two short stories on each trial, while tweeting other information, such as: "Five of six jurors are women. Not sure ethnic background. They were very focused on the testimony."

In July 2019, Judge Alan S. Fine decided Aledda should serve no jail time. He was sentenced to one year on probation and 100 hours of community service. The judge ordered him to write a 2,500-word essay on communication and weapon discharges.

Fast-forward to 2020. Katherine Fernandez Rundle, who had been the Miami-Dade state attorney since Reno went to Washington in 1993, was facing a serious election opponent for the first time in many years: a staffer of the American Civil Liberties Union who accused Rundle of ignoring police brutality cases.

Rundle responded by charging officers in several incidents called "rough arrests." In each case, the charge was backed up by video.

In January 2020, Miami-Dade Police Sergeant Manuel Regueiro went on trial on a misdemeanor battery charge for slapping a handcuffed teenager, Bryan Crespo. The case had been percolating for almost two years, after television stations broadcast video of the arrest.

Officers had gone to the house to arrest Crespo on a charge of stealing airbags. Unknown to them, a surveillance camera was in the living room. Crespo testified that he was being led away when he heard his name shouted. "I took a glimpse, a look, and I felt a slap. A real hard slap on my face." He said the officer told him: "This is for all the airbags you stole." He said the slap left him with "a busted lip."

Regueiro testified that he slapped Crespo because he saw Crespo "gathering phlegm in his mouth.... Before he could spit on me, I had to stop that spit from leaving his mouth."

When pressed by the prosecutor on cross-examination, he said Crespo pursed his lips and inhaled. "That's a telltale sign that someone's about to spit." The sergeant said he had to slap Crespo. "You don't duck. Then you're a coward."

The jury of six included two black residents. They deliberated almost three hours, slightly longer than the McDuffie jury did.

Verdict: Not guilty.

A juror said afterward that he was astounded that prosecutors went after an officer trying to control a criminal. "I don't even know why they charged this. They didn't even have evidence, other than the video."

And so it goes 40 years after McDuffie: Prosecutors put on a case against a police officer because of perceived public-political pressure. A jury — this one in Miami with two black members — once again sided with police. How long does it take to learn a lesson? There are certainly times in America when police officers should to be charged with brutality, but history makes clear that prosecutors would be better off if they ignored public pressure and be damn sure they have a solid case, preferably endorsed by a grand jury. *Chapter Notes

Chapter 41
Essay: Look at the Kickstand

After listening to five lawyers who were in the courtroom and several more lawyers who had an outside perspective, after reading six print reporters, watching news clips of one television station, and after digesting official reports and a bunch of other interviews and analyses, I am struck most by the observation of Frank, the homicide commander:

The Kawasaki was resting on its kickstand.

Officer Gerant studied the bike because he had one just like it. He saw it upright, on its kickstand. He worked for a different police department and was not smeared with accusations of bias or self-interest. Officer Gotowala, who arrived when the officers were done pummeling McDuffie, recalled seeing an officer knock over the motorcycle, meaning it must have been upright. Hanlon on the witness stand admitted he knocked over the bike after the melee. That meant it had been on its kickstand when he did so.

"If McDuffie had parked his motorcycle on its kickstand, that indicated intent to surrender," Frank wrote in his memoir. "It made no sense that McDuffie would give up, then throw a punch at a uniformed officer. More likely, Veverka's adrenalin had pumped to overload."

In his sworn statement to the detectives, Veverka said, "I pulled him off his bike and put it in park. I hit him with my fist, but he didn't go down." Was "park" referring to the transmission or the kickstand? How did he have time to do either when he was battling a man who was supposedly resisting mightily?

McDuffie stopped of his own accord. That seemed reasonable to Frank. And to me, too. Maybe McDuffie heard shots, as some suggested — or thought he heard shots. Maybe he just figured he'd had enough. This wasn't a thug with a long rap sheet. He was ex-Marine, ex-military police, gainfully employed, with nothing more than unpaid parking tickets and a suspended license. Why would he stop his motorcycle, put down the kickstand and then throw a punch at Veverka?

If McDuffie was the one to put down the kickstand, he'd have immediately encountered a bunch of angry cops. Even two of the Tampa defense attorneys acknowledge that. "There's no question that the police officers were sort of angry at McDuffie," Kogan told me. "He had taken them for a long chase in the middle of the night, and when he got to where he was apprehended ... the police officers were angry as hell and started beating on him. That was the whole thing." Carhart said cops naturally got riled during high-speed chases. "It's life-threatening to the officers. They get all worked up. Testosterone flows. These are pretty macho guys in the first place as police officers, and it did not surprise me that at the end of this heated chase there was a confrontation."

Even Del Toro, a co-defendant, said after his acquittal: "It wouldn't have been a total surprise if some hit [him]. It is stupid, but it happens."

What about Meier? He testified he saw McDuffie stop and surrender. That could very well have been true even if, as the defense charged, he came up with the "I give up!" later to help the prosecutors who were keeping him out of jail. Meier said he didn't see Veverka hit McDuffie. Perhaps he was helping out the colleague who persuaded him to come clean to investigators.

Veverka testified he hit McDuffie as hard as he could. It's likely that McDuffie resisted at that point, trying to protect himself. The other cops arrived, saw Veverka and McDuffie struggling with each other, and the pummeling began.

Even Prince, the Miami cop, wanted "to get a lick in." The first blows dispensed "street justice," but then Marrero smashed Mc-

Duffie's skull with such extraordinary force that at first the medical examiner couldn't imagine that a human could cause such blows. By this point, McDuffie wasn't battling, the examiner concluded: His head was on the pavement or resting against the wall. Marrero — the cop who'd gone to the ER four times because of confrontations while on the job, the cop who applied four times to be transferred out of the Combat Zone — had taken his rage out on McDuffie, whose autopsy showed no wounds on his hands or arms to indicate that he had resisted in any way.

That makes for some easy paragraphs for any journalist to write, including this one. It's a far cry from the "beyond a reasonable doubt" that the law insists jurors use.

Now, let's look at all the second-guessing. From a perspective of four decades, many of the criticisms seem like common sense – but they didn't from the political perspective of 1980. In his commentaries for this book, James Lees wondered why Internal Affairs wasn't allowed to proceed with the case, rather than homicide. He wrote that, in almost all police departments, Internal Affairs is set up to be an insulated, independent, fact-finding body. The problem was that the PSD's Internal Affairs had a horrible reputation. The media had reported time after time that Internal Affairs investigators found nothing wrong when others found outrageous behavior, such as happened with motorists' charges that Watts beat them after pulling them over for traffic violations. No one had faith in Internal Affairs, especially not Bobby Jones, the PSD's acting director, who called a meeting of top brass within hours of Edna Buchanan's story coming out and said he wanted Marshall Frank, who had done hundreds of homicide investigations, to lead the McDuffie investigation.

Lees thought it would have been much better if an outside, independent investigator had been brought in. As an ideal, that made a lot of sense. But the political reality in 1980 Miami was that both Reno, state attorney for less than two years, and Jones, the acting director, felt that they had to prove their mettle by conducting their own investigations. Those decisions led to cascading problems.

What about the rush to judgement? To this day, Yoss maintains that yes, the prosecutors rushed, but going slower wouldn't have made difference because "our case wasn't going to get any better."

Still, it's obvious that Reno later had second thoughts about how her office handled McDuffie. The clearest indication of that comes from Laeser, who went on to be her chief assistant. Following McDuffie, Laeser said, Reno established new rules on how to handle police shooting/brutality cases: Move methodically, no rushing.

"It is an important case," Laeser said of McDuffie, "because the world changed for my end of the profession as soon as the case was over. We changed everything in terms of protocol."

Reno and police agreed on a new way of handling any police-related homicide. As soon as such an incident occurred, specific people in Reno's office were to be notified immediately, as were designated teams of detectives and crime lab people. In other words, no more haphazard assignment to a rookie Internal Affairs sergeant.

Rather than a rush to indict, the teams planned regular follow-up meetings. "There was like a 72-hour meeting of everybody, a one-week meeting," Laeser said. "How have we progressed, someone getting charged, someone not getting charged, you know. Let's all sit down and brainstorm this."

Another change: After McDuffie, Reno was more likely to send difficult cases to the grand jury for a decision. "When it suited her purpose," said Tom Petersen, the Reno top assistant who handled the grand jury material for years after McDuffie, "she'd send cases to the grand jury. 'It wasn't me. It was the grand jury.'"

Yet another change: It was the last time that a Dade judge allowed the verdict in a major police brutality case to be announced on a weekend. And it was the last time that such a verdict would be announced without squadrons of riot police ready to move.

••••

ABOUT THE IMMUNIZED witnesses, Yoss remains adamant to this day: Prosecutors didn't have any choice. Before Veverka cooperated, Frank had statements from two Miami city police officers. The two were certain that the county cops smashed McDuffie when he was on the ground and not resisting. During their first interviews, neither was sure who struck the blows.

Veverka knew. He got Meier to cooperate. Looking back, it certainly would have been better to polygraph them. And if they failed the polygraph? Well, that might have been better than failing the Tampa jurors' lie detector test. The prosecutors desperately reached for Hanlon because they knew they had "baffling contradictions" with the first two. And Hanlon just compounded their struggles in Tampa. "These were just bad witnesses," Yoss said

Certainly, in retrospect it would have been much better to send the case to a grand jury. Del Toro would never have been charged. Perhaps Watts would have escaped too. Perhaps Veverka would have been charged with the cover-up, since he wrote seven false reports. Perhaps other cops, with less baggage than Veverka, would have decided it best to cooperate under grand jury pressure. Perhaps a grand jury would have picked up on Carhart's suggestion to indict Marrero by himself. That's a lot of perhaps. This is one of those 20-20 hindsight hypotheses: Whatever the grand jury did couldn't have been worse than what happened in Tampa.

But it might not have been better either. This brings us to the next big problem in the McDuffie case, or any case with an officer as the defendant. Even if the state had multiple witnesses, each with an impeccable story, and the stories confirmed each other, the defendant-cop could have walked free because it's so difficult to convict an officer who says he feared for his life.

One astounding admission of how much defense lawyers counted on public support for police came when McWilliams, the lawyer for Diggs in Tampa, was defending Willie Thomas Jones, the Florida Highway Patrolman who pleaded no contest to lewd and lascivious or indecent assault upon a child. When the case became public, there was a huge outcry that the white officer was doing no jail time for molesting a black girl, when a black officer would never get off molesting a white girl. In court, McWilliams objected to interjecting race into the case: "Judge, the reason that everybody wants to stick up for the man is because he is a police officer, not because he is white."

• • • •

NEXT BIG QUESTION: What if there had been no change of venue? What if Reno herself had marched into Judge Nesbitt's court, as critics suggested, and said this trial must remain in Miami?

After the verdicts, many believed that a Miami trial would have resulted in convictions. It became a mantra for many, including some of my Herald colleagues: Trial in Miami, blacks on the jury, stay away from those Tampa bigots and convictions were inevitable.

"A case should be held where people can relate to the problem," Miami police Sergeant Mike Gonzalez told a reporter shortly after the verdict. "In another town they feel it's none of their business, or maybe they don't have the courage to do the right thing. It should be tried in the city that bears the responsibility for what happens."

Yoss said of staying in Miami: "I don't know if it would have made any difference in the end, except we might have been able to get some blacks on the jury. It was a very difficult case to win." Later, though, he acknowledged that the jury was "one of the biggest problems we had in the case... But I don't blame it on the jury. The evidence and the testimony presented was not great."

With dozens of McDuffie stories in the Miami newspapers and dozens of reports on the television news, how many black or white residents of Miami could say honestly that they had an open mind on the indicted cops? As Neal Sonnett, representing Hanlon, told Judge Nesbitt, finding people in Dade who knew nothing about the case would mean getting "a jury of deaf, the blind and the completely ignorant."

Defense lawyer Kogan suggested that prosecutors in a Miami courtroom would have had the same conflicting witnesses and picked the same type of law-and-order jurors they did in Tampa, resulting in the same verdicts. He also wondered: If it took three weeks in Tampa to find six apparently impartial persons, how much longer would have taken in Miami?

What's more, there were — and still are — plenty of indications that Miami jurors are as sympathetic to cops as jurors elsewhere. A couple of years after McDuffie, a Hispanic officer killed an Overtown youth in a video arcade. That led to riots. The trial stayed in Miami. The verdict was not guilty.

Moving farther down this hypothetical rabbit-hole: What if the trial had stayed in Miami and the state managed to get convictions, at least on some charges? What were the chances that these convictions would have stood up on appeal?

Perhaps none. Carhart and many other attorneys believed an appellate court would have thrown out any convictions obtained in a Miami courtroom. "The climate in the community was so poisonous," Carhart said. "There was no way you could select a fair jury." A prime example was the post-verdict statement by Athalie Range, the Miami black activist: "The trial should have been here and the jury would not have had the audacity to adjudicate in the same manner."

Dunn agreed with the change of venue: "I urged that the trial be transferred to Tampa. I was afraid if they were tried in Miami, they would win on appeal," because of the overwhelming pretrial publicity against the defendants. "The problem was that the jury was all white." If there had been a black on the Tampa jury, "I don't think there would have been a race riot."

• • • •

NEXT QUESTION: HOW could the defendants been found not guilty of all charges? As Sergeant Gonzalez told a reporter, "I'm especially surprised that they didn't at least recognize a coverup took place."

James Lees, in his commentaries for this book, emphasized several times that the prosecutors should have started by focusing on the blatantly false police reports as way of showing jurors clear, indisputable examples that crimes were committed that night. As it was, the cover-up became a minor theme compared with immunized witnesses testifying who struck the deadly blows.

There clearly was a cover-up. Veverka filed seven reports, all false. Of course, his immunity agreement meant he wasn't going to jail. Del Toro was charged with aiding a cover-up, but no evidence supported that charge.

That left Diggs and Evans with cover-up charges. From almost all reports, Evans arrived at the scene after the beating was over. Carhart defended Evans by claiming that his client wrote an erroneous report because of what he was told by those who witnessed the incident. The lawyer persuaded the jury that the paramedic, the Jackson doctors and the medical examiner had all thought at first the head wounds were caused by an accident, so why couldn't Evans have been fooled as well?

But what about those pesky keys to McDuffie's Kawasaki found on the roof by a lab tech, exactly where Veverka and Hanlon said Evans threw them? That keys-throwing didn't really aid a cover-up, but it certainly showed that Evans was not simply an innocent sergeant taking notes on what others told him. The defense never did anything to refute the key-throwing testimony. Under different circumstances, those keys might have led to a conviction, but in this case the defense so completely discredited the immunized witnesses that the jurors didn't believe anything they said. And so they ignored the keys.

That left Diggs. If jurors had been paying close attention to each charge against each defendant, Diggs should have come closest to conviction — not on manslaughter, but on the cover-up charge.

No witness testified that Diggs struck a deadly blow. The prosecution's theory was that Diggs, as the supervisor that night, was responsible for not stopping Marrero, but multiple witnesses said Diggs was on the ground writhing in pain.

Still, he had signed a use-of-force report on Dec. 23, six days after the incident, about a motorcycle crash that didn't happen. While Veverka's first report said Diggs was one of the first to arrive at the scene, Diggs wrote that he was one of the last. Yet he managed to see a lot: "The subject's motorcycle hit the curb upon attempting to turn. The subject had no chin strap on his helmet, which flew off during the accident. The subject landed on his head and was bleeding profusely as officers arrived." Then Diggs saw McDuffie jump up and battle Veverka. "The subject continued to fight violently."

By the end of the trial, no one was claiming there had been an accident. The report was clearly false. Bowlin, the Central District commander, told jurors he'd asked Diggs how he could have seen a helmet flying and cycle crashing from two blocks away. Diggs insisted it was true.

By necessity, Diggs took the witness stand to explain his report. He gave jurors various desperate-sounding explanations: He wasn't absolutely certain; others had told him; he'd been ordered to write a false report; he signed a blank document.

What's more Gotowala, the non-immunized city cop, testified that when someone jumped in a squad car and ran over the Kawasaki to give it more damage, Diggs had a clear view of the incident.

If Diggs' cover-up charge had been tried on its own, it's quite possible a jury could have found him guilty. As it was, this was a secondary charge that became lost in the defense theme of the politicized investigation. Bowlin supposedly saw Diggs's quixotic application for PSD director as a threat, the defense argued, and that's why Bowlin was out to get Diggs. Perhaps the jury bought that idea, or perhaps, amid all the other charges, Diggs' cover-up just got overlooked.

• • • •

FINALLY, THE VERY NATURE of the incident made it difficult for jurors to comprehend. The confrontation lasted less than three minutes. Marrero said it was even less, maybe 45 seconds. Ten to 16 officers were on the scene, many of them hitting McDuffie. Many of this group said they didn't see anything wrong. Some were fired but not indicted.

There was so much confusion about what witnesses saw that I asked Yoss if the scene was poorly lit. No, he said. He and Adorno visited the intersection at night. There were strong lights on nearby buildings, and the lights of several squad cars would have been on as well.

"The difficulty of the situation," said Carhart, "is when you have like a mob committing a crime, how do you figure out — this is before video cameras — what was done and who did the actual deed. I respected the state's difficulty in mounting a credible case — and they fell far short of doing that," but even if they had, the key question remained, "Who did what?"

That's a crucial question, said Laeser: "If a lot of people have responsibility, then nobody's responsible. I've got to convince jurors that this person and this person alone committed a crime beyond a reasonable doubt…. I'm willing to bet that if there was a video camera on what's now called McDuffie corner, it would still be hard to figure out, and in which order. And just getting it from testimony, I thought was close to impossible."

In other words, despite all the tactics that could have been tried, perhaps the case just wasn't winnable.

In his memoir, Frank wrote that he was convinced a bunch of bad cops punished McDuffie with "street justice," but the problems with the immunized witnesses were huge. "No independent witness could say that any one cop committed a specific act that murdered Arthur McDuffie. Had I been on that jury, I might have had those same doubts."

• • • •

LET ME VENTURE ONE last hypothetical, based on the lawyers in the case.

For this book, I spent considerable time with Carhart in two lengthy interviews. When I was at the Herald, I devoted more than a month to a Janet Reno profile, including an interview in her attorney general's office in Washington. Both Carhart and Reno were admirable people with major achievements. But Carhart was a brilliant trial attorney. [See the Addendum on the Jones trials for one of his most astonishing achievements.] Reno avoided courtrooms.

And so here's a final if: If Carhart had been appointed to succeed Gerstein, he would have handled the McDuffie case completely differently, starting by going to the grand jury. Like Gerstein, Carhart himself would have led the trial team. It's likely the trial still would have moved to Tampa, because a change of venue seemed inevitable. What would have happened?

Carhart would have had at least one major advantage over Adorno: Carhart the prosecutor would not have had to face Carhart the defense attorney. And perhaps the result could have been different. *Chapter Notes

Chapter 42
Essay: The Media: My Cousin Vinny

Why were people so surprised by the verdicts? More than surprised, really. Astounded. Shocked. Four decades after the trial, it's obvious that the state's case was floundering from its very first witnesses. The defense knew it at the time. The prosecutors knew it. Jurors knew it. The public didn't.

Afterwards, that made a lot of Miamians angry. "The truth is the Miami Herald and the local media did a very poor job in covering that trial," said Merrett Stierheim, Dade County manager at the time, in an interview for this book.

"Quite frankly," said Kogan, the Del Toro attorney who went on to become chief justice of the Florida Supreme Court, "I believe the news media were really to blame for getting the community inflamed."

Even while rioters were still burning buildings, Joe Davis, the county's chief medical examiner, who had a good working relationship with the press and had postponed a Christmas vacation to make sure his office got the McDuffie autopsy right, said: "My impression of the newspaper is that anything that is highly flammable is published and anything of a stabilizing influence is not. I see a very irresponsible leadership by the news media."

Davis and Kogan were likely thinking of more than just trial coverage: They were looking back at the early days of the case, when newspapers and television were filled with reports based on the investigators' first interviews with eyewitnesses, while the defendants and their lawyers were silent.

Still, it's clear that the media coverage of the trial did nothing to alert Miami that acquittals were a distinct possibility. "It was a shock to everyone," said Maurice Ferre, the mayor of Miami. "I don't think we were prepared." Certainly, he wished police had been ready to deal with the explosion on the street. "We see it with hindsight, but we didn't see it with foresight. I think we were all guilty of that: the Miami Herald, CBS, the mayor of Miami, the police chief, none of us can claim we saw it coming and raised warning signs. Nobody raised warning signs."

Well, almost nobody. Of the seven reporters I examined who covered the trial daily, all but one did very little to reveal the problems with the state's case.

As could be expected, television had the shortest, simplest accounts. The Herald's were generally the longest, most detailed and best written. They were the work of Gene Miller, a two-time winner of the Pulitzer Prize and superstar of Miami journalism. His stories usually gave the most information each day, not only about what the prosecution was doing but also the defense's actions and questioning.

Still, the reporters generally covered each day's testimony without a broader perspective. That meant Veverka and Meier each said Marrero swung the deadly blows, without pointing out the "baffling contradiction," as CBS Reports later put it, between Veverka's version of McDuffie fighting ferociously at the beginning and Meier hearing "I give up!" Day after day, most reporters were not relaying the subtle nuances or offering a step-back analysis that might give a sense of how jurors were interpreting the proceedings.

There was one persistent exception: Verne Williams, 60, a veteran reporter of the afternoon paper, the Miami News. He nailed the courtroom chaos on several occasions. Even before opening arguments, he revealed the potential problems when the defense discovered that Prince, the city cop, admitted to kicking McDuffie in the head "just to get a lick in." The headline on that story was "McDuffie case in disarray." When Gerant named Watts as the one who smashed McDuffie in the head, Williams wrote that his "candid answers just may have wrecked the prosecution's case." Williams also foresaw Del Toro's acquittal in a story about how Del Toro was the forgotten man at the defense table.

When the state rested its case, Williams wrote, Judge Nesbitt said she realized there were "inconsistencies" in the prosecution's case, which Williams described as "beset by witnesses who had to admit having lied before turning state's evidence or whose memories differed from one another."

On the morning the verdicts were announced, the Saturday edition of the News ran a Williams story on 3A that noted, "No one really knows what the jurors are thinking," suggesting that convictions were far from assured. In the middle of that short story, he wrote, "The defense attorneys have raised havoc with the many discrepancies in the testimony" of the state's main witnesses.

Williams' stories were not seen by many. They generally ran inside the A section of the News, which had a Monday through Saturday circulation of 59,000 (it had no Sunday edition). As in most cities in 1980, the morning newspaper was the big dog. The Herald's circulation at the time was 421,750 on weekdays and 547,000 on Sundays. In most middle-class neighborhoods, well over half the homes were getting the Herald. Its news and editorials had by far the most influence on the county's politicians and civic leaders, but many regular people picked up their news from the three main television stations, those connected with the CBS, NBC and ABC networks.

Howard Kleinberg, editor of the News at the time, thought both Miller and Williams were simply doing their jobs. He agreed that Miller was Miami's preeminent reporter at that time—and perhaps of all time. In Tampa, "Gene was the AM cycle," meaning he got the first take on what happened for the morning newspaper. "So Gene was able to pick up every kernel, and Verne had to be more analytical, because that's where the Miami News had to go, what we call second-day lead."

• • • •

STEPPING BACK A MOMENT: I spent 42 years working for the Herald, much of that time with Tropic, the Herald's Sunday magazine. I know that newspaper journalism is by its very nature far from perfect, done quickly on deadline. Journalism may be the first draft of history. But first drafts tend not to hold up well over time.

Here I'm second-guessing coverage of other newspaper journalists. I'm sure that if intense insight was applied to my own work, it could be pretty embarrassing. I made plenty of blunders myself even when I wasn't on deadline pressure. I once wrote a story on "Killer Bees" rushing to the United States from Brazil up through Mexico that many thought meant disaster (though I noted some thought the danger was overrated). I once did a story on Y2K that, in retrospect, was completely unnecessary. If I looked back through the archives, I'm sure I could find a bunch of cringe-worthy material carrying my byline. I'm not enough of a masochist to do that.

In early 1980, when much of the newsroom was consumed with McDuffie, I was doing profiles like "Fearless 'Fang' Feinstein: the world's most expensive warrior," about an Air Force F-4 pilot. For that, I got to ride in a fighter jet. That spring I also wrote a semi-investigative piece on Scientology's foray into a Florida city, and followed it up with a fluffy look at the old-timey tourist attractions along Highway A1A.

If I'd been covering that Tampa trial, I'm sure I wouldn't have done as good a job as did Gene Miller.

Miller was 51 at the time of the McDuffie trial. He'd been with the Herald 23 years. He won a Pulitzer in 1967 for two investigations into people convicted of murder, Joe Shea and Mary Catherine Hampton, aka the "Hillbilly Lolita." His stories caused both to be released from prison. He then worked for eight years investigating the case of two black men, Freddie Pitts and Wilbert Lee, sent to Death Row after being convicted of killing two gas station attendants in the Florida Panhandle. Miller's dogged work led to the Florida Cabinet granting them clemency. For his Pitts-Lee work, Miller won another Pulitzer, in 1976.

When Miller died, editors asked me to collect quotes from journalists, civic leaders and people who knew him. The quotes ran alongside his obituary, which he'd written himself and placed in a sealed envelope years before, with blanks to be filled in with the details. It's certainly a measure of the respect editors showed him that they allowed him to write his own obit.

The lead: "Gene Edward Miller, 76, newspaperman, died at 9:12 a.m. June 17, 2005, at home. Cause: cancer, the family said. Noted Gene: 'Excellent health... except for a fatal disease.'"

• • • •

OF THE SIX PRINT REPORTERS, only Yvonne Shinhoster, now Yvonne Shinhoster Lamb, is still alive. She was 26 at the time, a black reporter assigned to cover a trial with plenty of racial implications, and she was careful to maintain a decidedly neutral coverage in almost all her stories. So did Marcia Slacum, 27 at the time, a black reporter from the St. Pete Times who sometimes referred to the "all-male jury," but almost never "all-white."

Shinhoster came under pressure on the first day of jury selection when lawyers criticized her trial-opening story, which began: "Arthur McDuffie's alleged crime was running a stop sign. His penalty was death." She remembered that "when I walked in, the defense looked at me funny." The lawyers complained to the judge that her story had tainted the jury pool. Like any professional journalist, Shinhoster always tried to be impartial, but feeling the pressure of the defense, she said she felt extra-vigilant in this case to be absolutely neutral.

Perhaps Miller felt that too. We don't know. His widow, Caroline Heck Miller, said she's not aware of any written personal reminiscences that might shed light on what he thought of the trial. We know he avoided giving anything close to his own opinion. Even after the trial, when two other reporters ventured personalized analyses, Miller chose instead to do a reported piece, interviewing lawyers about what they thought happened.

We do know that he was hearing the Herald bashed daily in the courtroom for supposedly pressuring prosecutors and investigators. At one point, the defense subpoenaed Edna Buchanan in an attempt to learn her PSD sources, and she dodged process servers in Miami. Carhart told the judge that perhaps her sources had witnessed the events of December 17 and could help Evans, his client. The Herald had to send an attorney, Sandy Bohrer, to Tampa to argue that Carhart was trying to use a Herald reporter as "his unpaid, private investigator." The judge agreed to quash the subpoena, but the defense kept up its criticisms of the newspaper throughout the trial.

During final arguments, the defense went so far as to blame the Herald for any possible attempts to cover up a legitimate use of force: The cops, they said, feared reporters would sensationalize the motorcycle incident like they had the LaFleur raid, and that's why they'd concocted an accident in an attempt to fool the Herald.

Jurors, too, were caught up in the anti-Herald fervor. When the riots erupted in Miami, Fisher, the jury foreman, told a Tampa's WFLA-TV that he thought the riots were caused by the Herald's coverage of the verdict. As Miller noted in a later story: "The first mob violence was reported around 6 p.m., about 45 minutes before the Herald's first edition was on the streets."

Perhaps with all of that, Miller chose to be as even-handed as he could, reporting on each day's happenings without attempting any analysis that could be viewed as opinion.

In fact, Yoss' criticism was exactly that: Reporters stuck to the facts without adding interpretation. "The trial itself and the facts we were able to present wasn't anything like the facts that were being presented, principally by the Miami Herald." He said the press coverage of the trial reminded him of the 1992 movie, "My Cousin Vinny," about two New York guys traveling in the rural South who were charged with murder. Vinny, played by Joe Pesci, was the lawyer who came down from the Big Apple to defend them.

Yoss described the movie: "They arrest these two kids for a convenience store robbery, and they're just shocked to find out they're being accused of this robbery and murder of the store clerk, and when [one of them] is being interrogated by the cop, he says, 'Why am I here?' And the cop says, 'You shot the clerk.' And [the kid] says, 'I shot the clerk?'" An emphatic question. "And the cop says, 'Yeah, you shot the clerk.'

"Well, in their trial, when the court reporter or the cop is reading the transcript of this conversation, ... he reads [the kid's reply] with no change in tone, no question mark: 'I shot the clerk.'

"Now, that's what the Miami Herald did," with witnesses like Veverka, Meier and Hanlon. "They never put in the intonation. They never put in the revelations.... Whatever it was, the Herald reported it happened exactly the way they said it on direct examination or whatever and never made it look like what it really was — which was terrible testimony by three cops. That's what the Miami Herald did. And everybody read the Herald, and everybody's reading about it in black and white what these cooperating cops testified about what these other cops did, and that's not the flavor that the jury was getting — nor us. We knew their testimony was terrible."

• • • •

ABOUT THREE MONTHS after the verdicts, the attacks against the Herald were the focus of a 99-page self-published book, "From Quiet to Riot," by Bob Hardin, an ex-Herald employee who preceded me as a staff writer of the Herald's Sunday magazine.

In 8.5x11-inch reproductions of typewriter pages, Hardin charged that the newspaper itself directly caused the riots by distorting the McDuffie coverage in its quest for a Pulitzer Prize. Major analyses by government agencies and academics thought the riots' causes were due to complex societal, historic and economic problems, but the pamphlet gained so much traction among Miami's movers and shakers that the Herald felt compelled to hire a law firm, which produced a 213-page report debunking the book.

Hardin blasted the newspaper at some points for ignoring defense arguments and at other times for reporting too much: "For the prosecution the trial was going horribly, but the newspaper coverage droned along, numbing the brain, extracting mere ounces of explanation for every ton of detail. Who was going to wade through it all, much less with a detective's eye to ask what was missing?"

Hardin clearly sided with the defense attorneys. He knew some of them well. After leaving the Herald, he became an employee of the Dade State Attorney's Office in the Gerstein era, where he associated with Carhart, O'Donnell and McWilliams.

"I never quite understood what he did," said Tom Petersen, a top assistant under both Gerstein and Reno. Sometimes, he was a speechwriter, but other times he just was hanging around and chatting with Gerstein.

Married to a daughter of the wealthy Keyes real estate family, Hardin moved in Miami's elite social circles, which meant that many of the city's leaders paid attention to his views, even though he printed only a few dozen copies of his book. His writing on the trials reflected the defense's views on the McDuffie trial and also his longstanding complaints about his former employer, the Herald, particularly its executive editor John McMullan, who Hardin thought treated Gerstein unfairly.

Herald staff thought the pamphlet was nonsense. Joe Oglesby, then a Herald reporter and columnist, viewed Hardin's work as "totally bogus. Not factually based at all."

In fact, Hardin's opinions were a mix of some legitimate problems in the McDuffie trial, such as the prosecution's rush to indict, with wild accusations about how every misstep by prosecutors and police could be blamed on Herald pressure, which was exactly what the defense maintained in Tampa.

Hardin blasted the Herald for ignoring anything that was pro-defense, and he gave the News no credit for its insightful Williams' analyses. In Hardin's view, the afternoon newspaper "marched in lockstep with the Herald." On the McDuffie case, "from start to finish, the pattern was that [anything] that didn't harmonize with The Herald's tune — to which everyone was dancing — was either minimized or ignored. The Herald wanted a bunch of cops tried and convicted for McDuffie's death, and damn any facts which might stand in the way of a mass inquisition."

In fact, after Del Toro's acquittal, Miller published an unusually long interview, much longer than any other reporter's, allowing Del Toro to express his anger at being dragged into a case he felt he didn't belong in. And when Marrero took the witness stand — the biggest moment in the defense's case — the Herald had the longest, most detailed account of what he said.

"After the trial," Hardin wrote, "the Herald said jurors 'couldn't be reached for comment.' Does anybody seriously believe that six ordinary citizens can elude the Herald for a month…? What explains this lack of newspaper instinct? The Herald didn't want to contradict its own conclusions."

In fact, the Herald was the only newspaper on Saturday to get comments from Fisher, the jury foreman, and Miller followed up the next day with a lengthy story on Fisher's views — again longer than any other reporter's.

In Hardin's view, "blacks, particularly, were conditioned that a verdict of guilty would exonerate the system of charges of racism. This was the message of the Herald editorial after McDuffie's death.

By all implication, if the verdict was not guilty, the charge of racism against the system was sustained. Thus, the difference between what was expected and what actually happened set off the riots. Shock and outrage erupted into rioting."

Certainly, there was a big gulf between expectation and result, but it's absurd to charge that the young blacks who rioted became enraged because they read a Herald editorial that raised their expectations.

Dunn, the activist, praised Hardin's work in 1980 as a "perceptive study," but to me he acknowledged that the rioters weren't Herald readers. In fact, the one rioter who talked to a reporter about media coverage said he and his buddies' source was television: "We had watched the trial every night. All those pictures and descriptions explaining how they beat the man to death, and they found those guys guilty of nothing?"

Edna Buchanan, too, pointed to television: "Gene Miller, the Herald's best, reported on the trial. His daily stories from Tampa covered both sides thoroughly. They were not all front-page. On TV, every story is front-page, and lots of people, particularly in low-income neighborhoods, get all their news from TV. What they saw may have convinced them that convictions were certain."

Kogan, Del Toro's attorney, saw for himself the simplicity of the trial on television: "When we went back to the hotel and saw the evening news, Wright was testifying about the autopsy. There was nothing about him first deciding it was an accident. They just had a 30-second clip saying [it was like] McDuffie was dropped from the fourth story of a building and that's all you see."

Later, a prominent Miami criminal defense attorney, Joel Hirschhorn, blamed the riots not on the Herald, but on television. Speaking at a meeting of the American Judicature Society in 1981, he noted that the McDuffie case was one of the first major trials to allow a television camera into the courtroom. Though no station broadcast gavel-to-gavel coverage, he maintained that the taped footage of key witnesses inflamed Miami's black residents. Eric Saltzman, who produced the CBS Reports show on the trial, disagreed. He said the most dramatic footage was of Eula Bell McDuffie wailing in agony after the verdicts. That happened outside the courtroom and had nothing to do with in-court cameras.

Other critics questioned whether television news should have been showing McDuffie's battered head in a morgue photograph, a photo that appeared on both Tampa and Miami television stations but not in the Herald.

Shortly after the verdicts, Carhart in Tampa told a reporter: "I don't blame the news media" for all the police brutality stories. "They did their jobs. They raise hell." But later, after the riots rocked Miami, he and the other defense attorneys, facing a public angry that their work caused the acquittals that sparked the riots, certainly did blame the media.

Carlton: "I think the media went a long way, without perhaps intending this result, to bring about the result that ultimately occurred to the detriment of the community. They sensationalized certain parts. They created race emotions over the victim" that sparked the riots. "That outbreak wasn't the fault of the defense team."

Shinhoster, the Tribune reporter, thought it preposterous that the media could have prevented the riot. Her brother, Earl, was the NAACP staffer in Miami, and he had a good handle on how people were feeling: rage that had been building up for a long time. "I think people would have rioted anyway. What happened was so outrageous, whether the papers had prepared them or not. People believed this was a good guy. What happened to him should not have happened. Particularly the violent nature.... It was almost a feeding frenzy, five or so people beating him. I think when people heard the details of that, they were outraged, and reporters could have no calming effect on that rage."

That assessment works for me. Clearly, the media didn't cause the riot. Still, with 20-20 hindsight, it's obvious that Miami's leaders could at least have been better prepared had they understood how badly the trial was going. As Stierheim, the county manager, put it: "Miami and Miami-Dade County was not prepared for that decision. It shocked everyone. It shocked me."

• • • •

IN THE NEXT CHAPTER, we'll explore more serious discussions of what really caused the riots, but before we leave this subject of the media, let's examine larger issues of journalists covering trials. Experienced lawyers, especially in criminal law, often say that newspaper reporting bears little or no relationship to what really happens in courtrooms.

A classic lawyer's protest came from Louis Nizer, a stellar lawyer in the last century. In 1972, he wrote in "The Implosion Conspiracy": "I am constantly astounded by the definite opinion people have about cases based on newspaper reports of a trial still in progress. At dinner tables, intelligent men and women, who would stoutly defend the presumption of innocence of any accused person, will condemn the defendant as guilty, substituting vehemence for their lack of knowledge, and holding forth authoritatively on testimony they have never heard, and of which the newspaper accounts give the most fragmentary version.

"Barest inferences and suspicions are elevated to incontestable truth. After the debate has raged for a while, someone, out of consideration for my supposed expertise, will turn to me and ask my opinion. I reply that I do not understand how they could have judgments when the defense has not even been heard yet, and when the evidence which has been adduced might fill five hundred pages of the record and of which they have read a diluted, selected version of ten to twelve paragraphs in a newspaper."

Certainly, with the McDuffie case, many people not at the trial had strong presuppositions about the cops' guilt. A headline of "I Give Up!" does a lot to rivet the brain, and all else becomes just noise.

Even the Herald, running the longest and most detailed stories of the daily media, was covering a fraction of what happened on any given day, and then in a nuts-and-bolts way, while the News analysis of events was read by only a few in Miami.

One suggestion is for a newspaper to assign one reporter to do straight reporting, and another to provide a flowing analysis. "I read the [New York] Times daily. You can do both," said Laeser, the veteran Dade prosecutor.

Hardin, too, raised this point: "The paper which can send three reporters to a football game couldn't spare anyone to analyze one of the most significant trials in the community's history, because it already 'knew' all it wanted to know?"

That last statement is an example of Hardin raising an important point, then slathering it with unfounded innuendo, with the underlying notion that the Herald was a monolithic entity, when in fact dozens of reporters and editors were working with their own ideas of what was important to cover, independent from the editorial page.

In 1980, and even more so today, it was a big deal for a reporter to sit through every day of a trial. To have two reporters sit at the same trial would have been unprecedented, and certainly Herald editors wouldn't have felt they needed a second opinion beside Miller to analyze the Tampa coverage.

In fact, the Tampa trial was unusual because it had at least a half-dozen reporters in the courtroom almost every day. Much of trial coverage in America consists of a reporter jumping in and out of a courtroom, perhaps covering the lead prosecution witnesses and the defendant if he testified.

Carhart, who went on to decades of top defense work, was familiar with reporters appearing briefly at his trials. "Journalists in the main don't have time to sit there for the length of the day and listen to the nuances that are so critical.... They have limited time, limited resources, limited space. So they have to give a limited picture. How many paragraphs do they have? How many inches? You watch the TV coverage of trials — it is all prosecution, is it not? You never see it from the defense standpoint."

The state's case is generally easy for a reporter to grasp. "The police media bureau hands you the fact sheet and you go with that," Carhart said. "I don't even recognize the case I'm trying when I read the newspaper or watch television. I mean they go to the flash point."

In his comments for this book, James Lees wrote that he was "intimately familiar" with the limitations of courtroom journalism during his career in both prosecutions and criminal defense. "Courthouse reporters generally write stories based upon the direct examinations of prosecutors and do not highlight cross examinations. Cross-examinations are more nuanced and more difficult to describe within the confines of a newspaper story. And cross examinations generally give readers an impression that a newspaper is favoring the criminal, an impression most publishers of local newspapers do not want to create."

That's a good description of missing nuances, but I must say that in my four plus decades as a journalist, I never experienced publishers telling me or my editors not to favor criminals, or anything else about covering trials, for that matter.

Still, there are plenty of examples in criminal trials, including the one in Tampa, of how daily journalists often struggle with cross-examination. "I give up!" makes an easy story. The long, meandering cross-examination of Meier — revealing that he hadn't recalled the "I give up!" statement for weeks — played out slowly, in complex questions, sowing seeds of doubts that don't lend themselves to short reports.

In fact, Miller offered considerable detail about Meier's cross-examination for readers who managed to get all the way through the story. Other accounts were much shorter.

Before and long after the Tampa trial, Carhart was known as a master of such cross-examination. He'd look "like he's pin-pricking you," said Oglesby, the Herald reporter who watched him when he covered trials, "and you turned around looked and your entire body was cut in pieces" with "a thousand knife cuts."

O'Donnell: "We know where we going, what we're trying to do, and maybe it doesn't make sense until closing argument when you try to take those pinpricks that Ed Carhart does – I'm more of a club guy, I guess – but then they just are sewn together and you see" in final argument everything come together. "That's not a disparagement [of journalists]. Even if they have law degrees, they're not Ed Carhart or even Ed O'Donnell when he puts his club down and tries to do that – and does it."

Carhart contrasted daily newspaper accounts, inevitably short and incomplete, with longer work. "If you read about the O.J. Simpson case in a book, or an article that The New Yorker might run, you get a much different picture."

Indeed, I know this first-hand. In 1986, I sat through a month-long trial for the Herald's Sunday magazine. Victor Posner, the wealthy owner of Arby's restaurants and Royal Crown soda, among many other businesses, was accused in federal court of criminal tax evasion. He was defended by Edward Bennett Williams, a legendary Washington trial lawyer, who was up against two much younger prosecutors.

Williams was in his last days. He'd have cancer treatments early in the morning, then come to court. Lawyers dropped by the courtroom just to see him in action. I didn't have to write a word until after the verdict — a conviction — and after interviews with many of the jurors.

That gave me the perspective of a rhythm of a trial perhaps similar to what jurors were feeling, rather than the quick hit on the witness of the day.

"Time after time," I wrote, "Williams appeared to outmaneuver his adversaries. The prosecutors came off as plodding and methodical, at times almost stammeringly deferential to the master litigator from Washington. But, slowly, as the trial progressed, Posner's great insulating wealth became a liability: Five years of his income-tax returns, every element of his private life was laid out for all the jurors to see. The figures were astounding, and the jurors reacted with a mixture of awe, envy and... ridicule."

Each day after trial, the jurors walked out of the courthouse and into the blistering summer heat. There at the curb were three black limousines waiting for Posner and his entourage, engines running to keep the AC going, as the jurors trudged blocks to a parking lot to get in cars they knew would be oven-hot. "Vic's limos," they called them.

If I recall, the city desk had a reporter drop in for a witness or two, but that was it until the verdict. I kept going. One juror told me she had gone out and looked at a property that was a key to the case; Posner was claiming a deduction on it that the government said was illegal. After my story appeared, the judge determined that her action was improper. Jurors are not supposed to do research on their own outside the courtroom. He threw out the verdict. Rather than face another jury, Posner pleaded guilty. He avoided jail time by agreeing to contribute $3 million to a homeless project.

Tropic Magazine, where the Posner story appeared, was killed off by the Herald in 1998. These days, outside of the New York Times and Washington Post, it's highly unlikely that any daily newspaper could allow a reporter so much time to do a trial story.

With such limitations, what could reporters do better? At the very least, they should interject a note of caution, especially into highly publicized stories where the pretrial publicity tends to virtually convict defendants. And that's even more true when it comes to police brutality cases.

It was only after the trial that the Herald mentioned the difficulties with cop cases, when columnist Joe Oglesby noted: "It is a recognizable lawyers' tenet that cops are more difficult to convict that anyone else. We all want to believe cops. And there is the almost impenetrable in-the-line-of-duty defense."

Indeed, if that idea had been inserted at least occasionally into trial coverage or editorials, it wouldn't have stopped the riots, but it might have helped alleviate the public's utter shock at the verdicts.

Still, perhaps the core issue isn't how the media covers the trials of police officers. Maybe it has more to do with how the everyday trials faced by black people in America aren't covered.

Mohamed Hamaludin is a veteran black journalist who worked many years for the Miami Times, which focuses on the black community. Hamaludin believed that rioting was going to take place after the acquittals no matter how the media covered the trial. But if the mainstream media had pointed out the bungling by the prosecutors before trial, that might have forced the state attorney's office to produce a better case — and perhaps convictions.

"But even more," added Hamaludin in an email, "the media could have played an important role even before McDuffie was killed by drawing attention to the socio-economic disparities in the city and the police brutality that African Americans were seeing as a byproduct of the neglect and which was a source of continued tension." *Chapter Notes

Chapter 43
What Really Caused the Riots?

The McDuffie case didn't happen in a vacuum, of course. As the trial plodded on in the spring of 1980, it became a secondary matter for most Miamians as an astonishing 125,000 Cuban refugees flooded the area in a matter of weeks.

The Mariel boatlift, as it became known, was just the latest onslaught. For two decades, Cubans and other Hispanics had been moving to Miami, climbing the economic ladder with considerable ease. Black residents often felt that they were becoming the forgotten minority. Add to this to the LaFleur wrong house raid and the white state trooper getting no jail time for molesting the black 11-year-old, and it was clear that anger in the black community was building. As if this were not enough, while the Tampa trial plodded along, an all-white jury in Miami convicted school superintendent Johnny Jones, the county's top black government leader, of second-degree grand theft for using school funds to purchase gold-plumbing fixtures for a vacation home. (See Addendum for a thorough look at Jones' struggles in court.)

Three weeks after the Jones guilty verdict, while the McDuffie trial was still going on, The New Yorker published an article by Calvin Trillin, "Judging Johnny Jones." Trillin reported the case was seen through the prism of race: Whites thought it was a simple case of corruption. Blacks viewed it as "the hounding of a black public official."

Trillin wrote: "The black community has sometimes felt itself almost literally forgotten. In recent years, when attention has been given to a minority group in Miami it has usually been given to Latins. There are not many visiting reporters who find the crumbling storefronts of black neighborhoods like Overtown more engaging than

Calle Ocho in Little Havana. In economics and political power, the blacks have over the years worked their way from second to third.... A black secretarial-school graduate who might have thought her handicaps in the job market would be limited to her color and an occasional problem with verb endings now has another handicap: she can't speak Spanish.

"In the past year or so, the black community in Miami has been shaken by a series of police-brutality incidents — most notably the death of... Arthur McDuffie," Trillin wrote. "Some people believe that Miami does not have the resources or the history to do much about easing the bitterness and mistrust caused by the gold-plumbing caper. 'There is no meaningful contact between races here,' one white human-relations professional said recently. 'There is no continuity of trust. What happened was a trauma. There's no other way to think of it except as a trauma. We may be a community that has trauma but no trauma-treatment center.'"

That statement appeared days before the McDuffie trial ended. The verdicts in Tampa were merely "the precipitating spark that blew the lid off the smoldering volcano created by dire problems of poverty, unemployment, underemployment, housing and functional illiteracy," wrote the Governor's Dade County Citizens Committee in its October 1980 report. McDuffie and LaFleur were "merely manifestations of long existing and deep-seated prejudices that existed between some white officers and black citizens," the committee wrote.

The panel also mentioned "inadequate youth recreational facilities and activities, political deprivation, hard core juvenile delinquents and failures of society" festering for decades. "If the McDuffie verdict had not ignited the explosion then it would have only been a matter of time before some other incident would have brought about the same result."

Indeed, the riot areas were poor and getting poorer. From 1968 to 1978 in Liberty City, unemployment soared from 6 percent to

17.8, as Bruce Porter and Marvin Dunn wrote in their insightful book, "The Miami Riot of 1980." By 1980, in the census tract where the worst violence occurred, 56.6 percent of families lived below the poverty line. Two-thirds of those over 25 didn't have high school degrees.

"But poverty alone does not make people riot," Porter and Dunn wrote. "If such conditions did in fact cause rioting, blacks in the United States would be in a continuously riotous state."

Porter and Dunn and Alejandro Portes and Alex Stepick, co-authors of "City on the Edge," point to the Kerner Commission, created by Lyndon Johnson to look at causes of the 1960s riots. Its report said there were immediate causes for riots — almost always a response to an incident of police brutality — but also underlying, deep-seated problems.

"Deep down," Porter and Dunn wrote, "the crowds do not react to what the police are doing in the current situation as much as they react to what police have done in the past — to what they 'always' do in a given set of circumstances."

Both the Porter-Dunn and Portes-Stepick books cite a seminal study by Stanley Lieberson and Arnold R. Silverman, who examined the causes of riots from 1913 to 1963. That analysis found that areas where riots occur generally share three underlying conditions: few black cops, few black-owned businesses and a lack of black elected officials.

All three conditions were present in Miami. "Thus, in their view," wrote Porter and Dunn, "riots are caused not so much by people being economically deprived as by those conditions that make them feel left out of the system, that make them feel victimized rather than served by the social order."

Indeed, this feeling of being left out, more than simple poverty, was the underlying cause of the Miami riots, the academics concluded.

"Miami fulfilled all three conditions amply," Portes and Stepick wrote, "but in addition the native minority confronted the reality of a changed city, where a new immigrant group was elbowing them aside. 'McDuffie' was, without doubt, the trigger for the riots, but the resentment of being always left out, of remaining invisible and forgotten as other groups marched forward, was the background against which the extremely violent actions of May took place."

The Commission on Civil Rights reported that Miami's black neighborhoods have "been isolated and excluded from the explosion of economic growth occurring all around [them] in the last two decades." Starting in the early 1960s, construction of Interstate 95 tore apart much of the black downtown area of Overtown, forcing many black residents to move to Liberty City, the commission reported.

At the same time, the first waves of Cuban immigrants were arriving. The 1980 census showed that Dade County was 46.4 percent non-Hispanic white, 35.7 percent Hispanic and 16.6 percent non-Hispanic black. The census was taken on April 1, meaning it would not have included the Mariel influx that was concentrated in late April and May.

Black residents had slipped to third place both demographically and economically, while the rest of the county was booming. Job creation and countywide revenue was rising faster than the national average, the Commission on Civil Rights stated. But "the black community has been notably absent from this economic success story. By all social indicators, blacks as individuals and as a community have been excluded from the economic mainstream in Miami. Their living conditions worsened as their families were dislocated by urban renewal and highway construction."

In 1960, Hispanic and black median annual family income was about the same: $3,777 for Hispanics, $3,367 for black families. Ten years later, black families were in a dismal third place. Median income was $8,091 for Hispanic families, $5,983 for black families, the commission reported. In 1979, with the national unemployment rate at 5.8 percent, Dade County's overall rate was 5 percent. In black areas, though, unemployment was three times that: 15.3 percent.

"City on the Edge" reported that Cubans were not necessarily taking black jobs directly. "There was, however, a new urban economy in which the immigrants raced past other groups, leaving the native minority behind. Hence, after decades of striving for a measure of equality with whites, Miami blacks found that the game had dramatically changed. Anglos were leaving, and other whites who spoke a foreign language were occupying their positions. As a result, most blacks were in a similar position as before."

"Miami was in the South," Stepick told me in an interview. "It had legalized segregation. My personal explanation that I have the most confidence is that the riots of 1980 are really caused by rising expectations and not being fulfilled. Through the 1970s, Miami, like the rest of the United States, was experiencing the outcome of the civil rights movement and new opportunities were opening up for African Americans, but they weren't opening up as fast as many people hoped. And then in the Miami case you have the juxtapositions of the Cubans."

In fact, Stepick said, Cubans were given benefits, boosted by "the Cold War politics at the time," that gave them much more federal help than Haitians, Mexicans or other immigrants received during that era. In the 1960s and 1970s, "on a per capita basis, they had received the most welfare benefits of any group in American history. Not surprising many of those fleeing a socialist/communist country were from the upper or professional classes. So that if you were a doctor or a lawyer or teacher or doctor and needed to be recertified, the U.S. government paid all those costs. They had never done that for anyone else."

Such help "allowed Cubans to progress rapidly," Stepick said, and that "gave the African American community the feeling 'we're being left out. We're being ignored.' So even though Mariel may not have been an immediate cause of the riots in Miami in 1980, the Cuban presence was certainly a contributing cause to it."

Stepick said he did considerable research into hotel and restaurants on Miami Beach, known as longtime employers of black workers. "There was lots of anecdotal evidence that Cubans came in and were able to take those jobs away. Actually, when you look at the census figures [for] blacks in low level hotel-restaurant jobs going back all the way to the 1920s up until 1980, it actually didn't change. They were the same percentages throughout all that time. So pragmatically what that meant was that blacks were holding steady."

That meant the job market grew, but the black portion of it remained stagnant. "The Cubans did progress in those industries and that progress again contributed to the blacks' frustration," Stepick said.

Dunn and Porter had a somewhat different take: "Much has been written about how the Cubans took away the service jobs and other clerical work from the blacks. And indeed looking at a comparison prepared by the County Planning Department between the kinds of jobs blacks held in 1968 and those ten years later is like seeing economic progress suddenly thrown in to reverse gear." The percentage of blacks holding clerical jobs fell from 13.3 to 11.1, machine operators from 10.3 to 2.2, service workers from 23.1 to 18.8 percent. White-collar jobs also fell, while "those doing general labor, at the bottom of the economic heap, rose dramatically. It went from 12.4 percent of the black population to 25 percent....

"Even more disastrous from the black viewpoint was the apparent ease with which the Hispanics rooted themselves financially in the economy of the city," Porter and Dunn wrote. "One study showed that black residents owned 25 percent of Dade gas stations in 1960. By 1979, that was down to 9 percent, while Hispanics during that period saw their ownership of gas stations climb from 12 to 48 percent.

The governor's panel shared the view of many that black residents were losing jobs to Cubans: "Our tourist industry, the hotels, motels and restaurants have a civic responsibility to once against make more jobs available to blacks. At the very least, blacks should be given non-contact jobs such as maids, porters, bus boys, etc., where language is not a problem. The industry should also take the lead in teaching non-Latins the few phrases that employees need to know to direct our Latin tourists to other Spanish-speaking employees."

• • • •

THIS FEELING BY BLACK residents that they were being left behind was well solidified by the spring of 1980. Then came Mariel.

For decades, even well into the 21st Century, it's been debated how much, if at all, Mariel contributed to the black anger that erupted in the riots.

The backdrop: In April, as the trial went on in Tampa, 10,000 Cubans jammed themselves into the Peruvian embassy in Havana and demanded safe passage out of the country. Banner headlines dominated the Miami newspapers: "Exiles cry: Let our people go," bellowed the Miami News, with a second banner headline: "Ferre: Cubans welcome here" while another head stated "Exiles plead for action by U.S." The Carter administration hesitated.

After halfhearted attempts to move Cubans in the embassy to other countries, Castro seized control of the situation by announcing that the port of Mariel near Havana was open to almost anyone who wanted to leave. Many Miami Cubans found any kind of boat they could rent or buy to make the 90-mile journey from Key West to Cuba to pick up relatives they hadn't seen in years. As the defense attorneys were making their opening arguments in Tampa, the News blared on Page 1: "Exile boats arrive Havana to take some Cubans to Miami."

The Carter administration continued to waffle: At first doing nothing, then welcoming the new refugees, then trying to stop the flow.

The boatlift drama consumed Miami media. On Thursday, April 24, as Meier in Tampa quoted McDuffie as saying "I give up!", the Herald's front page was dominated by a banner headline: "Ragtag Flotilla Ferries Exiles," with two accompanying stories: "Key West Hosts Chaotic Drama" and "Miami Cubans Vow to Continue Boatlift." That afternoon, the News' 1A banner headline declared: "Miami Cubans defy U.S.; exiles pour into the Keys," with two accompanying stories: "In Key West, a greeting of love and chaos" and "Freedom's road begins at Dade's Tamiami Park."

Indeed, the county had taken over the usual role of the federal government, which was utterly unprepared for the onslaught. At Tamiami Park, county employees set up a reception center, registering who was coming in, a task generally done by federal immigration officers. Soon, county police were involved too, trying to keep track of who was coming in as it became apparent that Castro was opening jails and mental hospitals.

The Miami media continued to cover the Tampa trial, but it became a minor matter on the local-section front or, as the trial went on, buried inside the local section. On the morning of Saturday, May 17, hours before the verdicts, the Herald's front page had four stories about Mariel, plus a box listing all the refugee developments on Friday. Adorno's final argument was on the front of the local section.

The first editorials responding to the riots suggested that Mariel was part of what fueled black rage. The Herald editorial listed LaFleur and Johnny Jones as causes. "Add to that embattled feeling the wave of Cuban immigrants — competitors for blacks' jobs —

and the ingredients for an explosion were all in place when the McDuffie returned its verdict."

Was there a link between Mariel and the riots?

Maurice Ferre, mayor of Miami at the time, believed so. "I don't think there is any question. I don't have any scientific evidence, but it's my considered opinion, there was a relationship. The black community was very, very upset" about the Mariel deluge. Ferre remembered trying to reassure Athalie Range, a onetime city commissioner, and other black leaders. "But we could not overcome the theme that in effect people were going to take over the jobs blacks initially had. I remember going to see Mrs. Range to help her calm down the community. 'This does not mean Mariel Cubans are taking over black jobs,'" Ferre told her. She wasn't convinced. She said, "I can name you people who have lost their jobs in Miami Beach because the Latins came in."

Howard Kleinberg, editor of the Miami News, is more cautious. "Well, I think there was a link" between the riots and Mariel. "Was that the main issue? "No. Was it something that led up to it? Absolutely."

Stepick, co-author of "City on the Edge," said of Mariel and the riots: "They certainly were very close in time and in geography. And so it seems natural that there is a connection between the two, and there are certainly people — particularly in the Anglo establishment — that have a perception, close to a presumption, that there was a connection between the two.

"I think it is critical to distinguish between the perception or assumption and the objective facts that would demonstrate the connections. And if you look for objective facts that demonstrate the connection you are never going to find those. That's impossible to show. There were no rioters on the street saying we're rioting because Cubans are coming to Miami."

There were no quotes from rioters on the topic, but Otis Denkins, who was at African Square Park listening to the police chiefs speak when the verdicts came in, told a reporter: "With all that has happened with the Cubans and the Haitians, we did not need that," meaning the Tampa verdicts. "There are going to be some horrible repercussions."

Dunn, co-author of "The Miami Riot" is emphatic: "The Mariel boatlift and the McDuffie riot were completely independent events. They were coincidental in the history. Blacks did not go out and kill white people because Cubans were coming in on the Mariel boatlift. Had nothing to do with it...."

"The McDuffie killing was distinct," Dunn said. "One was it involved a victim who had no criminal record, no reason for the police to harass, much less kill him. It happened at the end of a number of other events of police incidents —and it came at a time when the black community was very, very intense about a number of issues, including immigration, economic problems in the black community, etc. But McDuffie stood out because of the intensity of the beating, the public focus on it, the fact he was beaten by several police officers, all of whom are white ... beaten to death for no reason except contempt of cop, that he sped away, ran through a red light."

The riot was caused, Dunn said, by "the widespread perception, based in reality, that a great injustice had taken place and the system had failed. Mariel was an afterthought. It became a factor in the minds of the media, became a factor in the coverage that was projected outside of Miami in the national media, and so it became a truism. In the view of some public officials they were connected. But they were not...."

"I think at first immigrants, both Cubans and Haitians, were welcomed by blacks," Dunn went on. "I think there was a natural affinity between blacks and Haitians coming in. But that was in the early years. By 1980 the numbers had become so overwhelming and many of the people coming in were suddenly in or close to the black community, creating tensions for public housing, schools, public health care, so tensions were beginning to mount as more and more people came in. People began to resent all these people coming in, and they did begin to resent the encroachment on jobs, as they saw it. So the immigration issue had an overriding level of tension among the black people of Dade county in 1980." So while Mariel didn't cause the riots, "It might have been a subtext for it," Dunn said.

• • • •

SETTING ASIDE THE RIOTS, another major question has persisted for decades: Did the sudden influx of immigrants really hurt local black workers?

Over the years, Mariel has attracted many economic studies because, unlike most immigration, this was a sudden, large influx of newcomers in a single place: as many as 60,000 workers who settled quickly into the Miami area.

That's in contrast with the usual waves of immigration, which are blurred by many factors, including lengthy time frames and new arrivals generally heading to places where the most jobs are available, meaning their effects on native-born Americans are lessened.

Basic supply-and-demand theory states that if you increase the number of people who want to be janitors, for example, the wages of janitors tend to go down.

That theory didn't apply to Mariel, maintained David Card, who was a Princeton professor when he published a paper in 1990 that continues to be widely cited. "The Mariel influx appears to have had virtually no effect on the wages or unemployment rates of less-skilled workers," Card wrote. One big reason, he argued, was that the new workers created new jobs for those who had to service them in supermarkets, pharmacies, schools and the like. Card's study has long been cited worldwide by policymakers and the media as a major reason why people shouldn't be afraid of immigrants, including Mexicans entering the United States and Syrians arriving in Europe.

In 2015, a Cuban-born Harvard professor, George Borjas, declared he'd reached a completely different conclusion: Mariel caused a drastic drop in pay among those in a crucial demographic group. Unlike Card, Borjas focused on the native-born Americans most likely to face competition from the new arrivals: male non-Hispanic high-school dropouts aged 25-59. More than half of that group in Miami were black. The wages for this group, he found, "dropped dramatically, by 10 to 30 percent" after Mariel.

Spurred by Borjas' work, the Wall Street Journal, the Economist and many other publications revisited the Mariel issue. The New Yorker praised his "dogged research" for raising doubts about earlier studies. In 2016, Politico dubbed him the 17th most influential thinker "transforming American politics."

The pushback against Borjas from other academics was intense, with arguments about sample size and comparisons to other cities. For a while, Borjas engaged in the lively debate. Then, in 2017, his research was weaponized by Stephen Miller, President Donald Trump's senior advisor on immigration, when he cited the professor's work to argue for drastically reducing immigration of low-skilled, low-education immigrants. The outcry became so intense that Borjas dropped out of the debate and has been mostly silent on the topic since then.

Afterword
By Patrick Malone

Forty years after the McDuffie case, two memories stand out for me. The first: sitting in Dr. Ron Wright's cramped office looking at the skull fractures delivered with such lethal force they seemed beyond human strength. The second: driving home on a Sunday morning in May 1980 from a weekend trip to the Gulf coast and seeing from miles away the plume of smoke rising above the city that signified the riots.

I was the Miami Herald's medical writer then and wrote a detailed piece about the autopsy. It ran the same day as the indictments were reported. I left a year later for law school and a new career as a trial lawyer based in Washington, D.C. I've never done any criminal case work but have stood in front of juries many times in complex civil trials, teasing out intricate evidence about injuries to the human body and what or who is responsible for them.

Dr. Wright's careful documentation in his autopsy report was always to me the heart of the McDuffie case: The lethal blow that started between the eyes and cracked the skull from front to back through the skull base, then two more skull fractures from direct blows on the back of the head; no injuries to the hands or forearms. His conclusion: These wounds were delivered to the head of a person who could not use his hands to shield himself from the blows, and their impact was so powerful that the head had to have been supported by the ground or a wall, not free to snap back and absorb the energy. The force of the lethal blow was 90 times the force of gravity, he told me in his office, echoing his testimony at trial that it was equivalent to falling four floors and landing on one's head. This was no street justice fight that went a little too far. It was just murder, plain and simple. That was my conclusion, not necessarily his.

So as I read the passage in John Dorschner's account where the usually voluble defense lawyers were left speechless as Wright testified at the trial, unable to challenge his meticulous work, I wondered why the prosecutors didn't call the medical examiner, their strongest witness, first.

If Wright had testified first, the jury would have learned that hard science backed the prosecution and put the lie to defense claims, notably by defendant Marrero, that the blows were delivered in a fight to subdue a defiant motorcyclist.

Other witnesses worth calling early: the crime scene technician who found the motorcycle keys on the roof of a nearby building and other forensic investigators who proved the damage to the cycle was staged and not from any collision.

This alternative order of witnesses would have set in motion a completely different narrative — a shocking crime and a bungled coverup — than the one the defense lawyers were able to seize when the immunized witnesses came first.

Of course, sooner or later, witnesses had to appear at trial to link the defendants to the fatal blows and/or the coverup. And here the "rush to judgment" that Dorschner lays out so well was likely fatal to any chance to convict someone of the McDuffie killing, at least in my view. Was it really necessary to immunize, without even a polygraph test first (although the scientific reliability of such tests is doubtful), the first guy to walk in the door seeking a deal?

Why not first exhaust the investigative tools at your disposal – grand jury testimony that locks in the stories? That would have enabled a more sober consideration of whom to indict and who gets a "Get Out of Jail Free" card.

These what-ifs are easy enough to dispense at a 40-year distance. Could I have done any better? My 20-something-year-old self in 1980 definitely could not have. My current self, with scars from the times I have lost jury trials that I thought I should have won, probably yes. Most definitely I would have made many different decisions. To take one small example: My lawyering self with three and a half decades of trial experience would have examined the potential jurors as rigorously as the defense counsel did, if only to show that I cared. I know how easy it is to convey the wrong impression, as the young McDuffie prosecutors did by their indifferent juror questioning. My current self would likewise have taken far more time to get the indictments right and have the evidence locked down and make the witness order more effectual.

Would different decisions have mattered? We ask not in order to hunt down scapegoats but to learn to do better. When law enforcement officers become law breakers, failing to bring them to justice can tear at the social fabric that holds all of us together, as I saw in that plume of smoke rising above the city that distant afternoon a day after the McDuffie verdict.

These are hard, very hard cases, but necessary to pursue and important to win. They require the utmost in thought and preparation and sheer lawyerly craft, qualities that were sadly lacking in the McDuffie prosecution.[*Chapter Notes]

Epilogue

In the decades since the Tampa trial, notoriety continued to dog some of the players in the Tampa courtroom while others soared to prominence. One witness and one defendant were later charged with drug dealing. Both immediately sought immunity deals. One ended up doing 19 years in prison. A lawyer had his law license suspended because of the way he handled a case. A witness went to law school but was barred from practicing law, though he appealed all the way to the Florida Supreme Court. Another witness got a police job and was charged with police brutality.

Here's what happened to the major characters.

Adorno, Hank: Lead prosecutor. He and George Yoss created a hugely successful law firm, Adorno & Yoss, which grew to almost 300 attorneys in 17 locations throughout the United States and Latin America. In 2010, Adorno's law license was suspended after it was revealed that he got a $7 million settlement for seven clients — and $2 million for his law firm — by ignoring the claims of several other thousand claimants in a class-action lawsuit. The law firm collapsed. Adorno eventually got back his license to practice. He went to work for a Miami real-estate developer.

Buchanan, Edna: Herald reporter. She won the Pulitzer Prize in 1986 for her police beat reporting and went on to write many mystery and nonfiction crime books.

Carhart, Edward: Former chief assistant for Dade State Attorney Richard Gerstein and defense attorney for Sergeant Herbert Evans. In his last years, he was paralyzed from the neck down because of a progressive nerve disease that had afflicted him for years. Still, he continued to practice law from a wheelchair. In 2013, he defended a man accused of wounding a Miami-Dade police detective investigating a marijuana grow house. He died in 2016 at age 78.

Carlton, Philip: Defense attorney, represented Michael Watts. He had a long legal career. He was always a deeply religious Catholic, and in his later years, he became a prison chaplain. "The law has been very good to me. I've given my life to the law. When my wife and daughter went home to the Lord, I said it's time for me to give back to God for what he has given me." He worked in jails three or four days a week from 9 a.m. to 5 p.m. "I preach. I counsel. I pray with them. I do what I can to show them a better life. I think I'm called to do this work." He died in 2019 at the age of 89.

Del Toro, Ubaldo (Eddie): Defendant. After the judge ordered a directed verdict of acquittal, he told the Herald: "Now, I look at police work as the dumbest job any intelligent man could take." In 1983, he sued the county to get his job back so he could resign with a clean record. "They have ruined me in law enforcement" by putting a "do not hire" on his personnel record, he said. With no income, he was living with his parents. The county reinstated him, gave him $20,000 in back pay. He resigned. For many years, he worked for the Hialeah Police Department. In 1998, he received a master's degree in criminal justice from Florida International University. He left law enforcement in 2003 to teach at Miami Dade College's School of Justice. He died of brain cancer in 2006 at age 52.

Diggs, Ira: Defendant. He sold his home shortly after the trial to pay for his expenses and began looking for a police job anywhere in the country. Diggs settled in Texas, where he started a security and investigations business. For the past 35 years he has been a process server. "I can handle the difficult cases."

Evans, Herbert "Skip": Defendant. His wife gave birth to a boy on May 28, 11 days after the verdicts. Evans moved out of Dade County for three months because of threats against his life. He achieved a master's degree in prison management from the University of Miami. He became a security consultant and then a branch manager for Wackenhut, a security firm, then went to work for the

Miami Beach Fire Department. "I spent 14 years as a paramedic... and retired 24 years ago with a good pension and the joy of having spent those years providing care and comfort to those in need, plus fighting some dangerous high-rise fires on the Beach and saving trapped citizens," he wrote in an email in 2020.

Draper, David: Juror. After his employment at Stromberg-Carlson, he worked from home as a small-business consultant and helped with his wife's printing business. In 2007, he moved to Shelter Island, New York, where he became a volunteer at the historical society and created puzzles for the local newspaper. He died in 2013 at age 72.

Edgecombe, Phil: The black state attorney investigator who assisted prosecutors in Tampa. Not too long after the trial, a city of Miami police officer pulled him over on Interstate 95. "I had a three-piece suit on. I had a police radio. I had my gun in the glove compartment. My jacket was off. My badge was in my jacket. He put a gun to my head and said get out of the car. I said, 'I'm an officer what's wrong?' Let me show you my badge.' He said the car was stolen. I said it was a state car.' The city cop forced him to sprawl on the trunk of the car. Edgecombe knew what could happen to black motorists when dealing with white cops. "I was shaking." Finally, the cop allowed him to show his badge. The next day, at the suggestion of Janet Reno, Edgecombe went to the city police station to file a complaint. His boss at the state attorney's office, Ray Havens, chewed him for doing that without notifying him. Edgecombe quit on the spot. Reno asked him to reconsider. He refused. He went on to have a lengthy career as a private investigator, including some examinations of professional football players.

Frank, Marshall: Homicide commander. A year after the trial, he was shuffled off to be a captain in the Civil Process Bureau by Division Chief Dale Bowlin, the Central District commander at the time of McDuffie. "My knowledge and skills in homicide investigation were put to waste." The homicide pro of 1,000 investigations ended his career by spending one year in Civil Process, two years in Staff Inspections, four years as a district commander and two years in charge of the transit police. After retiring from the PSD, he worked several years for a security firm. He's written seven fiction and five nonfiction books. His 1999 novel, "Beyond the Call," is an interesting fictionalized account of a McDuffie-like case.

Gerant, John "Jerry": The witness who said Watts, not Marrero, struck the deadly blows. After testifying against county officers, Gerant was ostracized by fellow City of Miami police officers. He said he was "dumped in Sector 10," Liberty City, where police patrolled in two-man cars. No one wanted to ride with him. Colleagues told him he had to quit. He did. Eventually, he got sucked up in the drug culture that permeated Miami at the time. He became a pilot for drug smugglers. When he was arrested in 1987, he quickly agreed to cooperate, saying he was a minor player who could talk about the kingpins. He was granted immunity and testified against three drug dealers in 1988. In 1991, the feds withdrew the immunity deal, saying Gerant had lied to them: Instead of being a low-level pilot, prosecutors charged, he was really a high-level figure who paid the gang members who transported and stored the cocaine. In 1992, Gerant was convicted of operating a continuing criminal enterprise while living a "lavish lifestyle" in Boca Raton, Florida. He was released from federal prison in 2011.

Gerstein, Richard: Dade County state attorney before Reno. Perhaps most famous nationally for his work on Watergate. His prosecutors convicted Bernard L. Barker, one of the Watergate burglars, of fraudulently notarizing check. Became a criminal defense lawyer after resigning in 1977. He headed an American Bar Association task force on crime in 1982. He represented comedian Paul Reubens — television's "Pee-wee Herman" — against public indecency charges in Sarasota, Florida. He died in 1992 at age 68.

Gilder, Bob: Black activist who attended many sessions in the Tampa trial and the former president of the Tampa NAACP. He led black voter registration drives in the 1960s and led the effort to desegregate Tampa General Hospital. A eulogist at his funeral said Gilder could "in five sentences either stir up a crowd or calm down a stirred-up crowd." He died in 2003 at age 72.

Hanlon, William: The immunized witness dubbed "Mad Dog" by colleagues. He got a real-estate license in October 1980 and became an agent in Hollywood, Florida. For at least four years, he was paid $28,000 a year by county police but did no work. (A county attorney said he couldn't be fired after being immunized.) In his mid-40s, he went to law school at Nova Southeastern University, where he did 300 hours of pro bono work. He passed the written bar exam. He was never admitted to the bar, despite many appeals. In 2006, the Florida Supreme Court ruled that his conduct on December 17, 1979, was too egregious to forget. The justices concluded "that under the totality of the circumstances, the grievous nature of the misconduct mandates that (Hanlon) not be admitted to the Bar now or at any time in the future."

Harms, Ken: City of Miami police chief. He was fired in 1984 in a 2:47 a.m. phone call by a city manager he was feuding with. Harms has spent many years as a law enforcement consultant and expert witness.

Jones, Johnny: Dade school superintendent. For the "Gold Plumbing Caper," Jones was sentenced to three years. He appealed. In October 1980, a second trial was held, concerning charges he had accepted kickbacks from a book publisher and tried to cover it up. In the second trial, he was convicted of two misdemeanors. For each, he was sentenced to a year in prison, to be served consecutively. Jones appealed those convictions too. Out on bail, Jones took a job directing a self-help center for the Congress of Racial Equality. CORE was not happy with his results and asked him to step down. In 1985, the

3rd District Court of Appeal reversed his conviction in the plumbing case because the judge failed to hold a hearing to ask prosecutors why they excluded black potential jurors. A new trial was ordered, but the state dropped the case because two major witnesses refused to testify again. A judge ordered him to serve two years in prison for his two misdemeanor convictions. He served about a month in jail, with a provision for a six-day work-release program in which he could leave from 9:30 a.m. to 11 p.m. to work in a restaurant he managed. Several leading politicians pleaded for clemency, and Judge Ellen Morphonios changed his sentence to probation. He died in 1990 at age 60.

Jones, Willie Thomas: The Florida state trooper who pleaded no contest to

lewd and lascivious or indecent assault upon a child. In June 1980, Richard Gerstein issued a report requested by a judge. He called the case a "miscarriage of justice" bungled by police investigators and prosecutors. A federal grand jury indicted Jones on two counts of violating the girl's constitutional rights. Jones fled. For more than four years, he was a fugitive. In 1985, he turned himself in and pleaded guilty. He was sentenced to one year in federal prison.

Kogan, Gerald: Defense attorney for Ubaldo Del Toro. Shortly after the Tampa trial, Governor Bob Graham appointed him a judge in the Dade Circuit Court. By July, he was presiding over criminal cases that sprang from the McDuffie riots and the Mariel refugees. He served on the Florida Supreme Court from 1987 through 1998, including a term as chief justice from 1996 to 1998. In recent years, he's been practicing as an arbitrator and mediator.

Laeser, Abe: A major prosecutor in the Dade State Attorney's Office in 1980. He remained there throughout his career. He retired in 2009 at age 62. He supervised every homicide case for a decade. The Herald said he was credited with sending more men to Death Row than any other Florida prosecutor. For many years, he was

Reno's chief assistant. That ended in 1990, when during a long trial, a female jury consultant for the defense said he unzipped his fly in front of her. He said he meant it as a joke to a male defense attorney and didn't realize the woman was close by. "A 15-second mistake," he called it. Reno demoted him, but he continued prosecuting all death penalty cases for years afterward. His last case was sending two Orlando men to Death Row for kidnapping a high school couple on South Beach and robbing and gang raping the girl before killing her. Her boyfriend lived to testify.

LaFleur, Nathaniel: The Miami sixth grade teacher who was the victim of a wrong-house raid in 1979 that caused much consternation in the black community. He filed a $3 million lawsuit against the county police and five of its officers. In 1981, a jury of five white members and one black member awarded him $20,000.

Marrero, Alex: Defendant. He and his wife, Lourdes, separated a day after the verdicts. He became a self-employed private investigator. "In bars, strangers walk up to him and pay his tab," the News reported a year later. "On the streets, people shake his hand. Alex Marrero says his notoriety has brought him more friends than ever." In 1989, he was arrested by federal agents and charged with conspiring with a DEA agent to distribute cocaine and to commit bribery, after offering to take a job for $300,000 to give protection to a drug dealer. He pleaded guilty to one count of conspiring to defraud the federal government and agreed to testify in hopes of getting a lighter sentence. In 1991 he became the main witness in a trial against his former DEA partner. The prosecutor in that Herald story described Marrero as a "criminal and co-conspirator."

McDuffie family: The county paid $1.1 million to settle the lawsuit. After attorney fees, the remaining money went to Eula Bell, McDuffie's mother; his son, Marc; and two daughters, Shederica and Dewana. Frederica, his ex-wife, worked for many years in the library of North Miami High School. In 1984, Eula Bell moved to Georgia, where she died. Shederica eventually married a county police officer, had two children and divorced. Dewana, with a criminal justice degree from Florida A&M University, applied to the Miami-Dade Police Department but wasn't accepted. In 2019, she was working for a Miami high school.

McWilliams, Terry: Attorney for Ira Diggs. He died in 1995 at age 52.

Meier, Mark: Immunized witness. At the time of the trial, he was working for an air freight company. He was fired after the verdicts and became a private security officer.

Miller, Gene: The Miami Herald reporter at the trial. His later career was mostly as an editor of major projects. He took a buyout in 2001 for $287,365.28 (he listed the amount in his self-written obituary), then continued working as a "vendor." He died in 2005 at age 76.

Nesbitt, Lenore: The judge. She was appointed a federal judge by President Ronald Reagan in 1983, the first female judge in the Southern District of Florida. She died in 2001 at age 69.

O'Donnell, Ed: Attorney for Alex Marrero. He went on to have a long career as a criminal defense attorney. In some of his most well-known cases, he represented a Miami judge charged with bribery, a county homicide detective charged with murdering his wife and a Hollywood actor accused of trafficking in cocaine.

Petersen, Tom: Chief administrative assistant for Reno. He took a leave of absence from 1984 to 1989 to run an experiment in public housing projects trying to lower crime rates. He was appointed to the circuit court in 1989 and assigned to the juvenile division. He took senior status in 2000 and taught sociology for several years at the University of Miami. He retired completely in 2016.

Reno, Janet: After the riots, she kept meeting with black groups to reassure them she was concerned about their needs, and she appeared before several government panels to vigorously oppose accusations her office was racist. She wasn't afraid to push back. When she appeared on a radio show of her longtime critic, Marvin Dunn, he asked her: "What do you think the problem is?" She shot back, "Well, Marvin, it's people like you." In 1993, Bill Clinton appointed her attorney general. In Washington, she described herself as a "awkward old maid." The Washington press corps viewed her as a loner with dowdy clothes. Unknown to the public, she was a regular guest at the small dinner parties held by Washington Post publisher Katharine Graham, which included the top movers and shakers in the city. She ordered an assault on a religious compound in Waco that left 80 dead. "The buck stops with me," she famously told Congress. In 2000, she ordered agents in Miami to seize 5-year-old Elian Gonzalez and return him to his father in Cuba. Many Florida Democratic leaders say that action caused Al Gore to lose Florida in the 2000 presidential election. After returning to Miami, she ran for governor in 2002, losing in the Democratic primary. In her later years, she suffered from Parkinson's disease but continued to live in the home that her mother built. She died in 2016 at age 78.

Shinhoster, Yvonne: Covered the trial for the Tampa Tribune. Later Yvonne Shinhoster Lamb, a reporter and editor at the Washington Post, retiring in 2008. She's the author of "My Soul Rhythms: Prayer Stories to Ignite Your Spirit." She taught journalism at Howard University and Trinity Washington University. She later received a master of divinity degree from the Wesley Theological Seminary and moved to Dublin, Georgia.

Slacum, Marcia: St. Petersburg Times reporter for the trial. Later Marcia Slacum Greene. She went on to become a Washington Post reporter and editor, rising to be city editor. She died in 2010 at age 57.

Sonnett, Neal: Attorney for William Hanlon. He continues to practice criminal defense, now specializing in white-collar and corporate crime.

Tetreault, Joseph: Juror who served 20 years as a chief petty officer and another 20 years as a maintenance man at the VA Hospital in Tampa. For his last 11 years, he lived in St. Augustine, where he enjoyed bowling and golfing. He died in 2018 at age 86.

Veverka, Charles Jr: Lead witness at the trial. Acquitted of violating McDuffie's civil rights in December 1980. He became an officer with North Bay Village in Dade County. He tipped prosecutor Yoss to some cops who were secretly doing a drug business on the side. In 1983, he was charged with kicking a teen suspect in the groin. The charge was dropped. He resigned from the force.

Watts, Michael: Defendant. Lead subject of a major Herald story on police brutality in 1979. He attempted suicide a week after the riots. Watts found a job building custom bodies for vans, then worked for the North Lauderdale Police Department between 1985 and 1988.

Williams, Verne: The Miami News reporter who covered the trial. Williams' byline kept appearing in the News into 1988, the year that the Herald closed the afternoon newspaper as part of a clause in the newspapers' joint operating agreement. He died in 2004 at age 84.

Wright, Ronald: Deputy chief medical examiner for Dade County. Became chief medical examiner for Broward County (Fort Lauderdale) in 1980. In the early 1990s, a law firm sued him for allegedly destroying evidence, a staff member brought a sexual harassment lawsuit against him and a newspaper reported he was earning large sums as an expert witness. In 1994, Governor Lawton Chiles, who controlled the Broward appointment, decided to select someone else. Wright continued as a professor at the University of Miami medical school through 2001. In ensuing years, he has spent much of his time as an expert witness, working out of Tennessee and Broward County.

Yoss, George: Prosecutor. He became Reno's chief assistant in 1980 after Adorno left and served in that capacity for seven years. He recalled that the months after Tampa were a nightmare as Reno's office struggled to prosecute the worst of the rioters, mostly the murder cases. "We lost prosecutors who couldn't stand the pressure.... Every case was political. Every case was a problem.... We had prosecutors being threatened by members of the community, friends of the defendants." Reno's office dropped most of the minor charges. "People got arrested just for being out on the street, just being next to somebody who stole a TV. There were too many cases to deal with." About the era of McDuffie, he says: "In terms of Miami as a community, where we are now, as cosmopolitan as we are, as international as we are, it was a hiccup. Living through the hiccup was a nightmare." Yoss eventually went into private practice to help form Adorno & Yoss, which grew to 17 offices before collapsing when Adorno's license to practice law was suspended. Yoss continues to practice law.

Addendum

The Johnny Jones Trials

After the riots, Reno said the violence was sparked by "two inconsistent verdicts" five weeks apart, the other one being the trial of Johnny Jones, superintendent of Dade County schools who stood trial accused of what the press called "the Gold Plumbing Caper," while the Tampa trial plodded on.

In the McDuffie trial, the prosecutors lost a case against white police officers with an all-white jury. In the Jones trial, her prosecutors won a case against a prominent black leader with an all-white jury.

In fact, there were two Johnny Jones trials in 1980. Both were uncommonly interesting: for their historical importance to riot-ravaged Miami, for showing how Reno's prosecutors operated in racially charged cases—and for demonstrating how a defense attorney could make spectacular difference.

Ed Carhart was supposed to be Jones' attorney in both trials. The Tampa trial forced him to bow out of the first, with disastrous results for Jones. For the second trial, Carhart was there, facing what many thought was an insurmountable challenge: Jones was caught on tape, talking about getting kickback payments from a major school vendor and discussing how to hide such payments from Reno's prosecutors, who were already investigating him.

Jones was the highest-ranking black government official in Dade. He was highly compensated, and he enjoyed a sterling reputation until it was revealed he used school funds to buy expensive plumbing fixtures that a contractor said were intended for a vacation home Jones was building in Naples, Florida. Many white residents felt they betrayed their trust. Many black residents thought he had been framed. A hundred people went to the Herald building to protest the newspaper's coverage. "The media degraded him with just circumstantial evidence," said one protestor. "Nothing is logical, and nothing proven."

Carhart knew it was going to be a tough case. "I used to run cases by the patrons of Sally Russell's to see what the community reaction was. It was a restaurant bar across the street from the Dade County courthouse. It had court reporters; defense attorneys; not many prosecutors; some police, not many; secretaries and whatnot, and I'd run cases by there in the cocktail hour and see what kind of reaction I got. Johnny Jones got a big reaction. I knew [he] was in big trouble before he walked in the courtroom. The community was very hostile to him, sort of this syndrome [that] so much hope and faith had been put into him, and he turned out to disappoint them."

Carhart agreed to represent Jones, but Judge Thomas L. Scott refused to delay the Jones trial until Carhart was finished in Tampa. Scott had the same mindset as Judge Nesbitt: Let's get these racially divisive cases behind us.

Bill Frates ended up leading a team of five defense lawyers. He had a national reputation because he'd represented John Ehrlichman, Nixon's onetime aide, on a criminal charge, but most of his career was in civil cases. "Frates was not an experienced criminal defense lawyer," Carhart said. "He just wasn't."

In my interviews, Carhart refused to analyze the first trial, either Jones' guilt or innocence, or Frates' performance. He said he was too busy in Tampa to follow that trial closely. "I never actually looked at all the evidence in the case." After he died, his daughter allowed me to look through his storage boxes. There were large scrapbooks containing press clippings from the first trial. Perhaps he'd never taken the time to read them.

Unlike Nesbitt, Judge Scott refused to move the trial out of Miami. In April, just before the Gold Plumbing trial was to begin, Reno indicted Jones on three new charges, alleging he had accepted bribes from a Baltimore man who sold a remedial reading program to Dade

Schools. The man taped his conversations with Jones. On one of them, the school leader suggested the man raise his price from $25 a student to $70 a student so he could afford the bribe. The charges and their details were published in the newspapers and broadcast on television just before jury selection began. The defense howled about the timing.

Picking the jury took a mere two days. The state used five of its six challenges to exclude black jurors. For the sixth, they knocked off a Hispanic woman. The final panel consisted of four white women and two white men. While one Reno team in Tampa worked to get a single black person on the jury, the Reno team in Miami was hell-bent on keeping black jurors off.

Frates objected vigorously. "We're kidding ourselves if we say Dr. Jones will get a fair trial with an all-white jury."

The first witness, Aldo Delgado from Bond Plumbing Supply, said Jones and Solomon Barnes, principal of MacArthur South High, came to examine gold-plated fixtures. Delgado said Jones introduced himself as the superintendent of schools.

Frates. who had said in his opening statement that he'd prove Jones never went to the store, tried to shake Delgado's identification by getting Delgado to guess that the man in the store was about 6 foot or 6-1, about 225 pounds with "extremely gray hair." Jones was 5-10. Frates asked Jones to stand up, with his lawyer noting that he was "a long way from 225 pounds."

A school purchasing officer testified that Jones telephoned him "alerting me to the fact that a requisition was coming forward from MacArthur South" and he wanted it handled promptly. Barnes brought the order to the department.

Another Bond employee, Bonnie Blackstock, testified that a person who identified himself as Barnes placed the order by phone in mid-January. She asked him if he knew some items were 24-karat gold. He said yes. She testified that she handled the school system's plumbing orders for years, always dealing with plumbers, not school principals. This was the first time that the school had ordered a fixture in something other than white.

Thinking that the voice on the phone wasn't really a school official, Blackstock called the schools' purchasing department, which told her not to deliver the items.

When Barnes appeared to pick up the order, the store told him to call school purchasing director Leo Kerr. Kerr testified: "I asked him if he was aware some of [the fixtures] were gold-plated. I told him that we could not allow the purchase order."

Defense attorneys let much of this testimony slide, focusing only on those witnesses who said no plumbing class was planned at MacArthur South. The high school's curriculum director told the jury he didn't know about a planned plumbing class, but under cross-examination he acknowledged that Barnes often did things without telling him.

A black plumbing teacher at a local high school then took the stand to say he'd never used gold-plated fixtures to teach students.

The state's star witness was contractor Craig Meffert, who was building Jones $120,000 vacation home in Naples. He testified that after the original plans were drawn up, Jones gave him new drawings, made by a high school teacher, showing changes to the house's plan to include a bidet and other upscale bathroom fixtures, along with a Bond store brochure showing photos of the new items. At one point, Jones asked him to stay late in his office because Barnes was driving over with the fixtures. Barnes never showed up.

After stories broke about Jones seeking gold plumbing, Meffert testified, a "very nervous" Mattye Jones, the superintendent's wife, went to Naples and insisted on taking back the Bond pamphlet and the revised plans for the plumbing. She said her husband wanted to go back to the original plumbing.

Under cross-examination, Frates got Meffert to admit he lied at first to two Herald journalists, Jim McGee and Jim Savage, because he wanted to protect his client. But "after I saw I couldn't convince them Dr. Jones hadn't done anything wrong, then I decided to tell them the truth."

The defense case relied on alibi witnesses who stated that Jones could not have visited the Bond store on either date Delgado said he had. In one instance, friends testified, Jones was out fishing with them. For the second, a black activist said he was at Jones' home at the time Jones was supposedly at the store. Barnes's brother testified that he, not Jones, went with Barnes to the Bond store. Nine character witnesses, including the president of the University of Miami and the black owner of a prominent funeral home, testified to Jones' honesty.

Jones did not take the stand in his own defense.

In closing, prosecutor George dePoszgay said, "There is no way anyone could find any of those fixtures could have been intended for a plumbing class."

Frates's closing: "For some reason, an overzealous prosecutor is attempting to take Solomon Barnes, a very decent, productive and wonderful person, and Johnny Jones, who has made contributions to this town, to this country and to this state, and is trying to railroad them.... The state hasn't proved one iota of evidence, unless you believe all these [alibi witnesses] were lying." Frates noted that no plumbing was ever purchased.

The jury deliberated two hours and 31 minutes: guilty.

Many black leaders put the blame on the "all-white jury," but several criminal defense trials told reporters the key was Jones not taking the stand. Sonnett, who represented Hanlon in the McDuffie case, said most jurors don't usually hold it against ordinary people who don't testify in their own defense, but they expect public officials or professionals to speak, and if they don't, jurors are suspicious.

Charles Whited, a Herald columnist: "He sat in that courtroom day after day, his life on the line, like a stone. He let hired white lawyers talk for him, lifting not one word of self-defense. He sat there and let it happen. If that was me in that courtroom, and a witness like Craig Meffert, contractor, gave the critical testimony... and he was lying, I'd have fought like hell." He noted that Jones was known generally as "one of the most eloquent of men."

Judge Scott sentenced Jones to three years in prison. He remained out on bail for most of the time while his lawyers appealed. Five years after the trial, the state's Third District Court of Appeal ordered a new trial, concluding that the judge should have held a hearing to question prosecutors to explain why they had excluded five black potential jurors. Reno's office chose not to retry the case.

• • • •

JUDGE SCOTT WANTED the second Jones case, about the alleged kickbacks, tried soon after the first, on the same theory that the community was better off getting such racially charged cases over with as soon as possible.

Carhart objected. He needed a rest. "I was young and foolish, inexhaustible energy and whatnot. I was wrong. When the Tampa trial was over, I just had a meltdown. I moved out of my home, went to an apartment, just holed up for a couple of weeks. It was brutal."

When Scott pressured him for a quick trial, Carhart went to Ed Cowart, chief judge of the criminal courts. "I said, 'We've already had one riot. Scott's pushing me into trial. I am not going to enter the case until he agrees to set a reasonable trial date. Jones is out on bond and there is no need to railroad this case.' Ed Cowart listened to me very sympathetically. Next thing I knew, Scott issued a continuance."

Jones faced a charge of unlawful compensation for taking $70,000 in kickbacks from a publisher who had received $1.3 million from Dade schools for an at-home study program. Because he'd been caught on tape plotting with the publisher on how to hide the payments and asking the man to lie to investigators, he was also charged with witness tampering and suborning perjury.

Though the taped statements had been widely publicized in Miami, Carhart insisted the trial not be moved. "We feel we have a right to be tried in the community where the charge is laid, and that we shouldn't be run out of the community by a barrage of publicity or the state's conduct," he told Arnold Markowitz, a veteran court reporter who covered the trial for the Herald. Neither Carhart nor Markowitz mentioned that he'd taken the opposite position in the McDuffie case.

In many criminal trials, Carhart often felt like a lone gunslinger coming into town to defend an unpopular client. That was especially true in this Jones trial: "When I walked into the courtroom to defend him... I said to my trial partner, Jamie McGuirk, 'I have never felt so much hatred as I feel in this courtroom in all my life. Never. It was palpable.'... You know, he was the great black hope as school superintendent. And many white people who vigorously supported him over years were really crushed when Johnny ran off the tracks."

While Jones' first trial had taken less than two days to pick a jury, this selection process stretched over 10 days. Black observers watched carefully. "All day long, black people trickle in and out of the courtroom," wrote Tom Dubocq, a veteran reporter who covered education for the News. "Some are dressed in their Sunday best with their sleepy children in tow. Others come in their work clothes. A few stay the entire day, but most remain for just a few minutes."

Patricia Miles, a onetime PTA president of an elementary school, kept up a vigil at the back of the courtroom during jury selection. She watched as the prosecution kept knocking black residents off the jury. "It's depressing.... The more time I spend in there, the more hostile

I become." Outside the courthouse, a man protested daily that black people were being excluded from the jury.

Of the first 12 black residents in the jury panel, the prosecution excluded 11, including some who said they thought Reno was a racist but whom the judge wouldn't excuse for cause, forcing prosecutors to use peremptory challenges to remove them. The judge excused one black woman with severe arthritis. When the state was almost out of challenges, prosecutor Bill Richey asked Judge Scott to transfer the trial elsewhere: "The very process of attempting to select a jury in this case is further dividing our community."

The judge gave each side one more challenge. The lawyers next interviewed a black woman who said the Jones prosecution was racially motivated and the state attorney's office was prejudiced against blacks. Still, she said she felt she could set aside those ideas, and the judge refused to throw her off for cause. Prosecutor Bill Richey then rejected her.

That meant the prosecution had to accept the next prospect, a black, part-time cleaning woman who had no children. "Color wouldn't make any difference," she told the lawyers. Also on the jury was a white man with unusual connections to the case: Allan Margolis, president of WMBM, the black-oriented AM radio station. Margolis wrote a letter of recommendation for Jones when he was up for the superintendent job, and the station broadcast editorials criticizing the charges against Jones. Still, Margolis stated he could be objective. Neither side chose to remove him.

In a 52-minute opening statement, prosecutor George dePozsgay described Jones' relationship with David Rouen, a Maryland publisher of the At-Home Learning Program, aimed primarily at students doing poorly in arithmetic and reading. "Once you hear this evidence, you will find that you're looking at a very greedy man.... Johnny Jones would take his own mother down with him. I'm very sorry to tell you that, but that's the kind of man he is. That's how desperate he was to cover his crime."

Carhart deferred his opening statement until the defense's turn to present its case.

The first state witness was Jones' mother, Lucy, of Greenville, N.C. She testified that she opened a joint bank account for her son into which she deposited nearly $30,000 in bond interest coupons that Jones mailed to her.

Next up was Mattye Jones, his wife, who was asked about payments to a joint checking account, especially a $30,200 deposit that included $6,000 in cash, a $6,000 check from the School Employees' Credit Union and cashier's checks for $10,000 and $8,000 bought the same day from two savings and loan companies.

Crying at times, Mattye Jones said the money came from a late great-uncle in Mississippi who hid the money in his living room fireplace. "You'd have to be black to understand," she said. "Anytime you're dealing with cash, you're subject to... someone might think you stole it."

She said she'd accepted delivery at her home of seven boxes from a Maryland wholesaler. The cartons contained $7,941 worth of stereo and television equipment that were placed in Jones' den. She said she never asked her husband what was in the boxes or where they came from.

On cross-examination, Carhart elicited that she had a master's degree and considered herself bright enough to create a better lie, if a lie were needed, than the chimney money story. "Wouldn't you agree with me that a story of finding money in a fireplace sounds a little far-fetched?" Carhart asked.

"Yes, if you don't understand certain cultures.... I wouldn't have told my husband if I had known it would have gone to these extremes of ridicule for myself and my family."

Rouen, the publisher, testified that in the summer of 1978 Jones called and asked him, "Can you put anything together for me down here?"

Rouen asked: "When do you need it?"

Jones: "As soon as possible."

In September or October, Rouen brought $3,000 or $4,000 in $100 bills and gave them to Jones in a white envelope. That school year, Dade school system paid him $300,000 for his program.

Rouen kept paying Jones, including more than $30,000 in interest coupons from public utility bonds he owned. On the witness stand, he identified the coupons, which had been deposited by Jones' mother. There were more cash payments: $5,000 left for Jones at the front desk of a Washington hotel and $4,000 or $5,000 left at another hotel front desk during a trip to Miami. He testified that he purchased the stereo and TV equipment delivered to Jones' house and jewelry for Jones' wife.

After the gold plumbing deal was uncovered, a Reno investigator examined all of Jones' finances and found Rouen, who agreed to cooperate to avoid prosecution.

In taped phone conversations played to the jury, Jones warned Rouen that the investigator and dePozsgay were "big and grotesque." He asked Rouen not to mention him to the investigators or say anything about the bond coupons. "You know that'd just destroy me." He advised Rouen: "Just don't remember.... There's nothing wrong with amnesia."

On cross-examination, Carhart treated Rouen gently.

"Carhart, as well regarded for his cross-examination skills as for his jury speeches, had deftly turned Rouen into a defense witness," Markowitz wrote after the trial. "Instead of stripping the witness bare, Carhart let him sell his At-Home Learning Program to the jury. He let them tell how he had sold it, entirely on its merits, in the schools of Austin, Memphis, Philadelphia, New Orleans, Chicago and West Palm Beach. He got him to say that he never paid off anyone in those school systems and, most important to the defense, that Jones himself never insisted on being paid back part of the $1.3 million he [Roeun] was paid by the school board."

Carhart got Rouen to say he didn't consider his gifts to Jones to be kickbacks, but informal loans. Jones never threatened to kill the At-Home project if he didn't make payments. He said he cooperated with investigators out of fear of facing bribery charges. He had been granted immunity.

Carhart's defense consisted of a lone witness: Jones himself. After sitting "like a stone" at his first trial, Jones talked to the jurors, admitting that he had accepted money from Rouen and tried to get Rouen to lie about the deals. He said he viewed the payments as favors from a friend, and he helped Rouen's business by touting his program during speeches at conventions. He also offered Rouen advice on how to improve the programs. Near the end, they discussed making the payments look like loans, because he was afraid that the money might look bad if discovered.

Carhart: "Did Dr. Rouen ever tell you when he wanted you to pay the money back?"

Jones: "No, sir."

"Did you ever ask him?"

"No, sir."

"Did you ever ask for that money for a bribe, for keeping his program in the school system?"

"No...."

"Did you tie the money and your request to your position as superintendent?"

"No, sir."

"Did you think there was anything wrong with that?"

"I thought about a conflict of interest."

"Did you take the money anyway?"

"Yes."
"Did you pay him back?"
"No sir."
"Did he ever ask for it back?"
"No."

Jones denied receiving two cash payments totaling $10,000 that Rouen said he left for Jones in envelopes at hotel front desks. He stood by the story of the money found in the Mississippi chimney, and he said Rouen had given him a catalog from a Maryland store and told him to feel free to order from it at Rouen's expense.

He admitted urging Rouen to lie to investigators. Those conversations happened when a grand jury was deciding whether to indict Jones for the gold-plated plumbing. "I was under extreme pressure."

About the tapes: "I'm embarrassed by them. I'm empty inside. I'm extra embarrassed."

The prosecutors closed by using Jones' own words. They made accusing statements, then punched a button on a tape recorder and the jurors heard Jones confirm what the prosecutors alleged.

That put Carhart in an extraordinarily tough position. In his closing, he focused on the specifics of the main charge, accepting unlawful compensation, which carried a maximum of five years in prison.

"Repeatedly," Markowitz wrote, "he quoted from the jury instruction most critical to the charge of unauthorized compensation: 'It is not the crime of unlawful compensation to request, solicit, accept or agree to accept something of value by a public servant if it is not done corruptly and with the intent or purpose thereby, to influence the public servant in some way in the performance... of his public office or employment.'"

Rouen and Jones agreed, Carhart told the jury: Jones never threatened to stop the At Home program. Criminal activity "never really came to pass," under the definition of the law, he stated. Repeatedly, Carhart claimed that Jones was a victim of entrapment. He decried the state for humiliating the Jones family, forcing his mother and wife to testify in front of him.

Carhart pointed out that Jones didn't ask for money until two years after the program started. He didn't ask for a percentage of what the school board was paying. "No, he comes with his hat in his and hand and asks for a favor.... I submit there is no bribery in that situation. You don't have to accept Dr. Jones' word for that. Dr. Rouen said so.... Did he have evil in his mind? He certainly did, and I don't deny that. Did evil exist? No. It was entirely the creation of the State Attorney's office."

The jury deliberated three hours and 29 minutes. Not guilty of the most serious charge, unlawful compensation, which was a felony. Guilty of two misdemeanors: witness tampering and soliciting perjury.

Margolis, the radio man, was jury foreman. The easiest count was soliciting perjury, he told reporters. Jones said it on the tapes and admitted it in his testimony. But on the kickback charge, the jurors agreed with Carhart's argument: There was a lack of evidence to prove intent. The charge was "not proven beyond a reasonable doubt."

Judge Scott sentenced Jones to two one-year terms, the maximum allowable, to be served consecutively.

Laeser, the veteran prosecutor, said Jones' second trial, coming after McDuffie and the riots, "should have raised everyone's hackles. No black juror had missed the May riots. Payback is a bitch, but that second trial needed to have a change of venue. After the Tampa trial in McDuffie, Reno would not consider that option."

Clearly, Reno's team was under pressure to have a black juror after the all-white jury conviction of Jones in the first trial. She knew a report was coming from a governor's panel, which had been holding hearings. The panel called prosecutors excluding black jurors solely on the basis of race "inexcusable.... The verdict in the Johnny Jones case would have been far more acceptable to this community if a black had been seated on the jury." The report noted the "improper abuse of the State Attorney's right of peremptory challenge. Whether intentional or not, such an act is racist."

In Jones' second trial, Laeser believes, "no one took a dive, but... there was much more wishin' and hopin' than devious trial strategy. And when Jones told some story in a pleasant and relaxed manner, he certainly got the benefit of a reasonable doubt. Why someone from WMBM is on the panel is beyond me, but my instinct is that he had an agenda from the minute he got the jury notice. Can the head of that station find a reason to be excused? After all, a jury has been described as 12 [or six] persons unable to get out of jury duty. He must have known the 'magic words' to get excused."

To Laeser, it was obvious that jurors in both the first and second Jones' trials expected the eloquent superintendent to testify: "Every public figure who is not inherently offensive has a huge advantage in front of a trial jury. Unless they are incredibly guilty, they MUST testify. The jury hears the instruction about not taking a failure to testify into account — then makes their own decision."

Laeser concluded: "As fine a lawyer as Carhart was, this analysis about testifying had to be self-evident and easy to sell to the client who made the opposite choice in his conviction. Evidence only persuades the mind, and seldom impacts the heart."

Indeed, in the February 2020 trial of Harvey Weinstein, the movie producer once known for his eloquence and ease dealing with the media, "sat like a stone" as women accused him of rape. His lawyers said the sex was consensual. Weinstein said nothing. He was convicted of two charges.

Acknowledgements

First and foremost, I'd like to thank Patrick Malone, former colleague at the Miami Herald who went on to become an accomplished lawyer and author of many books. Without his encouragement, this book probably would never have been finished. Patrick read a draft that was almost twice the length of the final manuscript. It was wordy and meandered and had a much different focus. He urged me to keep trying. Thanks to Patrick's advice, the book took on a clearer, structured and (I hope) more readable shape. He continued to give sound advice through two more drafts, including directing me to legal resources, such as the theory of "Sponsorship Strategy," by Robert H. Klonoff and Paul L. Colby." He also wrote a thoughtful Foreword and Afterword. And he suggested that I seek out James Lees for expert commentary from a veteran criminal defense attorney.

Jim was the perfect person for commentary: A onetime police officer and a veteran prosecutor of 44 murder cases, he understood the nuances of a big-time trial of police officers from all sides. And as a conductor of 1,400 focus groups he has developed a great sense of what jurors think in these courtroom dramas. His perceptive, often pointed comments gave an added depth to the narrative that it wouldn't otherwise have had.

I'd also like to thank Greg Aunapu/New Media Gurus. Greg not only designed a great cover and formatted the manuscript into e-book form, but also served as an advisor, warning me about the length of an early draft and coming up with the title.

Gigi Lehman was invaluable editor. I happened to be married to one of the world's great editors, Kathy Martin, but we've always kept our professional lives separate, and neither of us wanted dinner time spent sniping about the proper use of, say, a colon. Both of us simultaneously thought of Gigi, our onetime colleague at the Herald, as the perfect editor, and indeed she was. She not only copy-edited the manuscript superbly but also suggested deletions and gave advice on how the later part of the book could be restructured.

Having said all that, I should add that any errors in this book are entirely my own.

Sources

The core of this book is based on interviews and news accounts of the trial.

Four of the five defense attorneys talked to me: Ed Carhart, Ed O'Donnell, Gerald Kogan and Philip Carlton. The fifth, Terry McWilliams, died in 1995.

Prosecutor George Yoss sat for two interviews, and I am especially grateful for his time. It was easy for the winning defense attorneys to boast about all the things that led to their victories. I told Yoss that, as with the case of Super Bowl losers, the prosecutors of the McDuffie trial had a lot of second-guessing to deal with. He faced most of the barrage of criticisms straight on and explained the prosecution's thinking of how the case was handled and how the trial unfolded. His perspective was invaluable, especially in acknowledging how problematic the immunized witnesses were. His views added a depth to the narrative that it wouldn't otherwise had.

Hank Adorno, the lead prosecutor, did not respond to many requests for interviews. As far as I know, he has not talked to any journalists since 2011, when the Florida Supreme Court suspended his ability to practice law for three years. Still, earlier interviews of Adorno's views of the trial are available, including a substantial one he did for CBS Reports.

Marshall Frank, the homicide commander, was crucial in revealing the problems with the investigation and the state's case, particularly with the lead witness. We did phone interviews and email exchanges, and his memoir "From Violins to Violence" was insightful not only about the McDuffie case but the tensions and politics of being a PSD cop in tumultuous Miami.

I also interviewed two jurors, Joseph Tetreault and Kenneth Stover. Another juror, the foreman, David Fisher, gave interviews shortly after the verdict. A fourth, David Draper, wrote a lengthy letter to Gov. Bob Graham giving details about his perspective.

Abe Laeser and Tom Petersen, in the state attorney's office at the time, were extremely helpful into giving me an understanding of how Reno and her staff worked.

I also talked to two key witnesses: John "Gerry" Gerant and Richard Gotowala, the city of Miami officers who were at the scene.

Other important interviews were author-activist Marvin Dunn, co-author of "The Miami Riot of 1980"; Joe Oglesby, Herald reporter and columnist; Howard Kleinberg, editor of the Miami News; County Manager Merrett Stierheim; Miami Mayor Maurice Ferre and Miami Police Chief Ken Harms.

Much of the pretrial information comes from the archives of the Miami Herald, the Miami News and Miami's Channel 4, WTVJ. The news clips are available online through the Lynn and Louis Wolfson II Florida Moving Image Archives.

For the trial, I studied the articles of the Herald, News, the Tampa Tribune, St. Petersburg Times, Orlando Sentinel Star and Associated Press as well as WTVJ news clips. I also interviewed Yvonne Shinhoster Lamb, then of the Tampa Tribune, the only trial reporter still living at the time of my research.

Many primary documents no longer exist. Harvey Ruvin, the Miami-Dade County Clerk of Courts, said the court file was routinely destroyed in the 1990s. The Miami-Dade State Attorney's office said it does not retain such old records. None of the attorneys I interviewed had kept documents from the trial. I spent dozens of hours without success trying to locate a trial transcript, including trying to locate the records of the long-dead court reporter in Tampa.

Several important players in the McDuffie drama did not talk to me, including the five defendants. Alex Marrero and Ira Diggs did not respond to requests for interviews. I couldn't locate Michael Watts. Ubaldo Del Toro died in 2006. At one point, Evans agreed to talk to me. But, as I was finishing the final draft, he wrote in an email: "After talking with my wife, I have decided to just go ahead and live my remaining years without any more controversy either new or old."

Of the three state's immunized witnesses, Veverka said he was "not interested" in giving an interview. Hanlon did not respond to emails. I couldn't locate Mark Meier.

Janet Reno was alive when I started my research, but two former top assistants (Yoss and Petersen) said that, because of Parkinson's disease, she was no longer able to give interviews.

John McMullan, then executive editor of the Herald, didn't want to talk about the McDuffie case when I reached him by phone. Instead he gave me an assignment: Find out how McClatchy screwed up the Miami Herald. Also refusing to participate: Mike Baxter, then the Herald's city editor.

I also didn't interview Edna Buchanan, the Herald's famed crime reporter and my colleague for decades. In 2016, she and I got into a political spat on Facebook after she called Trump "a breath of fresh air." I reposted her comment along with a cartoon of sheep in a pasture looking up at a billboard where a wolf announced: "I will eat you." The cartoon caption had one sheep telling another: "He tells it like it is." Many former Herald colleagues responded to that post, many shocked at Edna's political stance. She unfriended me on Facebook. Still, her memoir "The Corpse Has a Familiar Face" and interviews she has given (especially one with pultizer.org) were helpful for my research.

Sources frequently cited in these chapter notes:

CBS Reports' hour-long report "Miami: The Trial That Sparked the Riots," appeared on August 27, 1980.

"Eyes on the Prize," a 14-part PBS series released in 1985 and 1988. Washington University has an archive of transcripts.

"From Violins to Violence," by Marshall Frank, originally published in 2007, by Fortis Books.

Governor's Dade County Citizens Committee, report released in October 1980.

"The Miami Riot of 1980: Crossing the Bounds," by Bruce Porter and Marvin Dunn. Lexington Books, Lexington, Massachusetts. 1984.

• • • •

NOTE: ALL DATES IN the source material below are in 1980 unless otherwise noted.

Chapter Notes

FOREWORD NOTES

Patrick Malone is an attorney in private practice in Washington, D.C., where he and his colleagues at Patrick Malone & Associates represent seriously injured people in lawsuits against hospitals, doctors, drug companies, government agencies and other defendants. He is the author of "The Fearless Cross-Examiner," "Win the Witness, Win the Case" (Trial Guides 2016), "Winning Medical Malpractice Cases with the Rules of the Road Technique Case" (Trial Guides 2012) and is co-author of the best-selling advocacy book "Rules of the Road: A Plaintiff Lawyer's Guide to Proving Liability Case" (Trial Guides 2nd ed. 2010). He also wrote a book for consumers: "The Life You Save: Nine Steps to Finding the Best Medical Care — and Avoiding the Worst (da Capo Lifelong 2009)." He is a member of the American Law Institute and the Inner Circle of Advocates and is a fellow of the International Academy of Trial Lawyers. He is on the board of trustees of the Pound Civil Justice Institute.

• • • •

CHAPTER 1

On the number of dead: 18 died in the riots. I used 19 here to include Arthur McDuffie.

Basic information on the incident and trial comes from Miami Herald, the Miami News, WTVJ and the Porter-Dunn riot book.

Interviews: Maurice Ferre, Merrett Stierheim, Marshall Frank.

The Dewey Knight quote is from Eyes on the Prize.

The Frank quote is in his memoir.

The list of "all-white jury" mentions in the Herald comes from a NewsBank search.

The quote from the juror comes from the Tampa Tribune on May 19.

"When Liberty Burns" is a Dudley Alexis film. See Libertyburns.com.

Edna Buchanan comment from "Winning Pulitzers" by Karen Rothmyer, Columbia University Press, 1991, 186-89, as republished on the website pulitzer.org.

The juror comment on "effrontery" comes from a letter that juror David Draper wrote to Governor Bob Graham.

The Williams analysis appeared in the Miami News on May 19.

The Slager account is based on several news sources, including the New York Times from December 7, 2017, "Michael Slager, Officer in Walter Scott Shooting, Gets 20-Year Sentence."

A more complete bio of James Lees: He is a 1974 graduate of West Virginia University and a 1977 graduate of Wake Forest University School of Law. Prior to and during law school, Lees worked as a police officer in Ocean City, Maryland, serving as both a uniformed and undercover officer. During the summer of 1976, Lees was on loan to the Drug Enforcement Agency and worked in the Fort Lauderdale area of Florida as an undercover narcotics officer.

After law school Lees spent over six years as an assistant district attorney in Pittsburgh, where his work included six death penalty cases. He also helped head the investigating grand jury of Allegheny County in investigations of organized crime and drug trafficking in Pittsburgh and the surrounding county.

Since 1984, he's been in private practice through his law firm, Hunt & Lees L.C., in Charleston, West Virginia, where he has litigated both civil cases and criminal cases throughout the country. In that capacity he has served on behalf of the State of West Virginia as lead counsel in the impeachment of then State Treasurer A. James

Manchin and as a special prosecutor tasked with prosecuting State Police chemist Fred Zain, who was charged with falsifying crime lab results to help obtain convictions in criminal cases.

Lees now resides in Venice, Florida, but actively practices law nationwide.

• • • •

CHAPTER 2

Veverka's police report as well as the portions of the Veverka, Gerant and Gotowala interviews appeared in the Miami News on January 30.

The Edna Buchanan scenario is from her memoir, "The Corpse Has a Familiar Face" and her interview at Pulitzer.org. Her profile in the New Yorker, "Covering the Cops," appeared in February 16, 1986.

The Marshall Frank material is from his memoir and interviews. A Herald story on January 30 confirmed his account that Acting Director Bobby Jones asked him to personally lead the investigation. An interview with Linda Saunders Finney gave her account of the story.

Interviews with Gerant and Gotowala confirmed their getting hauled in on the Christmas holidays for interviews. Gotowala's explained to me why he quit.

The Watts material comes from a five-part Herald series in July 1979, headlined "Police Brutality: The Violent Few."

Information on the backgrounds of Watts and Marrero comes from Herald and Miami News stories in December 1979.

• • • •

CHAPTER 3

VERDICT ON TRIAL 341

Interviews with Frank, Yoss and Dean form the bulk of the narrative, plus Frank's memoir. The Meier account comes from testimony he later gave at trial.

Additional information from the Herald and News.

• • • •

CHAPTER 4

The LaFleur saga and the Purdy problems are based on Herald and News stories. When Purdy was fired, some blamed Stierheim for bowing to Herald pressure, but Stierheim told me he had his own gripes with Purdy.

The Reno section is based on Herald profiles (including one of my own, from Tropic Magazine, April 5, 1998), plus interviews with Yoss, Tom Petersen and Abe Laeser. Perhaps the best Reno family portrait can be found in the obituary of her mother, Jane, written by Margaria Fichtner, in the Herald on December 22, 1992. It began: "Jane Wood Reno, honorary Indian princess, prize-winning journalist, gator-wrestler, peacock-raiser, certified genius, carpenter, skunk-trapper and mother of Dade State Attorney Janet Reno, died early Monday at the sprawling South Dade home she had built almost single-handedly decades ago."

• • • •

CHAPTER 5

Interviews: Yoss, Laeser, Frank, Petersen, plus Herald and News stories and Frank's memoir. The Neal Sonnett quote comes from the National Law Journal article in July by Tamara Levin. The Adorno and Yoss profiles are based mostly on News and Herald articles.

The Mark Lane reference is to his 1966 book, "Rush to Judgment: A Critique of the Warren Commission's Inquiry into the Murders of President John F. Kennedy, Officer J.D. Tippit and Lee Harvey Oswald."

CHAPTER 6

Interviews with Yoss, Carhart, Laeser, Petersen, plus the governor's panel report.

The federal reports on the Ferguson shooting can be found on the website of the Office of Public Affairs of the U.S. Justice Department.

The New York Times: "Grand Jury System, With Exceptions, Favors the Police in Fatalities," December 7, 2014, by James C. McKinley Jr. and Al Baker.

CHAPTER 7

Interviews with Laeser, Frank and Dunn.

Articles from the Herald and News.

The Bowlin quote is from the Eyes on the Prize. He went on to say: "I don't think that this is just endemic to the Public Safety Department. I think, all around this nation in police departments, there are punishment areas. And many of them are in the black areas where we should have the best police officers."

CHAPTER 8

Interviews; Stierheim, O'Donnell, Kogan, Yoss, Carhart.

Media sources: The Herald, the News and WTVJ.

About what happened in the state trooper case: The judge, defense attorney and prosecutor later claimed that they understood that the trooper touched her only outside of her clothing. According to the Herald, the lead police investigator, Captain Irving Heiler, said that was untrue: "He rubbed her feet and fondled her breasts, there was skin-to-skin contact.... The trooper then instructed the child, already partially undressed, to remove her trousers. She became hysterical and he relented. He placed his hand on her vagina, outside the clothing."

Bowlin's comment is from Eyes on the Prize.

Tom Petersen, one of Reno's top assistants, recalled attending a meeting in which Reno listened to Bill Perry and other black community leaders. "I know there was a sense among civil rights activists who were saying Janet was not sensitive to civil rights issues. In my experience, she was. If anything, her affect in general could be kind of rigid, and I guess could be interpreted by blacks as being insensitive. She tended that way to all situations. She wasn't singling out blacks."

• • • •

CHAPTER 9

Interviews: Yoss, Laeser, Carhart, Dunn, O'Donnell, Frank and Eric Saltzman, the Harvard law professor, plus the Frank memoir. The Dunn quote is from a Herald story.

The Hialeah shooting and the Jones cases are from news accounts in the Herald, News and WTVJ.

In one pretrial motion, Carhart argued Evans was denied equal protection under the law because the state wouldn't admit him into a pretrial intervention program. He was rejected because "they said he was not a youthful offender," Carhart told the judge. "And in the program is an 89-year-old man, a policeman who forged a drug prescription and a school board clerk who stole money."

Richard Katz, who was working with Carhart on the case, said they knew there was no way Reno's office was going to allow Evans' case to be diverted. "I'll call it a stunt. We were back in his office on Flagler Street, and Ed said, 'Evans has never been arrested, right?' It was a rhetorical question. I said, 'Yeah.' I didn't know where he was going. And Ed said, 'And he's charged as the mastermind of a coverup, but not charged with any physical or violent act himself, right? Isn't there a program for first time nonviolent offenders? PTI? Pretrial intervention." So the next day, the lawyers went with Evans to the PTI office to apply. "Tom Petersen ran that office. He's a very good man — always the in-house bleeding-heart liberal."

When Petersen heard about the Evans application, Katz said, he called up Carhart, a good friend, and said: "God damn it! You're going to destroy the whole pretrial intervention program." Carhart replied: "Tom, what are you talking about? He meets all the guidelines."

Petersen said he has no recollection of this exchange, "but it sounds about right."

• • • •

CHAPTER 10

Interviews with O'Donnell, Carhart, Yoss, Oglesby, Shinhoster and Ferre.

U.S. Census data. The voter numbers come from a Herald story. The Hundley trial was in the Tampa Tribune. The Tampa black activist comments come from a United Press International story that appeared in the Herald in March. Many Miami black residents had negative views of Tampa, including Sergeant Linda Saunders, who did the Internal Affairs investigation of the officers. Her brother lived in Tampa and found the city "ultra-conservative."

• • • •

CHAPTER 11

News reports from the Herald, News, Tampa Tribune and WTVJ.

• • • •

CHAPTER 12

Interviews: Carhart, O'Donnell, Kogan, Carlton, Yoss, Laeser, Saltzman and Petersen.

Print sources: Various lawyer bios. During the trial, the only article examining the legal teams and contrasting the youth of the prosecutors versus the veteran defense attorneys was in the Miami News, by Marilyn Moore on March 31. That's where the black activist and Mrs. McDuffie quotes come from. After the trial, Verne Williams did portraits of the trial lawyers.

The Tampa Tribune was the only print source to do a profile of Judge Nesbitt. It ran on 1A on March 31 under this headline: The Judge: Colleagues Rate Her Honor as "Fair, Competent, In Control."

On McWilliams getting a conviction of rocker Jim Morrison: In 2010, long after both the prosecutor and rock star were dead, the Florida Clemency Board pardoned Morrison.

• • • •

CHAPTER 13

Interviews: Yoss, Carhart, O'Donnell, Kogan, Carlton, Edgecombe, Laeser and Shinhoster.

Media sources: The Herald, News and Tampa Tribune.

After the jury was selected, a problem popped up that revealed how hard it was to get ordinary folk to serve on juries in lengthy trials. Robert Heilmann, one of three alternates, asked the judge to be excused because his employers at the small company he worked for, Aluminum Service, told him they couldn't afford to pay his wages while he was on jury duty. Heilmann said he couldn't support his family on the $10 a day the county paid jurors.

Judge Nesbitt was incensed. She excused Heilmann but ordered his bosses to appear in court. Nothing in state statutes required employers to pay jurors, but Nesbitt fined the bosses $150 for contempt of court. A lawyer for the company said he could win on appeal, but the legal costs weren't worth it, and the bosses agreed to pay the fine. This incident underlines Laeser's comment that major trials get jurors only from large employers.

James Lees, the ex-officer and prosecutor, had this anecdote about jury selection: "I once defended a man who shot his drunken, unarmed wife directly through the heart from four feet away and killed her. His defense was mistaken self-defense: 'I thought she had a gun, I thought she was going to shoot me, so I shot her. Oops!' In jury selection I asked individual jurors when it would be OK to kill another human being. One juror replied, 'Only when you knew for sure the person was going to kill you.' A housewife on the panel, when asked the same question, replied: 'Threaten me, threaten my kids, or threaten my dog, and I'll waste you.' It does not take a rocket scientist to determine which of these jurors would be predisposed to convict my client and which juror I might have a fighting chance with. I chose jurors correctly and the jury acquitted my client of all charges."

Lees also noted this: "By the way: Only two states in the entire country use six-person juries in serious criminal cases: Florida and Connecticut. All other states and the federal courts use 12-person juries. In 1970 the U.S Supreme Court ruled that Florida's use of a six-person jury in a serious criminal case was constitutional."

Six years after the McDuffie trial, in 1986, the U.S. Supreme Court ruled in Batson v. Kentucky that prosecutors violated the equal protection clause of the 14th Amendment when they rejected jurors because of their race.

In Florida, the standard on excluding jurors because of race was set by the state supreme court in 1996 by Melbourne v. State, says Abe Laeser, the career prosecutor. That case "and its offspring have evolved into a complicated dance within the courtroom," Laeser wrote in an email. "That is true because — in spite of all protestations of fairness — it does make sense in any case with racial overtones to want more of 'yours' and none of 'theirs.' It is not pretty, but it is giving your client the best representation. So what happens today? Party #1 tries to exercise a peremptory challenge, for which no reason need be given. Party #2 makes a Melbourne challenge by claiming that the excusal was made for an improper reason [race, religion, national origin]. Once the challenge is made, the judge has to ask #1 to explain why it was made.

"This is where the 'fiction' now arises. #1 claims that the juror was inattentive, or sneered, or was overly nice to opponent by smiling — or just about any other stupid thing that would justify a peremptory challenge. The judge then has to decide if the claim is facially reasonable. If so, the juror is excused. If the claim is deemed to be a pretense, the juror is 'forced sat.' Most lawyers spot the bad jurors early and concentrate on getting some snarky answer to a dumb question, which they can later use to rebut the Melbourne claims.

"Since it is considered that the juror has the right not to be discriminated against, the Melbourne claim can be made by either party, under the guise of protecting juror rights. Almost every group is now protected: race, origin [do Cubans hate Columbians?], gender [LGBTQ?]. Strangely, age is not subject to a Melbourne claim, as long as it is applied uniformly. For example, one could claim to hate young jurors and exclude every one under 30 — as long as there are no exceptions. Melbourne applies to all parties in civil and criminal in order to give a juror equal protection."

• • • •

CHAPTER 14

Sources: The Herald, News, Tribune, Associated Press and WTVJ.

James Lees, the ex-officer and prosecutor, wrote that the "Prince incident again perfectly illustrates the need for prosecutors to have a complete investigation (preferably by a neutral agency) before any decisions are made about immunity. The problems that now were arising at trial were clearly predictable given the mistakes made in the first days and weeks of the investigation."

••••

CHAPTER 15

Sources: The Herald, News, Tribune, St. Petersburg Times, Sentinel Star of Orlando, Associated Press and WTVJ.

••••

CHAPTER 16

Sources: WTVJ, the Herald, News, Tribune, St. Petersburg Times, Sentinel Star of Orlando and Associated Press.

••••

CHAPTER 17

Sources: WTVJ, the Herald, News, Tribune, St. Petersburg Times, Sentinel Star of Orlando and Associated Press. On the "license to lie": Carhart interview.

••••

CHAPTER 18

Sources: WTVJ, the Herald, News, Tribune, St. Petersburg Times, Sentinel Star of Orlando and Associated Press. Frank says he has no memory of Meier's scenario of he and Bowlin playing the "good cop, bad cop"

••••

CHAPTER 19

Sources: The Herald, News, Tribune, St. Petersburg Times, Sentinel Star of Orlando, Associated Press and WTVJ. On the quality of the witnesses: Yoss interview.

Further comment from James Lees: "I cannot speak to 1980 in Florida, but I can tell by the mid- to late-1980s attorneys were using 'shadow juries' in courtrooms in both criminal and civil trials to get real-time feedback as to how the case was progressing. Shadow juries are nothing more than focus groups made up of the type of people who would normally serve on juries. They are organized from the outset of the trial. They usually believe they are working for some university research project and sit in the courtroom each day and watch and listen to exactly what the real jurors see and hear. At the end of each day each shadow juror is individually debriefed and the results of those debriefings are shared with the trial team who is, unknown to the shadow jury, using them to get meaningful feedback. It does not appear from the various accounts of this trial that anyone was using this valuable tool in this case, least of all the prosecution."

• • • •

CHAPTER 20

Sources: The Herald, News, Tribune, St. Petersburg Times, Sentinel Star of Orlando, Associated Press and WTVJ. Interviews with Carlton and Gerant. Juror Fisher's statements come from the Herald and Tribune.

• • • •

CHAPTER 21

Based on various news accounts and interviews with the lawyers. The detail of Watts reading the Edna Buchanan book comes from a Herald story. Yoss gave the Kogan anecdote about reminding jurors who he was and then sitting down. Yoss considered Kogan's strategy "the best."

CHAPTER 22

Sources: Herald, News, WTVJ, Tribune, Times, Sentinel Star and Associated Press. Interview with Gotowala.

CHAPTER 23

Interviews: Carhart, Frank and Kogan.

Media sources: Herald, News, WTVJ, Tribune, Times, Sentinel Star and Associated Press.

James Lees' comment on Frank's testimony on Del Toro: "Given the actual testimony of Commander Frank, one must ask what was the point of calling this witness? What did he add to the government's case? Virtually nothing."

CHAPTER 24

Sources: Herald, News, WTVJ, Tribune, Times, Sentinel Star and Associated Press. The battery and McWilliams "Aw, shucks" was the kicker to Gene Miller's story in the Herald.

The crime techs went to the scene more than a week after the incident. Could that delay have been a factor not finding fingerprints? There's no indication that Turner was asked that in court. I asked Frank in an email exchange. He responded: "Under perfect conditions, it would be difficult to develop and/or lift any print from a key... much depending on how much smooth/flat area existed on the key." With a week's delay in finding the keys, "add weather conditions, etc., most unlikely."

CHAPTER 25

Interview: Linda Saunders Finney.

Sources: Herald, News, WTVJ, Tribune, Times, Sentinel Star and Associated Press. Only the Herald reported on Saunders testimony.

• • • •

CHAPTER 26

Interview: Carhart interview on wanting to hide under the table.

Sources: Herald, News, WTVJ, Tribune, Times, Sentinel Star and Associated Press.

Continuing with Lees' restructuring the trial: After the Wright and the tech witnesses: "Next comes Miami officer Gotowala, who identifies Marrero as one of the perpetrators and testifies he was so disgusted he quit his job. Officer Gerant then testifies to the multiple officers beating the crap out of Mr. McDuffie and identifies Watts, however flawed, as another perpetrator of this crime. The prosecution ends with Mr. McDuffie's mother, presumably to give chain-of-custody testimony but in reality to grieve for her dead son in front of the jury. Only defense attorneys for Marrero and Watts are involved in the case, and no officers have immunity. I ask therefore a simple question: Are the odds of obtaining a conviction on at least one of these officers now much greater than the odds of obtaining a conviction based upon this mess of a prosecution? And with a conviction of one or both officers, an attempt could have been made to deal with the convicted officers to give testimony against other officers in exchange for some leniency in sentencing."

• • • •

CHAPTER 27

Interviews with lawyers Kogan and Yoss and jurors Stover and Tetreault.

Sources: Herald, News, WTVJ, Tribune, Times, Sentinel Star and Associated Press.

• • • •

CHAPTER 28

Interviews with jurors Stover and Tetreault.
Sources: Tribune, Times, and Associated Press.

• • • •

CHAPTER 29

• • • •

INTERVIEW: O'DONNELL.
Sources: Herald, News, WTVJ, Tribune, Times, Sentinel Star and Associated Press.

James Lees on Adorno's performance questioning Marrero: "The art of cross-examination takes years to perfect, and few attorneys ever perfect this skill. Young prosecutors are generally terrible at cross-examination due to impatience, lack of understanding as to the purpose of cross, and a lack of skill in controlling a hostile witness. While the transcript of the cross-examination of Officer Marrero does not exist, the recollection of people there at the trial appears to indicate a lack of controlling questions and a defined purpose in the cross examination of this defendant. Each segment of a good cross-examination has a particular point to make to the jury, but before the cross-examiner can make the point, he/she must force cut off all means of escape by the witness from the point. Seasoned lawyers call this 'closing the corral gates,' meaning the witness is in the middle of a large corral with multiple gates, and one by one the skilled cross-examiner closes each gate until there are no more gates to escape. Then and only then does the lawyer slip the rope around the defendant's neck to make the point for jurors."

• • • •

Chapter 30

SOURCES: HERALD, NEWS, WTVJ, Tribune, Times, Sentinel Star and Associated Press.

• • • •

CHAPTER 31

Sources: Herald, News, WTVJ, Tribune, Times, Sentinel Star and Associated Press.

Adorno was so tough on his own witnesses that the Orlando newspaper's headline was "McDuffie prosecutor attacks 'despicable' state witnesses."

• • • •

CHAPTER 32

Interviews: Shinhoster, Carlton, O'Donnell, Carhart, Yoss.

Sources: Herald, News, WTVJ, Tribune, Times, Sentinel Star and Associated Press. Some of the mood comes from the post-trial analyses of the News and St. Petersburg Times.

Because of the rush of news after the verdicts, newspaper and television accounts of Carhart's final arguments that Saturday morning were brief or nonexistent. Here, perhaps more than any other place, the lack of a transcript is felt. Carhart had a brilliant reputation for closing arguments — so much so that other lawyers often dropped by to hear them in Miami, as Herald reporter Arnold Markowitz noted in Carhart's next trial. Based on the Tampa jurors' comments afterward, it seems apparent that Carhart must have discussed in considerable detail of the flaws of the immunized witnesses because several jurors said they came to view the "free ride" witnesses as worse than the defendants.

Lees on Carhart's final argument: "There is no originality in comedy and there is no originality in litigation. Or not much of any. Fifteen years before Johnnie Cochran and his dream team of defense lawyers walked O.J. Simpson out of an LA courtroom a free man, the words of Mr. Carhart were spoken out into the ether to reverberate down through America's timeline: A flawed, rushed investigation to meet howling protests. All that's missing from this argument was a catchy jingle ("if the gloves do not fit you must acquit")."

"The themes put forward in Tampa were not original, but they were effective," Lees wrote. "They were themes that had been effective for Cicero thousands of years before. They were themes that had been effective in countless trials throughout the history of America. They were themes that would work in an LA courtroom 15 years later. And they were themes that certainly would work in this Tampa courtroom. Why? Because they were themes based in truth. And any time the trial story/theme of a case argued by one side is imbued with the truth that side almost always wins. The sad case of the prosecution of the murderers of Arthur McDuffie was no exception."

The description of the jury room comes from the Herald, as does the Adorno-Yoss "sorry, boss" phone call. AP and Sentinel Star had the scene from the defense's barroom celebration.

• • • •

CHAPTER 33

Interviews: Ken Harms, Clarence Dickson, Lonnie Lawrence, Frank, Ferre, Dunn, Petersen, Stierheim, Carlton. Bowlin recollection is from Eyes on the Prize.

Print sources: Herald, News, the Porter-Dunn riot book, plus Frank's and Buchanan's memoirs.

The estimate of the crowd size listening to the police chiefs at African Square Park comes from the riot book. In an interview decades later, Ken Harms, then Miami police chief, recalled 400 to 500 in the audience.

The description of the Kulp brothers comes from the Porter-Dunn riot book, the Herald and News and in particular Herald reporter Earni Young, who was at the scene.

There were a few tales of heroism. Martin and Ruth Weinstock, a retired couple, had gone to a minor league baseball game and were headed back to their home when they were confronted by a crowd. He sped up, but the car was struck by a flurry of rocks. The driver-side window was rolled down, and he was struck by a large chunk of concrete that fractured his skull. He drove two more blocks and lost consciousness. A mob was approaching. Ruth locked the doors. Martin revived, drove two more blocks, then passed out again. Ruth screamed for help.

From the Dunn-Porter book: "At about this time a black chemist and his wife, Ron and Jackie Malone, were driving through the intersection and saw the Weinstocks in trouble. Malone came over, moved the badly bleeding man to the passenger side and then, with his wife following in their car, drove the couple" to a hospital. After six days at Parkway General, Weinstock was released.

• • • •

CHAPTER 34

Miami Herald and Miami News on Monday, May 19.

• • • •

CHAPTER 35

Interview: Shinhoster.

Verne Williams' excellent analysis appeared inside the A section on Monday, May 19. Slacum's ran on the local front page.

CHAPTER 36

Interview: Saltzman.

Block, head of the governor's panel, was the Miami attorney who helped in the long battle to free two black men unjustly sentenced to Death Row, Freddie Lee Pitts and Wilbert Lee — a crusade that led to Gene Miller winning a Pulitzer for the Herald.

The Saltzman comment is from an interview.

CBS' Ed Bradley got a rare interview with Marrero. Some of his comments: "After you become a police officer, you stay in your own little world. You become so alienated from even your former friends, you family, everybody." When he started, "four and a half years ago, if you worked that area, a combat zone, they came out straight and said it, 'Listen kid, out here, you know you're on your own.... You put aside everything you learned in the academy. Because it doesn't work here.' And I go, 'That can't be true.' And he says, 'You'll see.' Sure as hell, Mr. Bradley, it was true. I feel alone out there. You only learn on the streets. Nothing they teach you in the academy — sociology, humanities, psychology — I tell you I tried to apply it three or four times out there, and you know where I ended up? In the hospital....

"How much can you cope with every day, day after day, in an area where I'm not familiar with as far as their culture, their ideas, their thoughts, their beliefs. I'm not saying it's because it's a black area. It's predominantly a high crime area and it could happen anywhere. Whether it be in a white ghetto or black it doesn't matter but it's a ghetto there.... I spent two years there. I put in four transfers. I never wanted to go there.... I never got out.... If you have a predominantly black area — I don't care what you say — you have to put black officers there.... I would be a benefit to the department if I worked a predominantly Latin area, a Cuban area, which I worked prior to that.

What reason did they have to get me out of that district and put me on it [the Central District]? They themselves ask for trouble."

• • • •

CHAPTER 37

I interviewed Stover and Tetreault. The Fisher comments appeared in the Herald, Tribune and St. Pete Times. The Draper letter appeared in the Herald on July 27, after it became part of the court record in the Veverka federal case.

• • • •

CHAPTER 38

Interviews: Carhart, Yoss and Dunn. Adorno responded on 60 Minutes. The Nesbitt ruling is from Herald and News articles.

An excellent summary of the Baltimore trials appeared in The New Yorker, July 13, 2016, "What Have the Freddie Gray Trials Achieved?"

"Sponsorship Strategy: Evidentiary Tactics for Winning Jury Trials," by Robert H. Klonoff and Paul L. Colby, The Michie Company, Charlottesville, Virginia. 1990.

Diggs testified he was ordered to insert Watts name when in fact Diggs said he didn't see Watts do anything.

• • • •

CHAPTER 39

Interviews: Denis Dean, Laeser.

The pretrial material comes from the Herald and the News. The Dunn comments come from his November 10 New York Times column. The trial narrative is based on articles in the Herald, News, Tampa Tribune, St. Petersburg Times and Associated Press.

• • • •

CHAPTER 40

The Stinson quote about 1,000 dying each year at the hands of police comes from a column he wrote in the New York Daily News, "Charging a police officer in fatal shooting case is rare, and a conviction is even rarer," on March 31, 2017.

The death count in Afghanistan is from the New York Times, Dec. 22, 2019.

The Bowling Green data through June 24, 2019, can be found at the institute's website.

Ferguson federal reports are from the website of the Office of Public Affairs of U.S. Department of Justice.

The Chicago shooting case is well summarized in a Washington Post story "Justice for Laquan," on October 5, 2018.

The Oliver shooting in Texas came from an NPR report on August 30, 2018.

The Fullinwider quotes from an Associated Press story from August 29, 2018.

The Slager account is based on several news sources, including the New York Times from December 7, 2017, "Michael Slager, Officer in Walter Scott Shooting, Gets 20-Year Sentence."

The Miami cases all come from the Miami Herald, almost all of them written by David Ovalle.

• • • •

CHAPTER 41

Interviews, Frank, Yoss, Kogan, Laeser, Shinhoster, Harms, Dean and Oglesby, plus the Frank memoir.

Veverka's statement appeared in the Miami News. Del Toro's is from his interview with the Herald.

The McWilliams quote was found in Herald and News stories. The quotes from Sergeant Gonzalez are from a Herald story. The Dunn quote on change of venue is from Eyes on the Prize.

Many Miami black residents remain adamant that the change of venue was the real problem. Linda Saunders Finney, who did the initial PSD Internal Affairs investigation into the McDuffie cops, continues to maintain that change of venue often works to the disadvantage of the black community. She points to the 1992 trial in California of four police officers accused of beating Rodney King. That trial was moved to a white suburb. The jury acquitted the four and rioting ensued. "We just never learn," Finney said.

On how hard it was to convict cops in Florida:

Shinhoster, the Tampa reporter, cited two issues: "No. 1: Police are law enforcement authorities. If you're going to believe anybody, you're going to believe them. No. 2: Black men have been made such stereotypes and demonized that society believes that if anybody did anything wrong, it's the black male."

Ken Harms, City of Miami police chief in 1980 and a vigorous defender of law enforcement, told me he was "absolutely" convinced that charges should have been filed against officers in the McDuffie case. Still, he acknowledged: "It is difficult to prosecute officers criminally ... That's been a long-standing pattern where people come to the belief, rightfully so in some instances, that the last line of defense between the good citizens and the criminals who will steal from them, rob them or kill them is the police, and if there is any doubt that can be granted, it will go to the officers involved. It's a difficult job to do. Many people understand that. 'You couldn't pay me enough to do that job. I'm not going to convict him for... what he did in a given set of circumstances because he's out there trying to protect us.'"

Denis Dean, who for many years represented the Dade Police Benevolent Association and was co-counsel for Veverka's federal trial, said: "During the 20 years I was general counsel for the PBA, I had 25 jury trials involving police officers — 24 not guilty. Police were looked up to. The public would give police more of a pass, unless you got into corruption. In closing arguments, I would say, 'Put yourself in the police officer's place. It's midnight. He's alone, totally in the dark. He doesn't know what to expect.' I've had cases where a BB gun looks like a gun.... So you would have those situations where jurors would sympathize with the officers."

Note that Dean's trials were in Miami: Keeping the McDuffie trial in town wouldn't have made it any easier to gain convictions.

••••

CHAPTER 42

Interviews: Stierheim, Kogan, Ferre, Kleinberg, Shinhoster, Yoss, Carhart, Laeser, O'Donnell.

The Joe Davis quote is from a Herald story. The Miller obituary ran June 18, 2005. The 1980 circulation figures are from the Alliance for Audited Media.

Miller certainly knew the Reno family, right down to Jane's and Janet's housekeeping proclivities. Years later, when the Clinton Administration lost its first two choices for attorney general because they had tax or immigration issues involving household help, Reno's name came up. Miller wisecracked in print: "If anyone in Washington inquires, I can testify that no maid has been inside your house in 20 years." When Miller died, Janet Reno said: "Of all the reporters that I dealt with locally, in Tallahassee and in Washington, he was one of the very, very best. He had an intellect that was remarkable. He could grasp issues quickly. You just had to give your input, and you had to do it honestly."

Several defense attorneys in Tampa didn't like Miller's coverage of the trial but admired him personally and so they blamed Herald editors for shaping Miller's coverage. Joe Oglesby said that was nonsense: "I knew Gene Miller very well. Gene was in charge of how he did it. The editors were working for Gene. Gene was not working for the editors."

Kogan didn't like the Herald's coverage, but he and Miller didn't appear to have had any long-term animosity toward each other. In 1992, when Kogan was a Florida Supreme Court justice, he officiated at the marriage of Miller's daughter, Robin.

Miller was born in Evansville, Indiana, worked as a copyboy for the Evansville Press and graduated in 1950 from Indiana University, majoring in journalism. "Fired from The Wall Street Journal in 1954. Lacked respect for price of crude cottonseed oil," he wrote in his own obituary. "Reporter on The News Leader, Richmond, Virginia, 1954-57. Departed after motorist failed to pay 5 cent toll and guard shot at him. Managing editor didn't think it was news because publisher and his neighbors owned the bridge." He started at the Herald in 1957.

The other Miami reporter, Verne Williams, 60, was a veteran who covered top stories, including the courts, for the Miami News. Born in Kansas City, Williams was a World War II army vet, a photographer before he became a reporter. His father, Verne Orville Williams Sr., was a pioneer Miami photographer whose photos of the early city found their ways into postcards and historic collections.

A lanky six-foot-two, he was the type of star reporter "who did a lot of interpretive work for us," recalled Kleinberg, editor of the News at the time. "You don't tell Verne Williams what to do. He was that kind of a reporter. My greatest moment with Verne Williams was in 1977. I came in very early in the morning and they were saying it was going to snow in Miami. I knew it snowed in West Palm Beach. So Verne was in on the early shift. It was about 6:30 in the morning and I said, 'Verne, why don't you grab a chair and go out on the roof on the building and see if it snows.' He said, 'I've been on this paper a lot of years, and I've done a lot of things and there's no way I'm going to sit on the roof and wait for a snowflake.' He absolutely refused. That's how Verne was. I ended up sending Ian Glass, who I think saw more snowflakes than actually fell!" Kleinberg said this laughing. The News ran a headline that day: "Snow in Miami!" with cutouts of snowflakes.

The other print reporters at the trial:

Yvonne Shinhoster, 26, the Tampa Tribune reporter, was a graduate of the University of Georgia She started as a reporter at the Atlanta Daily World, a black newspaper, then moved to the Macon Telegraph before joining the Tribune about two years before the trial. She covered courts as well as some business and general assignment. She was the one reporter accustomed to working in the Hillsborough County courthouse.

Marcia Slacum, 27, the St. Petersburg Times reporter, was from Baltimore. Her mother died when she was 4 and she was raised by a grandmother in Virginia. She graduated from James Madison University and taught English for a while before joining the Times staff.

Jim Runnels, 31, of the Sentinel Star in Orlando. He was raised in Florida, served in Vietnam with Air Force, went to Gulf Coast Community College, started with the Panama City News Herald, then moved to the Sentinel in 1978.

Pat Reisner, 49, the Associated Press reporter. Raised in the Bronx, she graduated with a degree in journalism from Fordham University. Her newspaper reporting career started in Los Angeles. She went over to Associated Press in Fargo, North Dakota, then transferred to Fairfax, Virginia, before moving to Tampa in 1970. Florida newspapers often did not put bylines on Associated Press stories about the McDuffie trial, but when they did, it was Reisner's.

• • • •

"MY COUSIN VINNY" WAS a 1992 film distributed by 20th Century Fox.

"Miami: From Quiet to Riot — An alternative viewpoint of The Miami Herald's role in events leading to the riots of May 1980," by

Robert Allen Hardin, published by Keyes-Hardin Productions, Miami 1980. Available at the downtown branch of the Miami-Dade Public Library.

Re Hardin allegations: Interviews with Carhart, O'Donnell, Harms, Petersen.

On Sunday, February 8, 1981, the Herald ran a huge article on Hardin's charges, starting on the bottom of the local front and jumping to a full page inside. It was written by Tom Fiedler, a measured reporter who was to go on to become the political editor, editorial page editor and eventually executive editor of the Herald. Fiedler took the assignment after Carl Hiaasen refused.

The Marvin Dunn quote on Hardin being "perceptive" is from his op-ed column in the New York Times, Nov. 10. "Why Miami Blacks Might Riot Again." In fact, in the Herald's coverage after McDuffie's death, Dunn was often a leader in demanding more attention for police treatment of blacks. In a January 6 Herald opinion piece, he wrote: "A part of the problem is that cries of 'police brutality' have been coming from the black community for years. They are almost always dismissed as self-serving or unsubstantiated. When it boils down to the word of an individual citizen versus that of a police officer, the officer is given the benefit of the doubt. Of course, the McDuffie case won't change that." When charges against Hanlon were dismissed, he said: "I feel insulted, but it doesn't surprise me. I've been saying these people are going to get off and Hanlon is the first one to do so. The black people aren't going to forget this."

The Edna Buchanan quote is from "The Corpse Had a Familiar Face."

The Hirschhorn exchange on the dangers of TV is from New York Times magazine: "Television's Day in Court," by Martin Clark Bass, February 15, 1981.

"The Implosion Conspiracy" by Louis Nizer, Doubleday, New York, 1992.

The Edward Bennett Williams story was entitled "An Embarrassment of Riches," Tropic Magazine, Miami Herald, August 31, 1986.

The Oglesby column appeared in the Herald on May 19, 1980, on page 1A.

• • • •

CHAPTER 43

Interviews: Dunn, Alex Stepick, Ferre, Harms, Kleinberg.

Print sources: Herald, News. The New Yorker story: April 21, 1980, "Judging Johnny Jones," by Calvin Trillin. The Governor's Dade County Citizens Committee. The Porter-Dunn riot book.

"City on the Edge: The Transformation of Miami," by Alejandro Portes and Alex Stepick, University of California Press, Berkeley, 1993.

The United States Commission on Civil Rights "Confronting Racial Isolation in Miami." 1982.

The 1980 census.

"The Impact of the Mariel Boatlift on the Miami Labor Market" by David Card, Industrial and Labor Relations Review, Vol. 43, No. 2. (Jan., 1990), pp. 245-257.

"We Wanted Workers: Unraveling the Immigration Narrative," by George Borjas. W. W. Norton & Company, New York. 2016.

• • • •

ADDENDUM NOTES

The Johnny Jones Trials

Interview: Carhart. The Laeser quotes are mostly from email exchanges.

Print Sources: Herald and News. The description of the second trial is based on Miami Herald stories by Arnold Markowitz and Miami News stories by Tom Dubocq. The Reno comment on the effect of the two trials appeared in the News in August 1980.

Printed in Dunstable, United Kingdom